BEHIND *the* PULPIT

Three Seasoned Lutheran Pastors Share Their Megachurch Stories

**Roger Eigenfeld,
Paul Harrington, &
Duane Paetznick**

Behind the Pulpit: Three Seasoned Lutheran Pastors Share Their Megachurch Stories © Copyright 2021 Roger Eigenfeld, Paul Harrington, & Duane Paetznick

First Edition
ISBN: 978-1-952976-23-0
Library of Congress Control Number: 2021913863

Published by Kirk House Publishers
1250 E 115th Street
Burnsville, MN 55337
Kirkhousepublishers.com
612-781-2815

TABLE OF CONTENTS

INTRODUCTION

Most folks have never been in a pulpit. But it is a place that pastors inhabit all the time. If you were to step into a pulpit, you would likely see all kinds of things. Maybe you would see a glass of water, a small book, post-it notes, a Bible, or various items used for sermon illustrations. Often those items have stories that go with them that you might find poignant, humorous, and insightful. This book will be a lot like wandering behind that pulpit and seeing the things that pastors see—things about pastoral ministry that are often poignant, humorous, and insightful.

There are three voices that you will hear throughout this book; the first two belong to senior pastors Roger Eigenfeld and Paul Harrington. Roger was senior pastor at St. Andrew's Lutheran Church in Mahtomedi, Minnesota, for thirty-three years. Paul was senior pastor and, later, pastor emeritus at Shepherd of the Valley (SOTV) Lutheran Church in Apple Valley, Minnesota—also for thirty-three years. Throughout the book, they each tell their stories.

The third voice in this book is mine. I am Duane Paetznick, and I am also a Lutheran pastor. I gathered the stories from Roger and Paul. In addition, I share my own perspective on occasion. You see, during my forty-one years of Christian ministry, I had the good fortune of being in a unique spot. I primarily served two church communities which were surging in attendance, programming, and mission. One of those churches was St. Andrew's, where I was the director of Christian education and where I worked with Roger for thirteen years. The other church was SOTV, where I served as a pastor for twenty-seven years. For much of that time at SOTV, Paul was the senior pastor. So I was able to see, up close and personal, two churches with ever-expanding ministries led by Roger and Paul—two long-term and dynamic, yet very different senior pastors.

Turns out, my experience was quite unique. My time with these congregations came at a time when many people who served in churches were experiencing something else—declining involvement. This was especially true in mainline denominations like the Lutheran church. Although some who served in ministry may have witnessed expanding ministry in one of their parishes, rarely has anyone been in my position, keenly witnessing dynamic ministry expansion at two different churches.

But *Behind the Pulpit* is not about me. It is primarily about how Roger and Paul led those two congregations from few or no people to thriving congregations that eventually became megachurches. How did they do that? How did those churches continue to grow while others declined? What happened in the pulpit and behind the pulpit? What lessons for pastors and churches today can be learned from our experiences? By sharing our stories, we hope to help the communal memory of the church and to help give some purpose, direction, and identity to the present and future church.

All three of us know that what happened at those two churches was not our doing. It was the work of the Holy Spirit. So, this book, then, is also about how the Holy Spirit guided us in leading our congregations through some marvelous and some difficult experiences.

As you read this book, please keep in mind that not every pastor's story is like our stories. We had the opportunity to be in ministry in the privileged locations where we were called: Mahtomedi and Apple Valley in Minnesota. These are suburban Twin Cities communities where most people are upper-middle-class folks. Undoubtedly, these locations, at this time in history, were ripe for change, growth, and development. That's not the case with many other churches. So we understand how our calls were unique. And we also think that these stories are worth telling.

Chapter 1

CALL

Duane: Call Stories

This is the story of two very different yet very exceptional Lutheran pastors, Roger Eigenfeld and Paul Harrington. They led their respective Minnesota congregations as they grew exponentially during the 1980s, 1990s, and 2000s. At one point, both of their churches, St. Andrew's in Mahtomedi and Shepherd of the Valley (SOTV) in Apple Valley, were among the top-ten largest Lutheran congregations in the United States. Their leadership was critical to that growth.

I had the privilege to work with both as a staff member in those churches. So I saw their leadership styles up close. I worked full-time with Roger for thirteen years as the director of Christian education at St. Andrew's while simultaneously attending seminary, seeking to become a pastor. Once I became a pastor, I worked with Paul for about twenty years before he retired from ministry. Both of these fine pastors were called to do the work they did, but it wasn't always an easy calling.

Everyone has a "call story." A call story is merely the story of how you got involved in what God has called you to do in life. That could be how you became a parent, a teacher, a salesperson, a spouse, or a volunteer. Most people think that pastors are the only people that are called by God. But that is not the case. Everyone is called. It's just that pastors are called to do something unique. And they often do it under a spotlight. So people usually are very interested in a pastor's call story. "How did you become a pastor?" is a question I have often heard over the years.

In order for you to become acquainted with Roger and Paul, let's hear their call stories directly from them.

Roger Eigenfeld's Call

It was June. It was the long-awaited weekend when I would join twenty other 8th graders from St. Peter's Lutheran Church in Milwaukee for our rite of confirmation. Two years of Saturday morning classes would finally be coming to an end. Two years of reciting memory work in front of other students every Saturday morning would soon be over. But, before the actual rite of confirmation could take place, there were still a few extra hoops we had to go through before the big event on Sunday.

First, on Friday, we had to go through the dreaded "exam night." Dressed in suits and ties and with parents, grandparents, brothers, and sisters looking on, we nervously waited for the pastor to ask us to answer questions from the list of one hundred he had given us to memorize. Nobody fainted, but a good amount of perspiration could be seen on the foreheads of many as they waited for their name to be called. Once that was over, though, we still had Saturday to look forward to.

On Saturday, the pastor had arranged for each of us to spend twenty minutes alone with him as he asked us a few final questions. Were we serious about being confirmed? Were we interested in becoming a part of Luther League, the senior high youth group? And then he asked the "big" question—had we ever considered becoming pastors?

Being a part of the church was just a natural part of life in the Eigenfeld family. My dad had served on the church council, he and my mother had taught Sunday school for years, and they always got us to church early enough so that on many a winter Sunday morning we found ourselves grabbing shovels and finishing off the last of the snow. We were also one of the last families to leave after worship was over.

So when the pastor asked, "Have you ever considered being a pastor?" the answer was easy: No! To which he simply replied, "Well, think about it! You might enjoy it!"

With those simple words, Pastor Christian T. Breest implanted in my brain an idea that I found impossible to shake. Could I become a pastor? Would I really like being a pastor? Maybe—just maybe—I might like it.

Pastor Breest's invitation, however, was just the beginning. You see, our congregation was a member of the Northwest Synod of the United Lutheran Church in America, and the synod was serious about recruiting young men for the ministry—so much so that they actually had an office at Northwestern Lutheran Seminary in Minneapolis dedicated to a project they called "Sons for the Ministry." It was a movement that included weekend retreats for high school students, invitations to come and look over Northwestern Seminary, a seminary professor who would keep in contact with each possible candidate for the ministry throughout the year, and even visits in college by current seminary students. The church and the seminary were dead serious about the mission, and they certainly made an impression on me—I started to think I might want to become a pastor!

There were bumps along the way. I started college thinking that pastoral ministry was the path I wanted to follow, but there were times when I thought other professions might be something I would like. Still, the ministry always ended up being the route I felt most called to follow.

A long time ago, someone said, "If you can avoid the ministry, avoid it. But if you can't, you're in for the ride of your life." I tried to avoid it, but in the end, I took it. And it's been quite a ride. One I'm so glad to have been on.

Duane: What it Takes to Get Ordained

There are many reasons that I am thankful I went to seminary and became ordained as a Lutheran pastor, despite incurring some significant debt. Among those reasons is the careful process through which people become pastors in the Evangelical Lutheran Church in America (ELCA). There are many things that a candidate for ordination goes through before becoming ordained. It is an obstacle course of things that help the church ensure the candidate is qualified. When I was in seminary in the 1980s, candidates needed to:

- *be approved by a number of formal committees;*
- *pass a psychological assessment;*
- *be able to read and write Koine Greek, the language of the New Testament;*
- *study Hebrew, the language of the Old Testament;*
- *take three to four years of full-time seminary classes;*
- *complete a three-month unit of Clinical Pastoral Education (CPE);*
- *do a full year of internship;*

- *have training on boundaries in ministry; and*
- *be carefully examined by professors, pastors, bishops, and lay people.*

If you will, this was the church's way of having consistency within the ranks of its leaders and the denomination's way of being accountable to the congregations—giving them a chance at getting a competent pastor.

Contrast that kind of comprehensive vetting in the ELCA with the method that some other churches use to call and ordain their pastors. Some of those other churches simply assign a person the title of "pastor" if the authorities in that particular church deem that person worthy of the title. No seminary training is needed. No committees. No specialized work. No testing. It's probably true that many of these people who become "pastors" in those congregations are gifted and faithful to the gospel. But still, there is almost no screening or accountability built into those call systems.

Paul Harrington's Call

To be honest, I cannot think of a time in my life when I did not aspire to be a pastor, even from my earliest years of childhood. I was born and raised in a family where the practice of faith was a top priority and where the church played a vital role in all our lives. Sunday worship was a joyful event and never seen as an obligation. My mother taught Sunday school all her adult life, and my dad taught an adult Bible study in every church we ever joined. And this was no small commitment as my father, through his employment, was transferred and promoted seven different times over a thirty-three-year period. So, my folks became very adept at finding healthy congregations to join in a wide variety of towns and cities. Consequently, even at an early age, I was exposed to some very competent and dedicated pastors whom I often grew to deeply respect and admire. Two pastors in particular during my formative teenage years, Arthur Holmer and

Glenn Wegmeyer, were very influential in further developing my faith life.

It happened in the old American Lutheran Church (ALC) denomination that every October, churches would observe Youth Sunday, wherein the youth of the church were asked to lead in worship on a given Sunday. For some reason, I was often asked to do the preaching (probably because no one else would even consider it). I recall being nervous at first (and perspiring a lot), but I also found that I was fairly good at it. I always got tons of affirmation afterward. A lot of people would say things like "have you ever thought about attending seminary?" And, of course, that thought was somehow almost always in the back (or front) of my mind.

Another profound exposure to good pastors was at our family's annual summer stay at Mount Carmel Bible Camp near Alexandria, Minnesota. We attended every summer without fail, and even though my dad was not a pastor, we most often showed up for "pastor's week" because some of the most gifted pastors in the Lutheran church were there as both teachers and preachers (Alvin Rogness, Olaf Hanson, Oswald Hoffman, Fred Schoitz, Paul Maier, Herb Loddigs, and Wilson Fagerberg among them). I was exposed to some of the best pastors and Bible teachers in the Lutheran church.

Next came a year at the Lutheran Bible Institute in Minneapolis. Here we studied the Bible intensely along with courses in church history, missions, doctrine, choral music, Old Testament and New Testament. Again, I got to know some really fine pastors who were great teachers and preachers—as well as encouragers!

Then came four years at Concordia College in Moorhead, Minnesota, where again, the Religion Department had a marvelous team of pastors such as Paul Sponheim, Jim Hoffrening, Jim Bergquist, and Lloyd Svendsby. It was here that I became involved with Campus Ministry, working closely with Carl Lee, a beloved campus pastor. I was given opportunities to assist with campus worship services, distributing Holy Communion and writing an article for the campus newspaper. It was also at this time that Luther Seminary sent out professors to our various Lutheran colleges to talk personally with any who thought of themselves as "pre-seminarians." I recall several great conversations with the likes of John Victor Halvorson and Bill Hulme.

By this time, if you haven't already guessed, I was so primed for the seminary that I could hardly wait for the fall of 1967. It seemed like my whole life had been one long exposure to some of the finest men and women that the church had to offer. I was hooked. My faith had grown exponentially over the years and proclaiming the Gospel of Jesus Christ as a vocation was now my life's goal.

It was also during this time that I met and later married the love of my life, Margaret, who also had a deep faith, had attended the Lutheran Bible Institute, and had taken the Parish Worker's course in case she should marry a pastor. I don't think our meeting or our marriage was some kind of accident. God's hand was surely involved in all of this.

Five years at the seminary sealed the deal. In addition to classroom work, I was invited to work part-time at Prince of Glory, an inner-city church. For a year, I worked as a chaplain, taking Clinical Pastoral Education (CPE) training at Fairview Riverside Hospital (my twelve-month internship), working in the Chemical-Dependency Unit at Abbott Northwestern Hospital with Phil Hanson (a truly amazing pastor), and working two summers at two different church camps (Emmaus, Menagha, Minnesota, and Minne-Wa-Kan, Cass Lake, Minnesota)—first as a camp counselor and later as a camp director.

You can see how blessed I was to be constantly introduced to the idea of parish ministry through association with literally dozens of men and women who were also called to serve the church and their Lord. Truthfully, I do not believe I ever considered another vocation.

Duane: Divine Radar

I once read that finding a call is like "divine radar." God has given each of us something like radar to help us find our true calling. This radar is simply our joy and happiness. When we are doing something worthwhile for the world and we are happy and enjoying what we are doing, that means our divine radar has kicked in, and we have found our true calling. Both Roger and Paul certainly had this divine radar working as they found their respective calls and churches. For Paul, that radar began very early. For Roger, the radar was a bit fuzzy. But eventually, both found their calling.

Duane: The Call to Serve . . . Somewhere

In the Lutheran tradition, there are two parts to every pastor's call. There's the "inner call"—the voice inside a person's head that says, "Yes, I want to be a pastor." But that's not enough in the Lutheran tradition. That inner call must be confirmed by an "outer call." The outer call happens when a church somewhere actually hires (or "calls") the person who has the inner call. Until that happens, the call isn't complete. It isn't verified. It isn't true. In other words, the call can't just come from someone's heart or head. The larger church must put its stamp of approval on it. And that's not a bad way to go about business in the church. In the Lutheran church, it prevents the Jim Joneses and the David Koreshes of the world from asserting their authority over people.

Getting outside input on critical decisions is always worthwhile—even as people consider their calls to other vocations. What is in a person's head and heart is likely not the whole story. It's always best to get a calling confirmed by some other voices, lest a person fool themselves.

Roger and Paul each have their own stories of getting calls to go someplace. Here are their stories of how they got to those key churches that we'll be looking at more closely in the chapters to come.

Roger Eigenfeld's Call to St. Andrew's

I graduated from Northwestern Lutheran Theological Seminary in Minneapolis (now Luther Seminary in St. Paul) in 1966 and was called by the Board of American Missions of the Lutheran Church in America (LCA) to develop a new LCA congregation in Apple Valley, Minnesota. After just over a year, Christus Victor Lutheran Church was born with a little over one hundred charter members.

My time at Christus Victor, however, would be short-lived, for in 1967, I received and accepted a call to serve as youth pastor at the 3,500 member Richfield Lutheran Church in Minneapolis. In 1970, I received a similar call to serve as youth pastor at Holy Trinity Lutheran Church in Minneapolis.

The call to Holy Trinity was soon to be cut short by a lack of funds. In 1971, with red ink flowing, the need to reduce staff was most apparent, so all three of the pastors were told to put their names in for calls. For some reason, I was the first to be approached by a congregation seeking a new pastor. It was then that the opportunity to serve at St. Andrew's came to be.

Quite interestingly, St. Andrew's did not appear to be that much of an opportunity. First off, I had no idea where Mahtomedi was—it sounded to me like it was somewhere close to the Canadian border. In fact, in a telephone conversation about St. Andrew's with Dr. Melvin Hammarberg, President of the Minnesota Synod, I blurted out that I was too young to go up north and die. Raising his voice, Hammarberg said, "It's not that far! In fact, many consider Mahtomedi and White Bear Lake to be the garden center of the Twin Cities. Get in your car and check it out!" And so, on a dreary, rainy November day in 1971, my wife Carolyn and I drove all the way from south Minneapolis to this little town of 3,000 called Mahtomedi. It wasn't that far, but it also wasn't downtown Minneapolis.

Later that month, I was contacted by the president of the congregation to set up a meeting to discuss the call to St. Andrew's. A brief meeting with the call committee followed, and then I heard nothing. Thanksgiving, Christmas, New Year's, and then January all came and went, and still, I heard nothing. What I didn't know was that St. Andrew's was trying to save money by delaying the calling of a new pastor. Finally, I called the president of the congregation and said that if they weren't interested in me, I would appreciate them letting the synod know so that my name could be released to pursue other opportunities. It was a phone call that got the ball rolling.

Soon a congregational meeting was put on the calendar, and the call to serve St. Andrew's was extended. And so, with five little kids in tow, the Eigenfeld family made the transition from urban living to life in a very small town. My first day in the pulpit was April 1, 1972, a day that also happened to be Easter Sunday, and I spoke to an overflowing attendance of 400. The next Sunday, it would go down to 220.

Little did my family know that St. Andrew's would end up being the place where I would spend thirty-three years as their senior pastor. We could not imagine that our children would grow up knowing Mahtomedi as their only home. And who could have guessed that St. Andrew's would also be a place where I would be privileged to experience a ministry so explosive in growth that each and every year it would present new and exciting opportunities to see the Holy Spirit at work.

Melvin Hammarberg was right! It wasn't that far, and much to my surprise, it was more of an opportunity than anyone could have ever imagined.

Paul Harrington's Call to Shepherd of the Valley

Following my seminary graduation and ordination in June of 1972, Margaret and I moved to Pontiac, Michigan, a suburb of Detroit.

Sylvan Lake Lutheran Church was my first call, and there we stayed and served for almost nine years. It was a small but highly active and caring church. We soon grew to love the members as well as the entire community. Two of our children were born in Pontiac, and we had a very fulfilling ministry building up a congregation that had struggled and suffered under the leadership of a former pastor. But by the spring of 1980, we were wanting to move back to Minnesota so that our children could get to know their grandparents, cousins, uncles, and aunts. Still, it was with heavy hearts that we left Michigan.

It happened that in the spring of 1980, I attended our annual district convention in Kalamazoo, Michigan, sitting across from a fellow named Donn McLellan. Donn was an associate editor and writer for the old *Lutheran Standard* magazine and was in Kalamazoo to cover our convention. I knew Donn quite well because Margaret was writing a monthly "for kids" piece for the magazine at that time, and I was both submitting occasional articles as well as editing the monthly Michigan district insert that came out with each issue of the *Standard*. While talking together over lunch, Donn asked me if I would be interested in coming back to Minnesota to interview for the position of mission developer for a new church in a place called Apple Valley, where he also happened to reside. I told him that we might be interested, that we would be back in Minnesota in July for our annual family vacation, and that an interview would be possible at that time. It also happened at this time that another friend from Augsburg Publishing House named Lowell Hake asked me if I would be interested in working as a liaison (PR person) between Augsburg Publishing and the many districts of the American Lutheran Church (ALC), promoting the Augsburg product line of publications, books, worship and educational materials, records, and tapes. It also happened at this time that the district president of southeastern Minnesota (Elmo Agrimson) somehow knew of my interest in coming back to Minnesota and asked if I would consider interviewing at Pine Island, Minnesota, just a few miles north of Rochester.

So, we came to Minnesota that summer, and I did three interviews in July. Shortly thereafter, I had three "Letters of Call" lying on my desk back in Michigan from Augsburg Publishing, Pine Island, and Apple Valley. What to do now? Pray like mad. To be honest, we rather quickly ruled out Pine Island as it did not feel like a good fit and Augsburg Publishing as there would be lots of time traveling all over the country and also because I knew that my heart was truly in parish ministry.

I should say something about the evening we interviewed in Apple Valley at the home of Arne and Judy Teigen. Things were going along quite smoothly when suddenly the sky turned green—and yes, I *do* mean green. I have never seen such a phenomenon before or since. Then came a bad storm with very high winds that blew down trees and power poles everywhere. Afterward, parts of Apple Valley were without power for four days. But the funny thing was, we never went to the basement, and the interview continued just the same. What were we thinking? Later, I thought this could be some kind of a sign from the good Lord, but I wasn't at all sure just what it meant. Likely nothing. Anyway, we "passed the test," got the call, said our sad farewells to some wonderful people in Michigan, packed up the house, and arrived in Minnesota in early November of 1980.

We did have a small core group of people already in place (about eight households) after an initial study and survey that had been performed by Pastor Howard Sortland two years earlier. This small group had already interviewed two other pastors who had turned them down. Basically, it was pretty much a start-from-scratch mission. We spent most of November and December getting moved in, setting up an office in our home to save the national church some money. We also met with community officials, found a school gymnasium for our first worship services, formed a steering committee, and did everything we could think of to be prepared for our grand opening in early January 1981. Some fifty-three people attended our first service in the Rosemount Elementary School gymnasium. Also, Margaret was just two months away from delivering our third child, Becca, who was also to become the first baby baptized in our little congregation on Easter Sunday of 1981. We were off and running . . .

Chapter 2

BEGINNINGS

Duane: Long Pastorates

It used to be that pastors frequently moved from congregation to congregation, about every five years. But that has changed over the past forty years because it has become evident that one of the keys to growth in a congregation is the stability of the leadership, particularly the senior pastor.

Both Roger and Paul had remarkably long pastorates. Roger was senior pastor at St. Andrew's for thirty-three years, while Paul was senior pastor at Shepherd of the Valley (SOTV) for about twenty-seven years. Talk about stability and continuity! Today, if you look at larger churches, that kind of stability in leadership is a common theme.

But just as every journey begins with a first step, all pastorates start with that first year. And for both Roger and Paul, their beginnings were not easy.

Roger's Early Days at St. Andrew's

April 2nd, 1972 was Easter Sunday. It was to become my introduction into the life and ministry of St. Andrew's as well as the community of Mahtomedi. My preparation for my very first day as their pastor was complicated by the fact that I was just coming off a week-long Colorado ski trip with forty youth from my former congregation, Holy Trinity in Minneapolis.

Arriving back at Holy Trinity on Saturday afternoon, it was a mad dash from our home in Minneapolis to the parsonage in Mahtomedi—where we would spend our first night in sleeping bags in a totally empty house. Putting the final touches on my Easter sermon was also done on the fly since my new office was nothing but a desk, a chair, empty shelves, and an old Remington manual typewriter that was to become my technological companion. It took almost a year before the church council would decide that maybe it would be a good idea to provide me with an electric typewriter.

Easter Sunday was a wonderful way to begin my ministry. The day was sunny and bright, the three-hundred-seat sanctuary was filled to overflowing with four hundred in attendance, and the addition of an Easter breakfast gave Carolyn and me the opportunity to do a very informal "meet and greet."

Duane: Thinking Homiletically

You might note that Roger put the finishing touches of his sermon together for that first Easter just before delivering it. My experience in working with Roger over the years was that he often put his sermon together on Saturday night. Sermon-writing that late in the week is not something that most pastors want to be doing. But for Roger, it was a hallmark of his ministry. I remember driving by the church many times late on Saturday nights and seeing the light on in Roger's office where he was putting together his sermon.

I once asked him about this rather unusual habit. He said that although he wrote his sermon at the last minute, late on Saturday nights, he would think about what he would be saying all week long. On Monday morning, at the beginning of the week, he would read the scripture texts for the following Sunday. Then, throughout the week, he would mull it over, read material related to his sermon, and digest the scripture texts in the context of his life. In other words, the upcoming sermon was always in the back of his mind. He called this sermon methodology "thinking homiletically" (homiletics being another name for the art of preaching).

I never waited until Saturday night to finish my sermons. But over the years, I took to heart his notion of thinking homiletically.

Roger's First Week

Coming off the high of Easter Sunday, my first week was like floating on a cloud. The congregation seemed enthusiastic about my arrival. The building was just a few years old. Surely this was going to be the place where I belonged. But reality quickly set in when a representative from Northern States Power dropped by to say that because we hadn't paid the electric bill for the past two months, he was there to shut off the power. I told him that I was the new pastor and that I knew nothing about any unpaid electric bills. Unmoved, his face turned determined, and he said, "Well, unless you can pay me now, I'm going to have to shut off your electricity."

I hemmed and hawed for a second or two, and then I said, "Okay! Turn it off! We'll have a candlelight service next Sunday. That'll let the congregation know we need some money."

His jaw dropped, and he said, "I can't do that to a church!"

"No, go ahead," I said. "You've given me a golden opportunity to show the congregation they have to give more. Candles will be just fine!"

Stumbling for words, he said, "Do you think you can make a payment next month?"

I said, "I'll work on it!" And then he left—without turning off our electricity.

The next week, in a letter to the congregation, I described the visit by the Northern States Power employee and explained that his purpose had been to turn off the electricity. "Shocked" at the news, the congregation came up with the needed cash to square us with the power company.

Roger's Early Struggles

One of the first challenges I encountered when I came to St. Andrew's hinged on the fact that the congregation was deeply in debt. The new sanctuary accounted for much of the debt because $21,000 of the annual budget of $50,000 went to service the mortgage on the new building. The remaining $29,000 had to cover light, heat, salaries for the pastor and a secretary, and whatever program the congregation could afford.

Negotiating my salary should have tipped me off to the fact that St. Andrew's was living on a very tight budget with little in the way of wiggle room. When I sat down with the president of the congregation to discuss salary, he was quite blunt in saying that the best they could offer me was $8,000 per year. "But" he said, "we do have a newly constructed parsonage that you can live in for free." That may have sounded good to him, but the problem for me was that my current salary at Holy Trinity was $13,000, which included a housing allowance. The move to Mahtomedi would leave me $5,000 short and with a Minneapolis house to sell in a down market.

Those first six months after I took the call to St. Andrew's ended up being a financial tightrope for our family. Not only were we $5,000 short, but we still had to make mortgage payments on a house we no longer lived in. Every week, I would take the trip back to Minneapolis to mow the lawn. I even painted the house and bought new carpet to make the place more sellable. To tide us over, we took out a loan from the bank to pay for the mortgage on a house that wouldn't sell. Eventually, it did . . . for only $400 more than we had paid for the house four years earlier.

Mahtomedi—the promised "garden spot of the Twin Cities"—had changed in my mind to a garden with wilted flowers and grass that our personal financial drought had turned brown. If serving St. Andrew's was a call from God, he must have dialed the wrong number. With a wife and five kids to feed and clothe, the luster had rubbed off, and I began to wonder what I could possibly do to right my financial and professional ship.

The questions began to pile up. "Do I leave St. Andrew's and seek another call?" I was thirty-two years old. "Maybe I should go into some other line of work that could more adequately provide for my family?" If God had some plan for St. Andrew's that included me, then God would have to somehow let me know. All I knew was that something had to change.

Once again, Dr. Melvin Hammarberg, the president of the Minnesota Synod, was there to offer help. Sharing with him my dilemma, he suggested that I take advantage of some career counseling at what was then Ramsey Hospital. I took him up on it, and after completing a battery of tests, the counselor called me in and said, "Sit down, I'm going to tell you who you are!" I wasn't sure if the news would be good or bad. Then he said, "Roger knows exactly what the church is not—and he is very articulate about it. In fact, he's quite angry about it. But if he ever figures out what the church is—he will be gang-busters."

He went on to say that there was no way I was called to be any-thing but a pastor. The forms I filled out and the questions I answered made it crystal clear to him that it was in my bones. He went on to say, "Don't waste your time seeking out some other career. Instead, figure out what this lover's quarrel you're having with the church is all about, get it behind you, and go for it." The upshot was that I was stuck. I couldn't run from being a pastor. St. Andrew's was where I had landed. I was just going to have to make the best of it.

Hammarberg was very helpful, but the immediate question was how to get more money into the Eigenfeld bank account. The answer came in the form of peddling newspapers.

A *Minneapolis-Star Tribune* newspaper route had just become available in Mahtomedi, and we took it. I say *we* because the route had to be in my wife's name. I couldn't have another job without go-ing through all the hoops of getting permission from the church council. So, the easiest thing was for Carolyn to become the "owner" of the route.

Every afternoon, the newspaper truck would pull into our driveway, drop off one hundred copies, and away Carolyn and the kids would go. With hindsight, the newspaper route turned out to be a gift from God—both financially and in getting to know the neigh-borhood. Quite simply, by delivering those papers, we discovered where most of the members of St. Andrew's lived.

Sunday mornings, however, were quite a different story. On Sunday morning, the *Minneapolis-Star Tribune* truck would show up in our driveway at 3:00 a.m. There was no way in good conscience that I could rouse my wife at 3:00 a.m. and watch her go off into the sunrise while I stayed in bed. So, Sunday morning became my time to do the route.

Crawling out of bed to greet the newspaper truck, I loaded the papers into my station wagon and began my three-hour journey to complete the route. Arriving back home at 6:00 a.m., I took a shower, ate my breakfast, and then headed off to church to lead three services at 9:00, 10:00, and 11:00 a.m. After a busy Sunday morning, I came home, ate lunch, and then headed back to church to lead afternoon and evening youth activities.

The newspaper gig lasted about a year until someone at a church council meeting piped up and said, "I understand our pastor has a newspaper route. I don't think he should."

My response was simply, "I agree! Give me a raise and the newspaper route will end today." Within minutes, someone on the council made a motion to raise my salary, and the saga of the pastor and his family delivering newspapers was over. Looking back, it was the fastest raise I ever received.

Duane: Starting from Scratch

Someone once told me that for the first year, the best thing a new pastor could do in a new congregation was to simply "love the people." No big changes that first year. No radical ideas. No paradigm shifts. At least not that first year. Rather, during that time, get to know the people. Listen to them. Try to understand the rhythm of the church. Find out about the culture. Then, after a year of loving the people, trust will develop. It is then, after trust has been established, that, if needed, the new pastor can work on change. Even so, there will always be obstacles and challenges in that first year or more.

Roger has spelled out some of his early challenges at St. Andrew's, an established congregation. But what is it like to start a congregation from scratch, as a mission congregation? It's a fact that not many mission churches succeed. Yet, Paul Harrington and Shepherd of the Valley were able to do it. How?

Paul's Early Days at Shepherd of the Valley

When I moved my family to Apple Valley, Minnesota, in November of 1980, northern Dakota County was on the cusp of an explosive expansion. Prior to 1980, the Cedar Avenue bridge over the Minnesota River was a narrow two-lane structure that actually had a wooden deck. It was said that when two trucks crossed traveling in opposite directions, their side-view mirrors often nicked each other and sometimes even shattered.

But all of that was about to change. Cedar Avenue (State Highway 77) was given a total make-over, including a brand-new multi-lane bridge, which had the effect of something like pulling the cork out of the end of a bottle. Because of this beautiful new highway, easy access was now available to Eagan, Apple Valley, Rosemount, Lakeville, and even Farmington. We were definitely at the right place at the right time.

Over the next few years, Dakota County grew at a dizzying rate. School District 196 was opening a new school seemingly every other year and is currently one of the largest districts in the state of Minnesota. At one point, Ridges Hospital's maternity ward was averaging twelve to fifteen births a day. And, of course, new houses and new subdivisions were popping up everywhere. If memory serves, the county grew by 15 percent in just one year.

In the months of November and December of 1980, and later in the warmer months, I did door knocking, flyer distribution, advertising in the local newspapers, and meeting with city and school officials as well as several area pastors. One pastor told me that Apple Valley did not need another Lutheran church. He did say that he would try to be cordial. His church had just built a new sanctuary and was heavily in debt, so I am sure I was seen as "competition."

An early task was to secure a place to worship. Jerry Cassem, a good Lutheran and a school official, was helpful in getting us into the

Rosemount Elementary School gymnasium on Sunday mornings. Almost all of the schools in the district were already in use on Sundays, which tells you that we were by no means the only new mission church in this area. Lots of denominations were represented in Apple Valley in the 1980s. We stayed in Rosemount for fourteen months until the Greenleaf Elementary school gym opened up in Apple Valley. This was much closer to what we thought of as our "prime location" for the future.

So it was on a very cold morning on January 11, 1981, that we held our first service of worship with fifty-three pioneering souls in attendance. These folks were not all strangers—some had met several times with Pastor Howard Sortland, who had spent a month or two in Apple Valley doing a feasibility study before our arrival. In the following weeks, we formed a steering committee, organized a Sunday school, put together an adult choir of eight members that met in the Austad home (Gene Austad and I comprised the entire bass section), started weekly confirmation classes in our home with three confirmands (Scott Solomonson, Julie Solomonson, and Scott Brunick), and started writing a monthly newsletter in my basement office. It was a very busy time, to say the least.

I need to give credit to those early pioneers who put up with all the inconveniences of not having a building to call our own. Most of us had a couple of boxes in the trunks of our cars full of things like hymnals, paraments, communion ware, choir music, Sunday school materials, welcome signs, and office supplies. But in a strange way, all of this "hardship" brought us together. Meetings were held in homes or in local restaurants. Sometimes we rented or borrowed rooms in other churches. But through it all, there was a bonding, a shared vision, a commitment to Christ and his church, and a real sense that this was worth all the time, effort, money, and prayers that we put into it. And, of course, it was. There was a standing joke that the congregation that sweats together also sticks together.

It should also be noted that a growing community does not guarantee a growing church. There must also be some intentionality. As one of our bishops likes to say, churches grow because of love, leadership, and location. I believe that Shepherd of the Valley had all three of these qualities. Another line I often quote is that churches are not museums for saints but hospitals for sinners. All are welcome.

I discovered early on in my ministry that people today can sometimes be desperate for community. It is quite possible for people, even in urban and suburban society, to live very isolated lives. There is a great line in one of Harold Kushner's books about his friend Goldstein, who goes to the synagogue each week for worship—but mostly to see his friends.

This is not all bad. It interests me that every picture of the church in the New Testament is relational: the vine and the branches, the hen and her brood, the shepherd and his flock, the temple of living stones all joined together, and St. Paul's great analogy of the human body. Christ is the head, but all the parts are connected, so the hand cannot say to the foot, "I have no need of you." And again, what is the first thing in all of creation that God speaks out against? It is not some great sin or abomination. It is loneliness. God said, "It is not good that the man should be alone." Bottom line, we were made for community, and where better to find this precious gift than in the church? Hospitality should always be one of the most prominent hallmarks of the Christian church. So a welcoming fellowship was a top priority as Shepherd of the Valley developed over the years.

You know, these days, I often hear young people say something like this: "I am a spiritual person, but I have no time for organized religion." I would argue that it is very difficult to maintain a vital, growing, and life-enriching faith apart from the community of faith we call the Church.

The early years of any mission church are a critical time. The mortality rate for new congregations in most national church bodies is nearly 60 percent. But we were fortunate. When we finally opened the doors to our new building in December of 1984 after worshipping in two elementary schools for most of four years, the response was almost overwhelming.

One of the most necessary parts of starting a new church is to develop a critical mass of people who are bonding with their pastor and with each other. If this doesn't happen—and it does not happen by accident—the church will not succeed. These early pioneers must be selfless people with a shared vision and excitement for this new ministry. I did have several families tell me that they would join once we had built our building and had "everything up and running." Thank the good Lord for those who were willing to stay the course for those nearly four years when we had no building to call our own.

Paul: Early Hurdles

I learned early on that mission churches tend to attract two kinds of people. One kind is the folks who come to share in the exciting beginnings of a new congregation. Wonderful people. I often told them that one day, they could look back over their lives and see that the sacrifices they had made had brought about a church that will continue to serve the community for decades to come, if not longer.

The second kind of person is the one who comes with an agenda of sorts that they could not get enacted at their last church. They are good people with good intentions that can sometimes be a bit misdirected. I recall one woman who told me almost as soon as we met that I, as a pastor, would "never have a vote on the church council," I told her politely that I did not need a vote on the church council and that if

I had one and a vote was so close that it needed me to be the tie breaker, I would not vote anyway. If any action taken by the council is that divisive (50/50 split), then someone needs to go back to the drawing board. For the record, I found out later that this woman had belonged to three other area churches before coming to us. Bottom line: mission pastors should be aware that a few folks come with real baggage that has to be managed with kid gloves.

This same woman, being somewhat persuasive and highly suspicious of just how I conducted my ministry, formed a small pastoral evaluation committee that met for over a year. Because I had my office in my home to save the church rent money, I mentioned in a Mother's Day sermon that while working at home, I sometimes also helped babysit our infant daughter when Margaret was off to work for a few hours. Again, this woman became convinced that I was sitting around the house all day and doing nothing.

At this point, I called in our synod bishop, who came to the rescue and put an end to this somewhat confused and misdirected effort. The committee soon disbanded upon the bishop's strong recommendation. In the wake of all this, about six families left the church—of whom, two later returned. What was most interesting is that after this, the mood of the church became much more positive, and the church took off like a rocket.

It was also during this time that Bishop Lowell Erdahl, who was a good friend and who had officiated at the wedding of Margaret and me ten years earlier, suggested we get some counseling courtesy of the ALC. He recognized that we were a little "beat up" by all of this. We got full psych evaluations and were declared healthy and well-suited for parish ministry. That was surely good news, as self-doubt can sometimes start to set in. Looking back on it now, I think it was a growing time for all who were involved.

Another challenge was having oversight from four different mission development directors in less than five years. The first two directors died somewhat unexpectedly, both of coronary-related issues. My third director was just filling in for the time being. The fourth director proved to be most helpful because he had, in fact, developed a new mission church. I was thankful for his advice, though by this time, we were up and running as a church.

Worship attendance shot up dramatically after each new building dedication. Apparently, people love to see such "brick and mortar" progress. Another issue that arose as we grew bigger was that some of the folks who grew up in small towns wanted their little, cozy church family to also stay small. It took me a while to figure out what was going on here. Their desire was that the birth rate and death rate would happen with some kind of parity. In other words, almost no growth. Well, this was, of course, totally unrealistic. Our county was growing by double-digit percentages every year. We actually had some families leave the church because we were getting "too big." I wrote about this matter in the church newsletter several times, reminding people that this is not like a faucet that you open or shut at will. Does not the Bible encourage evangelism and church growth? Who are we to think we should or could somehow stifle growth? Could we control the work of the Holy Spirit? Bob White, our youth director at the time, jokingly suggested a "Rude Sunday" where we would go about insulting anyone who looked like a prospective member. He also called for "Bad Breath Sunday" and "Ugly Tie Sunday."

Over time, people got the message that growth was going to be with us for quite some time, though I had personally always said that I would rather do a good job of ministry with three hundred people than a lousy job of ministry with three thousand. I recall the shocked look of a council member who asked me what we would do when a three-year pledge drive concluded and we still had a big mortgage. I told him that we would have another three-year pledge drive and another one after that until the mortgage was paid in full.

Related to all this was another challenge of getting the synod and the national church to understand exactly what was happening in our area. We had never planned on becoming a megachurch, but the numbers were just astonishing. At one point, our area of the county had 210,000 residents, one-third of whom were Lutherans or folks who would be comfortable in a Lutheran Church. That meant that, theoretically, we could have had seventy Lutheran churches of 1,000 members each! Instead, we had but a handful of churches, some of which were worshipping 100 or 200 a Sunday. I tried to tell officials that our county was unlike any other county in the nation in terms of speed of growth and density of Lutherans. It mostly fell on deaf ears. We needed several more churches in this unique area in order to handle the growth.

Duane: Bumpy Beginnings

As I think about Roger's beginning at St. Andrew's and Paul's beginning at Shepherd of the Valley, two things stand out for me: 1) they both had a bumpy beginning, and 2) they both got some counseling at a crucial time early in their ministries at those churches. This counseling helped them set out on a course of amazing ministry for years to come.

Being a pastor can be a lonely experience. Sometimes there is self-doubt. Sometimes there is conflict. Sometimes there is a need to find help. Thank goodness that both Roger and Paul were able to get help and support when they needed it. The whole church is better because they did.

Chapter 3

LEADERSHIP

Duane: Similarities in Leadership

John C. Maxwell, a pastor and author of several books on leadership, has written that *"people buy into the leader before they buy into the vision."* That's certainly what happened with Roger and Paul in their respective ministries. What was it about them that so appealed to people? How did they get the skills to be leaders? How did they see themselves as leaders?

Roger: Trust Is the Key

When I began my ministry and was still wet behind the ears, I had no clue what it meant to be a leader. In fact, I can't remember a single course in seminary that prepared us to lead anything. Our heads had been filled with facts about the Bible and church history, but we hadn't taken a single course on how to lead a congregation. That, apparently, was something that we were supposed to learn once we got a congregation of our own to lead. So, with minimal preparation other than a year of internship, I found myself stumbling into the future, not knowing where I was going. Someone once said, "If you don't know where you're going, any road will do." The only trouble is that many of those roads end up being dead ends.

By the time I arrived at St. Andrew's, I had, at least, acquired a few leadership tools in my toolbox. The experience of starting a congregation from scratch told me loud and clear that I didn't know very much about leading anything. Knowing that you don't know anything is truly a gift that, if embraced, can create a desire to fill your mind with new knowledge—in my case, with examples of leadership I might want to emulate.

And that's exactly what my second call at Richfield Lutheran gave me. Here, I had the opportunity to become a student, gleaning as much as I could from Harold Rasmussen, a gifted master at leadership. Rasmussen instinctively knew how to bring a congregation along with him, never getting too far ahead but still far enough in front that members were encouraged to want to take the next step. Richfield Lutheran's growth was the product of steady and well-thought-out planning that took the congregation from one level to the next. On the outside, it looked as if it was a well-oiled machine that rarely stumbled, but on the inside, you quickly discovered that the reason for rarely stumbling was the sense of trust that had been built between the senior pastor, the church council, and the members. Trust had become the major building block that allowed the congregation to move confidently into the future. What this sense of trust also created was an immense sense of pride in being a member of Richfield Lutheran Church—members who then became evangelists out in the community, inviting friends and neighbors to share in the experience that they were enjoying.

When I came to St. Andrew's in 1972, it was Richfield Lutheran Church that became the model I began to put into play. Richfield wasn't perfect, but they were a model I knew from having worked in their midst. In many ways, I came to St. Andrew's with an image in my mind of what we might become. Richfield and St. Andrew's were, of course, two different congregations. Richfield had grown from 450 to 3,500 and had developed a very mature ministry in a thriving urban setting with three pastors and a large staff. At St. Andrew's, we were at 800 members in a town of less than 3,000, with nothing more than a solo pastor and a lone secretary and part-time accountant. So, where did we go from there?

Roger: The Church Growth Movement

In the 1970s and 1980s, there was, throughout America, a movement centered on church growth. Places like Fuller Seminary in Pasadena and the Crystal Cathedral in Garden Grove, California, were leaders in providing workshops and leadership conferences that laid out the basics of how to grow a church. Like a thirsty prospector looking for water, I began to attend as many church-growth conferences as my time and budget would allow. Some were worthwhile, others less so, but it was through this process of finding out what other pastors and congregations were doing that gave me insight into just how large and dynamic St. Andrew's could become. And each conference and speaker ended up offering a nugget or two of valuable information that I could absorb and employ in my ministry at St. Andrew's. After each conference, I would come back with the certainty that if someone else had helped to grow a congregation, they had already proven that it could be done. And if they could do it, why not St. Andrew's?

Duane: Learning Something New

Perhaps by now, it is obvious that church growth was important to Roger. One of his great leadership gifts was his passion and his ability to focus. His focus often was on evangelism—reaching others with the Good News of Jesus Christ. But how to do that, how to do evangelism was something he learned along the way.

So Roger, as mentioned above, went to conferences and workshops to find out more. Not only did he, himself, go, but he thought it was important for his staff to do so, too. He strongly encouraged me to attend numerous events and workshops. In addition, he also thought that it was important to scout out other fast-growing churches to see what they were doing.

So I, too, was able to go to conferences at Fuller Seminary and Schuller's Church Growth Institute, as well as a number of other conferences and workshops. And I learned a lot. For instance, at Lyle Schaller's Yokefellow Institute, I learned that the nursery is the second-most-important room in the church for church growth after the sanctuary. Why? Well, it's the smell. With a straight face, Schaller said that, for newcomers, if the nursery smells like dirty diapers, they will go somewhere else. Who knew that?

Roger: You Can't Lead From the Middle

If someone is going to take on the role of leadership, they need to have some idea of where they want to go. Congregations have attempted to zero in on some of the "who, what, where, when, and why" by creating mission statements—short, easily remembered phrases that capture the essence of what the congregation is intending to do. But mission statements are only as good as the planning and execution that needs to accompany them. In other words, a desire to go on a trip to Paris remains only a desire unless a date is set, a ticket is bought, bags are packed, and you are in your seat ready to go.

And here is where most mission statements begin to break down. So often, mission statements are the result of well-intentioned ideas that have been put together by well-meaning leaders and staff members, but they never stick. The reality is that unless someone takes ownership of those ideas, begins to flesh them out, and creates a plan that will bring them to life, they will remain ideas but never actual ministries.

One of the lessons I learned over the years is that you can't lead from the middle. If you're going to be a leader, you need to begin to act and behave as one. What that means is that a leader needs to be willing to risk being wrong. Not every idea is a good one, but sometimes, there exists within that idea a kernel of possibility that just needs a chance to flourish and grow.

Roger: A Church in Slovakia

The need to get out in front and exert a degree of risk-taking leadership was sort of forced on me and St. Andrew's in an encounter I had with a Lutheran congregation in Slovakia that, under communist rule, had been meeting underground. When the Berlin Wall came down in 1989, they decided that now was the time to become a viable, visible congregation with an actual building. Amongst themselves, they had sacrificially collected some money toward the project. The crux of the matter, however, was that they needed a whole lot more help in accomplishing their goal.

We learned about their desire to build a church through the ELCA. In 1991, a trip to Slovakia was arranged wherein members of the congregation would be in attendance along with members of the city council—many of whom were recent former members of the communist party. In a room with a dozen members of the congregation on one side and a half dozen city leaders on the other, the conversation seemed to be headed toward a deadlock. City leaders were hesitant though somewhat willing to give permission to build a Lutheran church, but where would the money come from? It was then that I just blurted out, "St. Andrew's will pay for the building!"

Eyes quickly trained on me, my wife gasped, and someone said, "What did you say?"

"I said, St. Andrew's will pay for the building!"

There was a look of surprise and a sigh of relief from the congregation members and a look of shock from city leaders, but if St. Andrew's would pay for the building, the city would give permission.

Now what? And here's where the risk of leadership comes in. Going back to St. Andrew's and standing before the congregation the next Sunday, I announced that I had just promised folks in Slovakia that we would pay for their new building. The cost, I said, would be $190,000 (things were a lot cheaper in Slovakia in 1989.) So, the challenge was placed before them. And, amazing as it may sound, over the next two Sundays, all of the $190,000 was raised.

Today, if you take a trip to Prievidza, Slovakia, you will see a beautiful building that seats just over two hundred people, where in the entryway, a plaque says, "A gift from the people of St. Andrew's Lutheran Church, Mahtomedi, Minnesota."

Duane: Servant Leadership

One of the most important aspects of leadership, especially in the church, is the notion of servant leadership. Jesus embodied it in his life and death. He showed us how it is done. Likewise, to be a follower of Jesus means that pastors and other leaders in the church are also called to embody that style of leadership. It means getting your hands dirty, helping those who need help, being of service—all the while doing so with humility. Although Roger points out that "you can't lead from the middle," this idea is not mutually exclusive from leading through service, example, and humility.

Paul: Philosophy of Leadership

I must confess that I was not much of a philosophy student in college. It was all just a bit too abstract and ethereal for me. I am more of a hands-on, nuts-and-bolts kind of person. In the early days of a mission church, people join partly because they like you—at least enough to share in your vision and your future goals for the congregation. You are the point person for almost all matters of congregational life. But as the church grows and more staff is added, it has to become a shared ministry. This I learned early on. I believe I rewrote my job description at least a dozen times over the years. In other words, I kept giving away more and more work that I had previously done, just hoping that whoever took on this or that task would do a credible job. And for the most part, that was the result. In some ways, it was my job to minister to the staff so that they could minister to the congregation. I always told them that I wanted them to do well and to feel some real fulfillment in their work. In short, the better they looked, the better I looked. And the worse they looked, the worse I looked. I've always said, "A good leader does not create a bunch of followers. A good leader creates a bunch of leaders."

My vision for the church was simply that I wanted to do good ministry. Solid, engaging preaching (I worked hard on my sermons), good educational programs for all ages, a music ministry—both vocal and instrumental—that enhanced worship, youth programs that really excited and engaged kids, various events that strengthened the bonds of fellowship, mission trips and outreach programs for youth and adults alike, with generous benevolence giving, pastoral-care ministries for weddings, funerals, baptisms, divorces, and counseling in general. We were a full-service church in every sense of the word.

I recall a family that joined specifically because their child, big into sports, could not get confirmation classes at their former church that would fit their sports schedule. My pastoral assistant, Cris Ireland, assured the family that we would do whatever it took to make it work for this young person. I think Cris would have found a teacher for a 5:00 a.m. class if that was the only option. It was this kind of solid, traditional, caring, high-quality ministry that became the hallmark of Shepherd of the Valley for many folks.

Over the years of our development as a church, the American Lutheran Church (ALC), and later, the Evangelical Lutheran Church in America (ELCA) held some seminars, retreats, and conferences specifically for pastors of mission churches. But I soon noticed something. Not one of the featured speakers or consultants had ever done a mission church themselves. So I just quit going because they were not helpful. Instead, I called up some local Lutheran pastors who were in growing churches. I told them that I wanted to buy them lunch while I picked their brains. They all agreed. I chose them because they were maybe three to five years ahead of Shepherd of the Valley, and I simply wanted to know what was working and not working for them. No need to invent the wheel over again. These lunches went on for several years, and they were all very helpful.

Truthfully, I think there is a real bias in the Lutheran church hierarchy about larger, growing congregations. There is a prevailing feeling among some that if you are vital, healthy, and growing, you have somehow sold out to the world. And if you are shrinking and dying as a congregation, it's because you are being faithful to the gospel.

Paul: What About Church Councils?

Some years ago, a staff member at Shepherd of the Valley (SOTV) said to me that one thing he worried about a lot was the monthly church council meeting. When I asked why he felt this way, he replied, "It's a night when a group of well-intentioned people meet to make major decisions about an organization that they love but that they really know very little about in terms of its inner workings. And because of this, things can quickly go haywire if not very carefully managed." We all know stories of churches that, for whatever reason, were not well managed, and the results were disastrous. You know the old line: a camel is a horse designed by a committee.

Someone once asked me who has the authority in the local parish. My answer almost surprised me. I told this person that the senior pastor had some authority, as did the other pastors on the staff. Then the lay staff also has some authority. Add to this list the congregational president who has some authority, as does the church council. Then, too, the congregation has some authority when duly assembled as a voting body. Also, the local synod and the national church office have some authority. I have just listed eight potential persons or groups, all of whom have greater or lesser degrees of authority in the local church. Anyone can quickly see how messy this matter of authority is in the parish. I have often thought (quite honestly, with some degree of envy) about how different this is to, say, the military—or even corporate America—where there are very clear lines of authority. In these two settings, there is almost no ambiguity as to who is in charge and who is not.

Added to all this is the very biblical picture of the pastor as shepherd who is called to be a servant-leader. And what does that title and role imply? When should I be a strong leader, and when should I be a servant, simply implementing the will of others in the congregation? This gets very dicey sometimes. I also recall the line about a general who got so far ahead of his troops that they started to think he was the enemy, and he got shot in the back (or the behind). When is a person to lead, when to follow, and when to walk alongside?

So, here are some answers about what we did at Shepherd of the Valley. One, we relied heavily on our nominating committee to select the absolute best "team players" we could find to serve on the council—people who had the best interests of the church and community at heart. I would even bring a preselected list of names to the committee, and I would not be too bashful in wholeheartedly recommending them as nominees. Usually, the committee was grateful for the work that had already been done so that we were not just pulling names out of the air.

Secondly, we never nominated two people for the same position. This is a huge mistake made by many churches. Why do this when we have already decided who is the best person for the job and we know very well that all those not selected are going to go home that day thinking that their church has just rejected them? This is a silly and hurtful way to run a church. So, when the congregation gathered to vote, we always asked for nominations from the floor, and hearing none (or very few), we either voted on paper or moved a unanimous ballot. This way, we got the best candidate we could find to serve for a two-year term, with one opportunity to run for a second term. Some of our best and most committed people chose to re-up for another two years. We never wanted to "burn out" our people, something churches are notorious for doing! We also tried to keep council meetings to ninety minutes with a very tight agenda. It did not always work out, but people today really do appreciate it if we do not waste their time, which people value almost as much as their money.

Another important point: over time, as the church grew, the church council became less and less of a decision-making body. There were major decisions that simply could not wait thirty days until the next council meeting. Here is the beauty of a well-oiled staff. Suppose the senior pastor or any other pastor has a good idea. It gets discussed and vetted by the pastors and later by a staff of thirty, forty, or more. The council is kept in the loop via email, and the staff needs to fully justify its thinking and, eventually, its actions. Be careful to never overstep your authority, and never railroad anything! But by the time this decision gets to the council or to the congregational meeting, seven pastors and a staff of dozens have already given their tacit approval. Very few times did anyone challenge this process, and over the years, it served us well. In time, we even told the council that they were not a decision-making body. Their job was to provide oversight, to correct any wayward plans or ideas, and to help disseminate information to the whole congregation. They also voted on any major issues like the budget, buying or selling property, and calling a pastor. But their main task was to serve almost as cheerleaders for the staff and all the ministries of the congregation.

Last item. I had a standing policy that if we ever voted on anything in the church involving the staff, the council, or the whole congregation and we did not get at least a 75 percent approval (higher is even better), I would then ask to table the resolution for further study and input. The quickest way to split a church is to have a very divisive vote taken where half the people go home feeling alienated and unheard.

When proposing an idea that might get some push back, I would just briefly mention it at a council meeting as something to think about. A month later, I would bring it up again for some fairly brief discussion. The next month, I would ask for a straw vote that had no meaning other than to test the waters. At the next month's meeting, I would ask for a much more in-depth discussion on the proposal. Finally, a month later, it almost always passed, with some of the council members thinking it was their idea in the first place. Truthfully, if the proposal got shot down, likely it was not a good idea anyway. Patience can be important for leadership.

Duane: Group Wisdom

I knew that Roger and Paul were leaders when I worked with them. No doubt about that. But that did not mean that they made every decision all by themselves. They both respected and encouraged the ideas of others. They utilized the collective wisdom of those around them quite often.

For instance, Roger led lots of retreats. I mean lots of retreats. One of the main reasons for the retreats with decision-making groups like staff and church council members was to brainstorm ideas, build group consensus, and—most importantly—to build group ownership. In other words, Roger used these retreats as a way of getting at some group wisdom.

Similarly, Paul did not dictate what would happen at SOTV. Rather, he built harmony and accord. The way he did that was often through one-on-one connections—over a cup of coffee, in the office, or, often, in the hallways of the church.

Leadership means knowing when to get out front and be bold with decisions, when to build accord, when to empower, when to encourage, and even when to stop.

Duane: Pastoral Leadership Lists

Paul has told me that Lowell Erdahl was a mentor for him in his ministry. Erdahl has written a little book called "10 Habits for Effective Ministry." According to Paul, this book should be mandatory reading for every pastor and seminarian in the church. He calls it his "Bible" for parish ministry. It is that good. In the book, Erdahl has ten chapters that list the qualities of pastoral leaders.

Both Paul and Roger have their own "leadership lists." These are important items that every pastor who aspires to leadership should keep in mind. Paul has ten (as in the Ten Commandments) and Roger has twelve (as in the twelve disciples).

Paul's Leadership List: What a Pastor Needs

Every pastor needs:

- A deep and abiding faith in God;
- To be highly organized and a good motivator of people;

- To possess good relational skills;
- A supportive partner, if in a relationship;
- To have the ability to raise large amounts of money;
- Reasonably good health: physical, mental, and spiritual;
- A vision and the know-how to cast that vision;
- To be quite good at speaking, writing, and general corre-
  spondence;
- To see work as a calling (vocation) and not just a job; and
- A willingness to work long hours, especially during the early
  years of development.

Roger's Leadership List: How to Behave as a Leader

- **Not every idea is for the moment**—some need to be allowed
  to be planted and take root until the time is right.
- **Every call is an interim call.** The congregation will go on long
  after we are gone. That's the way it has always been.
- **Ministry is a lifestyle.** It is not something you can do on a
  part-time basis. You need to be planted with both feet for the
  long haul. Join hands with members of the congregation to
  develop the place you are at into something spectacular.
- **Work with leaders in the congregation** to create three-year,
  five-year, and ten-year plans . . . and make them public with
  measurable goals.
- **Learn how to delegate responsibilities.** Do those things that
  only you can do and allow others the opportunity to expand
  the ministry by utilizing their gifts and talents.
- **Learn to say no**. You cannot do everything, nor should you be
  expected to. Someone said, "Jesus died for the church so you
  don't have to."

- **It's okay to fail.** Some ideas are like trial balloons. Some work, others do not. You'll never know unless you try.
- **Give others credit.** It is amazing what can be accomplished if you don't care who gets the credit.
- **Say "YES" when you can** to an idea or a request from a staff member. Reserve "NO" for those times when you know it is inappropriate or not in the best interest of the congregation.
- **Create retreats** for staff members and council leaders. Give them and yourself the chance to get to know one another better and to allow ideas to simmer and grow.
- **Take care of yourself!** Take your day off! Go on vacation! Attend your kids' concerts and games! Take care of your marriage! Have fun! Enjoy life!

Duane: How Their Leadership Styles Felt to Me

There were many things that were similar about Roger and Paul in their leadership styles. Having worked closely with each of them, I saw them in action. Here are some leadership traits and skills that I observed in both of them:

- *Trustworthiness: In a profession where trust is essential, they were able to gain the trust of those around them.*
- *Integrity: They were both strongly ethical people. They walked the walk.*
- *People skills: They somehow made people feel good about being with them and about being a part of the church.*
- *Preaching: Over and over, from people in both congregations, I heard people comment about how they loved to hear them preach. Although very different in style, they both were connecting to people through their sermons.*

- **Remembering names:** *Paul, in particular, was renowned for this ability. But both worked hard at calling people by their names.*
- **Empowering:** *They had the knack of making staff people and volunteers feel that they mattered and that what they were doing mattered.*
- **Work ethic:** *They set an example for everyone else on the staff and in the congregation by working hard for the sake of the gospel.*
- **Faith:** *Although neither Roger nor Paul were "in-your-face" types, still their faith in Jesus Christ was evident by their joy in what they were doing.*
- **Sense of humor:** *Being with each of them was fun because they both were so playful.*

Despite these similarities, they also had different styles of leadership. Roger's leadership was always pretty assertive. He had a vision, and he simply encouraged people to catch that vision and take the ride with him. He once told me that soon after he became the pastor at St. Andrew's, a member came to his office and asked if they could leave a plaque with Roger. The plaque read, "Make Haste Slowly!" Certainly, Roger took the first part of that phrase to heart. Not so much the second part. A favorite quote of Roger's comes from Dwight Eisenhower, who said, "Leadership is like a piece of string. If you push it, it crumbles. If you pull it, it moves." Roger led by pulling.

In contrast to Roger, Paul's style of leadership was much more indirect and encouraging. An apt quote to summarize Paul's style comes from George Patton, who said, "Never tell people how to do things. Tell them what to do and they will surprise you with their ingenuity." Paul simply pointed us in a direction and let us go about doing our work, always encouraging and supporting us.

You might say that Roger's style was inspirational, and Paul's style was educational. Roger focused on youth ministry. Paul focused on ministry in general. Roger loved retreats and conferences. Paul would rather connect one on one. Roger thought stewardship should be high profile. Paul took a much more subtle approach. In other words, they were different types of leaders because they were different types of people.

Warren Bennis has said, "Becoming a leader is synonymous with becoming yourself. It is precisely that simple—and it is also that difficult." Paul and Roger have shown me that leadership means being comfortable and confident in one's own skin. However, their styles of leadership were different, their styles worked for them. I count both of them as great mentors to me in how, as a leader, the main thing is to be yourself. Lead with integrity and honesty. People will follow. In my opinion, that is something that will be helpful in any congregational setting for any pastor.

Chapter 4

STEWARDSHIP

Duane: Lots of Experience

As senior pastors in very large churches, an important role for both Roger and Paul was managing the finances of the church. Probably the most important aspect of this role was the leadership they provided in fundraising or, as it's called in the church, stewardship.

Both Roger and Paul led annual stewardship campaigns to help with the general budget. These usually took place sometime in the fall of the year. In addition, they were both leaders in numerous capital campaigns designed to help raise funds for special building projects.

These two men have vast experience in the area of stewardship. Each of them led forty or more stewardship campaigns during their ministries at *their respective churches. How did they do that? What did they emphasize? What did they learn?*

Roger: Stewardship Means "Blessed to be a Blessing"

In 1973, I was in my second year at St. Andrew's and had begun to put together a men's group that would meet on an occasional basis. Usually, a special guest was invited to come and share a bit of his life's story. Over the years, some pretty interesting folks addressed the group. One time, it even included a visit from Herb Brooks prior to his becoming the head coach of the 1980 USA Olympic Hockey team. Herb lived in Mahtomedi, and his fame as the coach who defeated the Russians in what was to become known as the "Miracle on Ice" was history yet to be written. So, many saw Herb as just a neighbor, and only about twenty men showed up for that event. If we would have scheduled his visit after that fabulous victory, we could have packed the place.

In that second year of my ministry in Mahtomedi, I invited a friend by the name of Cliff Fox to come and speak to the group. Cliff was one of the directors of Lutheran Social Service of Minnesota (LSS) and had a charm, charisma, and sense of joy about him that captivated anyone with whom he came into contact. While setting up the time to come and speak, he asked me what I wanted him to speak about. "Oh," I said, "just tell them about LSS and anything else you think they might enjoy hearing."

Well, it was the "anything else you think they might enjoy hearing" that opened the door to a complete change in my life and that of St. Andrew's. Cliff did tell an interesting story about the mission and message of LSS, but then he veered off into territory about himself and his family that ended up having a lasting effect on me and my ministry.

Somehow, and I don't know how he got into it, Cliff started to talk about the role of tithing, giving 10 percent of a person's income to the work of the Lord. He talked about how he and his wife would sit down on an annual basis and figure out how much they would give to God's work in the world. He said that the conversation extended to his children as well. Each one would figure out from their allowance and part-time jobs how much they would be setting aside as their tithe. Cliff went on with such enthusiasm about tithing and how much fun it was for their family that I expected that the family dog was probably tithing as well.

Well, after the gathering had concluded and most of the men had left, I thanked Cliff for his presentation, and then, in a sort of off-handed manner, I said, "Now, Cliff, you don't really give 10 percent of your income to the church, do you?" Cliff pulled back a bit, looked me square in the eye, hit me hard in the sternum with his index finger three times, and said, "Roger, nothing is going to happen in your life or the life of your family or the life of this church until you do!" Cliff had made his painful point—a point that I not only felt in my sternum but that caused me to seriously consider, for the very first time, the role of tithing in my life.

Roger: Bitter and Angry

The sting of having accepted the call to St. Andrew's with the reduction in salary that caused bills to pile up due to the mortgage we were still paying on the still-unsold house we owned in Minneapolis had taken its toll. This dream call to the garden spot of the Twin Cities had caused me to become bitter and angry with myself and with God. It was a bitterness and anger that boiled inside and even got me to the point where I wanted to just chuck this whole ministry thing and find something that could actually pay the bills. And, when it came to personally giving financially to St. Andrew's, my only thought was that I shouldn't be expected to give anything—the fact of the matter was that they owed me.

After suffering the three-fold index-finger sting to my chest from Cliff, I shrugged my shoulders, bid him adieu, and went home with my head still ringing with the words, "Nothing is going to happen in your life or that of your family or the life of this church until you do." As I walked through the parsonage door, my wife asked the proverbial question, "Well, how did it go?" I shared the index-finger message from Cliff about tithing with her, and she said, "We always tithed in our home when I was growing up. Do you want me to figure out what a tithe for us would be?"

"Yeah, go ahead," I responded, not thinking much about what she had just said.

The next day, she had a sheet of paper on which she had written two budget scenarios. One had the meager, miserly, and, as far as I was concerned, grudge contribution to the church. The other showed how much a tithe would be. But it didn't end there. With a matter-of-fact tone in her voice, she said that if we were going to tithe, we would have just $50 to make it until the next paycheck, which was a week away. That, quite frankly, was going to be quite a stretch with five kids, a dog, a gerbil, and three goldfish to feed. I wish I could say that I prayerfully considered which way to go, but I can't. Instead, I ignored the whole thing, shrugged my shoulders, walked out the door, and headed over to church, leaving my wife in limbo as to what we should do.

The answer came the next Sunday when I walked into the house after morning worship. She greeted me and then said, "Well, I did it!"

"What did you do?" I said.

"I made out a check for the tithe and threw it into the offering plate!"

We now had fifty bucks left in our checkbook, and God was going to have to figure out how we were going to make it to the end of the week. Most certainly, I had no clue.

But during that week, some miracles began to take place. Some of them I pulled off on my own by taking all the pop bottles that had refunds coming and cashing them in for a couple of bucks. I also filled my station wagon with newspapers and carted them off to get a huge $6.50 for them. I even found out that I could get milk and bread on credit at the local dairy, which I immediately took advantage of. But the most unexpected miracle was on Wednesday of that week when I went to the mailbox and pulled out a letter that contained a check from a magazine called *Alive Now*. I had completely forgotten that about six months earlier, I had sent them three articles in hopes that they would be accepted for publication. Well, they decided to buy them for a grand total of $60. So with the $50 in the checkbook, the refunds for the pop bottles, and the $6.50 for those piles of papers—and now, the $60.00 from *Alive Now*—we were able to rearrange a few things in our budget and from that moment on became tithers.

Roger: Everything Changed

There's a lot more to this story, but I can tell you that tithing changed everything when that first check was thrown into the offering plate by a wife with more faith and trust than me. What tithing has done is that it has automatically caused us to prioritize our spending. After all, if we're going to set aside at least 10 percent of our income as a tithe, we're naturally going to have to make sure the leftover 90 percent takes care of everything else we have to pay for. And we stuck with it. We continued to tithe even as this bunch of kids went off to college—all of them heading off to Lutheran colleges with the familiar names of Luther, St. Olaf, Gustavus, and Augsburg. It wasn't easy, but somehow God performed the miracle of giving our kids the college education we had hoped and dreamed they might have from the day they were born.

But there's another benefit when the pastor becomes a tither. It allows the pastor to boldly challenge the rest of the congregation to do the same. Not that you're bragging about your giving—rather, it's a telling of the blessings that come to a life that finally has its priorities straight. It also allows you, as the tither, to become a *giver*, a person who participates in being blessed to be a blessing, instead of a *getter*, a person who doesn't recognize that everything we have is a gift from God.

Roger: Don't Join If You Don't Want to Pledge

When someone walks through the doors of any congregation, they are guests and should be treated as such. After all, visitors have a lot of options and choices on how they are going to spend their days, and for them to choose to take the time to get in their cars, journey to your church, find seats, participate as best they can, and then go back home requires no less than three hours of their time. For that effort, they need to be thanked and invited to come back. As long as they are a visitor, the courteous thing is to give them the best welcome that we possibly can.

But once they decide to join, everything changes.

In new member sessions, I unashamedly challenged each prospective member with the words, "If you intend to join, we expect a pledge!" It is most certainly an attention-getter as heads pop up, eyes widen, and a strange sense of discomfort begins to come over the room. Some are not sure that they heard what I said, but it starts to sink in when I share the reasons for my expectation.

• You're in a building that was paid for by someone else.

- You are experiencing the talent of a staff that is bringing you the best in music, worship, education, youth ministry, and a whole array of programs and opportunities that are paid for by the gifts of those who are members and friends of the congregation.
- You're standing on the shoulders of those who have gone before. Their offerings and tithes made St. Andrew's what it is today.
- Now, if you become a member, you will be joining the ranks of those who are financially contributing to move St. Andrew's into the future.

In other words, we had expectations that you would be a companion with us in moving the ministry of St. Andrew's forward. Unlike American Express, which says, "Membership has privileges" at St. Andrew's, we believed that "Membership has responsibilities." One of those responsibilities, in addition to regular worship, prayer, and reception of Holy Communion, is to financially support the work of St. Andrew's. After explaining this to them, we would give each of them a pledge card to take home, pray about, and return the next Sunday. Interestingly, few decided not to join. Most everyone completed a pledge card. The dollar amount was up to them. We always challenged them to become tithers. We encouraged them to consider giving a percentage of their income to the work of the church. If they were not a current tither, I would encourage them to consider giving 2 percent of their income to start and then encourage them to increase that amount by 2 percent each year. In just a matter of five years, they would be at the 10 percent level of giving. It was a plan that worked. It was an eye-opener for many. But, if the church was going to succeed and meet the expectations of providing a ministry that intended to change lives and, indeed, the world, the challenge had to be presented. As in most things, if you don't ask, you don't receive. St. Andrew's was a church that asked!

Roger: Budgets are Based on Pledges

At St. Andrew's, an annual budget can be put together with confidence that the income will be there to support the financial spending voted on by the congregation at the annual meeting. This is possible because the entire budget is based on pledges that members make during the annual stewardship-commitment drive. Sticking to basing the budget on pledges-in-hand avoids the temptation to throw out to the congregation any old hoped-for budget number that is more pie in the sky than can ever realistically be achieved. Basing the budget on pledges not only makes it easier on the treasurer who is in charge of paying the bills, but also, what you end up with at the end of the year is a report that shows that the financial health of the congregation is in the black, a report that the congregation and leadership can celebrate as successful managing of its members' contributions—all because you were realistic in putting together your spending plan.

Now, this doesn't mean that you never challenge the congregation to reach for the sky with challenge goals that exceed your current grasp. But that kind of challenge should be done during the stewardship campaign itself through publications, videos, temple talks, and sermons. Then, if the congregation rises to the challenge and increases their giving through pledges, consider it a victory worth celebrating. But don't put the cart before the horse. Always base the budget on pledges and other historical income flows that you can justify as realistic and attainable.

Roger: Regular Annual Stewardship Campaign

Most congregations have an annual stewardship campaign that happens at the same time every year, and St. Andrew's was no exception. Each year, I would scratch my head and try to figure out how to make that particular year's stewardship campaign something that would cause the members to want to support the work of St. Andrew's with renewed enthusiasm and commitment. Over the years, we did our fair share of mailings, brochures, video presentations, temple talks, every-member visits, and dinners.

One particular year stands out because of something we called "Friendly Gatherings." These took place over a period of three or four weeks and included a host family that would open their home to about twelve or fifteen people for a chat about the life of St. Andrew's and our hopes and dreams for what we could accomplish in the coming year. We had about four thousand members at the time, so it worked out that we would need to schedule forty different homes to accommodate those who might respond to the invitation.

As crazy as it might sound, it was actually a lot of fun. I would head off to one home at 7:00 p.m., at which I would give my presentation and ask those present to fill out their stewardship-commitment card at that gathering. After that, the host would come out with some coffee and pie while I picked up the cards and shuffled on off to the next home—where the host had already served the coffee and pie and was waiting for me to arrive so that I could give my presentation along with the request that they fill out their stewardship cards at that time.

For twenty nights with two gatherings per evening, I shared the hopes and dreams of St. Andrew's. But I also gave those present the opportunity to share with me their own dreams, hopes, and concerns. The result was that I was able to touch the lives of more members on a personal level than I had ever anticipated. The fabulous thing about those "Friendly Gatherings" was that they resulted in an increase in the amount pledged by 25 percent over the previous year. It was work, but, as I said, it was a lot of fun.

Roger: Pledge Weekend

Sometime during my tenure at St. Andrew's, I attended a conference for senior pastors where one of the topics discussed was the annual stewardship campaign. One of the pastors shared how every year, they would attempt to come up with all kinds of gimmicks and creative ideas on how to present the need to provide for the financial health of the congregation. He then went on to say that as interesting as some of these variations might sound, none of them were as effective as the annual Pledge Weekend. His reasoning was that people were going to come to church on the weekend anyway. You don't have to jump through a bunch of hoops to make sure they'll be in attendance. So, he figured, use one of those weekends and promote it as the time when every member is invited to complete a stewardship-commitment card.

And he was right. So, at every one of our weekend services on the first weekend in October, members are given the opportunity to come down the aisle to place their pledge on the altar as a sign of thankfulness and commitment. The wonderful part of this practice is that it becomes a part of the regular flow of life in the congregation. After a while, everyone knows that the first weekend in October will be set aside as Pledge Weekend. And having Pledge Weekend early in the fall gives the church council enough time to prepare a budget in preparation for the annual meeting, during which it will be voted on and hopefully approved.

Roger: Managing the Budget

One of the jobs of a senior pastor is making sure that there is enough cash flow to service the bills. That means that there needs to be a regular, scheduled time during the week when the pastor, business manager, and accountant sit down and go over the budget in detail.

I have to admit that I wasn't always on top of the finances and probably could have saved myself and the church council a good bit of head-scratching if I had been more consistent in paying attention to the financial health of the congregation. It's a task that must be done.

Roger: Building Programs

One of the best ways to create enthusiasm in a congregation is to build something. The excitement of watching a building going up quickly becomes a source of pride for members. It's a physical thing they can point to and show to their friends and neighbors as proof that the congregation to which they belong is growing. But there's one factor in all of this that can turn out to be a congregation's Achilles' heel, and it's that it is easy to build but hard to come up with the money to pay for it.

Truth be known, evangelical, non-denominational congregations that stress tithing as an expectation for every member do a much better job at paying for what they build. Many congregations build multi-million-dollar campuses that are either completely paid for on the day the congregation walks inside or have planned to pay for the entire project in no more than three to five years. Lutherans, on the other hand, seem to have a difficult time wrapping their arms around the concept of getting rid of building debt as quickly as possible and are more than willing to commit the congregation to a twenty- or thirty-year mortgage, the servicing of which starves the rest of the budget for much-needed funds.

But there's something more that happens when you build. You now have a new monthly commitment to light, heat, air-conditioning, custodial service, and repairs that you didn't have prior to erecting your new building. That fact became crystal clear when we built and later occupied a $12 million, 1,800-seat sanctuary in 2000.

We had done a good job of putting together the plan for servicing the twenty-year mortgage for the new sanctuary. Our debt load for our 9,000-member congregation was $5 million, and we were confident that we could meet that monthly payment. Our annual program budget was just shy of $4 million, and another $4 million came in through programs that the congregation was offering such as retreats and mission projects. But what we never figured into our budget planning was that the cost of operating the new sanctuary along with snow plowing the new six hundred car parking lot was going to add up to close to $250,000 a year—a figure we did not have in the budget. Add in a recession that took place in 2000, and things got awfully tight. The result was that a lot of juggling had to be done in the budget, including a freeze on salary and hiring as well as letting some staff go.

Debt means less programming. Debt means fewer staff. Debt means less reason for people to join. As one council president told me, "The goal is to have fewer obligations so you can take advantage of more opportunities." Or, as another council member once said, "You can't borrow your way out of debt. You just end up digging a deeper hole."

Roger: Professional Fundraisers

Many congregations have the thought that they can do as good a job at raising money for building programs or debt-reduction as any outside fundraiser. In fact, some think that hiring an outside firm is just a plain waste of money.

Well, thankfully, the leadership at St. Andrew's was not of that mind, and over the years, we held many campaigns that raised millions of dollars that we simply could not have raised by ourselves. There are many reasons for hiring an outside firm to help with the task of increasing the level of giving for debt-reduction or new projects.

- They know what they're doing.
- They have experience with raising millions of dollars.
- They will provide the leadership for the campaign.
- They will guide you in putting together publications and other communication tools.
- They will help the organization to involve hundreds of members in the campaign.
- They will take the blame for things that go wrong.

One of the more important reasons for hiring an outside firm is that they will push the leadership, including the senior pastor, to make personal visits to members of the congregation for the "Big Ask." The Big Ask is sitting down with a family and boldly saying that "we'd like you to consider a gift over a three- or five-year period in the hundreds of thousands of dollars." I remember resisting that expectation of the fundraiser, but if the projects we were working on at St. Andrew's had any hope of succeeding, hundreds of our members were going to have to step out of their own financial comfort zone and contribute at a level few had ever thought of committing to. It's not easy to walk into a home and say, "We had a gift of $250,000 in mind for you." Some just smiled and showed us the door. Others said they would get back to us. But there were those for whom the challenge was something they were willing to accept, and it was their large gifts and those of hundreds of other smaller contributions that allowed St. Andrew's to construct the buildings that are so necessary for education, fellowship, worship, and mission.

Roger: Offer Many Opportunities to Give

Back in the old days, there was just the offering envelope. Today, it's apps on our phones, online giving via text, and even kiosks where members or visitors can utilize their credit cards to sign up for an event or fulfill their pledges.

One other avenue we pursued at St. Andrew's was mailing statements to members six times a year. In this way, the member or friend of the congregation was made aware of whether they were ahead or behind in their giving, and ample time was given them to catch up if they were in arrears.

Also, as many congregations have found, the opportunity for members to sign up to have their contributions taken out of their bank accounts or via a credit card has helped in taking care of the summer slump in giving that happens when people take off to enjoy the Minnesota summer.

One important note that we discovered was that those who use an American Express card consistently give more than users of other cards. Too often, congregations refuse to include the American Express card in the choices offered because Amex charges a higher fee to the congregation, but the higher fee becomes far less important when a higher rate of giving is taken into consideration.

Roger: Say "Thank You" A Lot

I once attended a seminar on fundraising at Fuller Church Growth Institute in California. For some reason, I missed reading the fine print that indicated that the conference was geared toward college foundation officers who would sit down with people in hopes of having them include the college in their wills and estate planning. These folks were talking about raising the expectations of alumni to give hundreds of thousands and sometimes millions and millions of dollars, and here I was, a lowly parish pastor in the midst of all of these high-powered experts. There was much that I gained and learned about the fine art of raising funds at this seminar, but the real eye-opener came when the professor leading the seminar answered one of my questions by saying, "The reason these people receive more money than you is because they know how to say thank you, and they say it a lot."

And he was right! There are dozens of ways college foundation officials let the alumni who contribute to their cause know how grateful they are for their continued gifts and support. Their names are listed in annual reports and magazines the college sends out. They receive phone calls and letters of appreciation from foundation officers who are adept at keeping up with their constituents. What he pointed out was that, as pastors, we actually have fifty-two opportunities to say thank you. Fifty-two Sundays when the faithful are gathered together where we can express our thanks to the masses—but we often fail to do so. Then there are also phone calls and letters—a simple thank you can make all the difference in an individual's level of giving.

Roger: It's a Matter of Faith and Prayer

George Mueller was a Christian evangelist in the nineteenth century. Mueller and his wife, Mary, dedicated themselves to providing for the many orphans in Bristol, England. More than 10,000 orphans came under the care of George and Mary Mueller during their lifetime. The two of them established 117 schools and created Christian education opportunities for more than 120,000.

What is remarkable about the Muellers is that they never made requests for financial support, nor did they ever go into debt. Instead, the Muellers were in constant prayer that God would touch the hearts of donors to meet the needs of the orphans. Many times, it is said, they received unsolicited food donations only hours before they needed to feed the children. On one well-documented occasion, thanks was given for breakfast when all the children were sitting at the table—even though there was nothing to eat in the house. As they finished praying, the baker knocked on the door with more than enough bread to feed everyone, and the milkman gave them plenty of fresh milk because his cart had broken down in front of the orphanage.

In Zechariah 4:6, we read, "Not by might, nor by power, but by my spirit, says the Lord of hosts." Or, as Paul writes in 2 Corinthians 5:7: "For we walk by faith, not by sight." In essence, the work of stewardship is a matter of a congregation and its leadership being willing to trust that God will provide for whatever is needed to accomplish all that God has in mind for that congregation. We just need to trust and believe.

Duane: Differing Approaches

Even though Paul and Roger were extremely successful as leaders in stewardship at their respective churches, they had some differences in methodology. In fact, for me, as an eyewitness to each of their ministries, the most striking difference between them was in the area of stewardship.

At St. Andrew's, we used to joke with Roger that he sent out so many pledge cards every year to congregational members that if they saved them, there would be enough to wallpaper their house. A stewardship campaign for Roger involved lots of publicity, repeated mailings, and special events. It was always high profile.

In comparison, for Paul, stewardship campaigns at Shepherd of the Valley (SOTV) were often quite understated. I remember one year when the full extent of the stewardship drive was that it was mentioned at worship on one Sunday only just before the offering was taken. Although Paul considered stewardship a cornerstone of his ministry, he also believed that "asking for money" could turn off some people. It could sometimes be counterproductive.

For some, their notion of the church is that it is "always asking for money."
So, Paul often emphasized other aspects of stewardship, which he lays out
below.

Paul: Stewardship Is an Opportunity

It may sound very strange for me to say this, but I actually enjoyed preaching about money and the old triad of time, talent, and treasure. I say this because I liked the challenge of doing it in such a way that it was invitational and encouraging while not producing some level of guilt or shame. So many stewardship sermons begin with a shopping list of parish needs ("We have to pay the heat bill or the light bill—or else!"), and then they quickly degenerate into something that has nothing to do with the biblical concept of living the joyful life of a good steward. I often told the congregation that I did not want anyone to give the church even one dime begrudgingly. And I meant it. Honestly, we did not need or want that kind of money. I even suggested on occasion that there may be some at worship who should take something out of the offering plate rather than putting something in. God loves a cheerful giver, and that was the only motivation I was interested in promoting. The Greek word for *cheerful* is *hilarios,* from which we obviously derive the word *hilarious.* When we give, we should all be laughing with genuine hilarity instead of looking like someone who was weaned on a dill pickle that had been dipped in lemon juice.

I also liked preaching on this topic because I truly believed that people were looking for help in this area of their lives. I read somewhere that the second most common cause of marital discord is money. If you look at society today, we have people with gambling addictions, people drowning in credit card debt, people making poor investments—people finding it hard to save anything for a "rainy day" and people who simply cannot resist purchasing (or hoarding) all the material goodies they find "on sale" at the local mall. There is an old joke reminding us that life is like a doughnut: you are either in the dough or you are in the hole. Our spending habits often determine which one of these we will find ourselves to be—in the dough or in the hole.

I also don't mind teaching and preaching on this subject because it was a very common theme in the ministry of our Lord. There are thirty-four parables found in the synoptic gospels. In over half of them, Jesus is talking about the proper use of our worldly wealth. This would include either our monetary wealth or our material wealth. So why did Jesus spend so much time teaching us about money? Because he knows just how easily we become possessed by our possessions. It is no accident that the first commandment deals with idolatry. Money, for some, has an almost hypnotic quality, and it can easily become the "god" of our lives. As a wise person once noted, money can be a valuable servant or a terrible master.

Paul: Stewardship Is a Lifestyle

For me, the word *stewardship* is not so much about money as it is about an entire lifestyle. And once a congregation embraces this concept, stewardship programs become something of a joy. There were a couple of guiding principles that I always tried to stress in my ministry regarding stewardship.

The first principle is that you and I own nothing. Absolutely nothing. This news comes as a shock to a lot of folks. We enter this world with nothing, and we leave it with nothing, and the only thing that really matters is what we do in the meantime with whatever amount of wealth God has entrusted to us. Someone has noted that you never see a hearse pulling a U-Haul trailer. Simply put, we take nothing with us when we go. Psalm 24 tells us that "the earth is the Lord's and all that is in it." It all belongs to our Creator. This news, however, flies in the face of all who live in this very materialistic world where we are encouraged dozens of times each day to buy, to own, to insure, to stockpile, and to protect all our wealth, be it monetary or material. I like that line that says that we buy things we do not need, with money we don't have, to impress people we don't even like. Some of our spending habits are truly nonsensical.

Here's my second principle: if it's true that we don't own a thing, then what is our relationship to this wealth? Answer: we are trustees, we are caretakers, and we are managers of this wealth, but only for a time. Jesus once told a parable about a man who entrusted all of his wealth to three of his servants before leaving on a lengthy journey. Two of the servants managed his wealth wisely and profitably. The third servant just buried his share of the wealth in the ground. When the master returned, he was not happy with the third servant. And why? Because instead of being faithful, he was mostly fearful. Instead of taking some risk and using the money for some good purposes, he simply stuck it away where it did no one any good at all.

Duane: Stewardship and Parenting

I have often passed along something unusual that I learned about stewardship from Pastor Paul. He once said that parenting is an act of stewardship. What he meant is that parents are given children as a gift from God and that it is a parent's task to take care of that child. In other words, parents are to be stewards of that child.

So, in many ways, stewardship and parenting both mean "letting go." For isn't that what parenting is? Parenting is a series of "letting go" of the child as he or she grows. Similarly, stewardship of all the resources that God has given us is simply constantly "letting go" of those resources in order to help the world grow up to become what God intended it to be.

Paul: Stewardship and Trust

Three of my favorite stewardship stories include the "Wedding at Cana in Galilee," the "Feeding of the 5,000," and the "Great Catch of Fish." In all three of these stories, Jesus asks his disciples to do something that seems just ludicrous. "Fill the six large stone jars with water." (John 2:1-11) "What? We don't need water, we need wine."

"Tell the people to sit down on the grass and give them something to eat." (John 6:1-14) "What? Where would we ever find enough food to feed this crowd?"

And "Peter, go out one more time and let down your nets." (John 21:1-8) "What? Lord, we have fished all night and caught nothing." Despite their skepticism, they all do what they are asked. In the end, it all comes down to one word—*trust*. They trusted Jesus to provide and provide he did. Please notice how Jesus utilized the resources of those around him, even multiplying those resources many times over. Twelve baskets of leftovers. About 150 gallons of very fine wine. And so many fish that their nets were ripping apart and they had to call for help to assist with the catch. Trust in God is the key phrase in any meaningful understanding of stewardship. I love that line from Psalm 23: "The Lord is my Shepherd, I shall not be in want." God always finds a way to provide. It has been said that you can trust God too little but never too much.

Paul: Giving Is Good for You

Another very important insight for people to understand is that we give not so much for what it does for others but for what it does for us. This is a profound insight into Christian living that many people never seem to embrace. But what a liberating thought! Every time I write out a check for church or charity, I have defeated once more those powerful innate selfish voices that say to me, "Don't do it, keep it for yourself." But if I don't ultimately own it, and I am here on this earth only for a time and mostly here to share it, then why be selfish with it? I have always liked these two acronyms: GOD'S and MINE, Giving Our Daily Share and More Is Never Enough. Discover the joy of giving it away! Wealth can sometimes be a real burden, but that is never what God intended for our lives. Show me a generous giver, and I will show you a joyous person. It has been said, somewhat jokingly, that when it comes to giving to church and charity, some people will stop at nothing.

Note that the most important gifts in life are not material gifts, they are spiritual gifts. Gifts that you cannot buy at the Mall of America. Think about it. How do you put a price tag on love, joy, peace, or hope? These are the building blocks of our lives, are they not? And they come from God alone. It's also worth noting that in the seven petitions of the Lord's Prayer, only one petition asks for a tangible, material gift, our daily bread. The other six petitions all ask for spiritual blessings. God provides both kinds of gifts, but despite what the world may think, these spiritual gifts are priceless indeed and to be desired most.

Paul: Stewardship Strategies at SOTV

So far, I have spelled out the theological basis for our many stewardship programs, which were almost always hugely successful. For several years, our annual budget hovered just around three million dollars. So we took this work very seriously. Since we strongly encouraged tithing to the church, as a church, we also tithed our budget, meaning that some years, we gave away about $300,000 to some twenty-five to thirty different ministries. We reasoned that as God had blessed us as a congregation, we should also bless others.

For a time, our national church offices promoted a program called Growth Giving, which we adapted very effectively at Shepherd of the Valley. Each time we had a stewardship emphasis, we simply asked our members to figure out what percentage of their income they were now giving to the church and then simply raise that commitment by 1 percent a year, with the eventual goal of a 10 percent tithe. It was, for many, a painless growing experience. And I think it was also a faith-building experience. People told me from time to time how they had actually reordered their finances around their giving to the church and found it to be to their benefit as much as to the church's benefit. I also came to believe that once people discovered the joy of such disciplined and thoughtful giving, they seldom, if ever, went back to their old giving habits. Our programs were always Bible-based, invitational, encouraging, and life-giving. Seldom did we hear complaints about "the church always asking for money."

We also hosted and promoted a campaign prior to each of our five building expansions. Our national church body offered something called a Resident Stewardship Program whereby a consultant from our national offices came for a month or so and walked us through a number of Bible studies, in-home coffees, congregational dinners, mailing blitzes, and finally, every-member visitations. They were a lot of work on top of all our other parish programs but well worth the time and effort. Without such programs, our expansions would never have been possible. I have always believed that people can be very generous, but you must clearly define the objective and then demonstrate a compelling need. My philosophy for capital campaigns is that you should always set three possible financial goals: a minimum goal, a challenge goal, and a miracle goal. We always wanted and needed to celebrate one of these three goals.

One thing I often did during stewardship drives was to find out the gross annual household income of the members of our church. This meant finding out what the median household income was for our county and then multiplying that number by the number of active households in our church. Believe it or not, that number very often surpassed $100 million. Why did I do this? Not to create any guilt, but simply to show the congregation the enormous financial potential we had as a congregation. I am sure that many churches have no idea just how wealthy they are. I merely pointed out that if we were all tithing, we would have a $10 million budget. If we were half-tithing, we would have a $5 million budget. And if we were third tithing, which was exactly the case, we would have a $3 million budget. Showing such potential had a way of quelling any criticism about the church asking for the impossible.

Paul: A Warren Buffet Quote

Here's a true story I shared in my preaching on occasion. One evening some years ago, Warren Buffet, one of the wealthiest and most generous men in America (and quite humble too), was giving an after-dinner speech. He began by saying to his audience, "Congratulations, you have all won the ovarian lottery." What in the world is the ovarian lottery? Buffet went on to describe six factors that all applied to his audience. They were all born white and born in America, they were all born with a reasonably high IQ with relatively good health, and they all came from homes that had some kind of a work ethic and placed some value on higher education. Buffet said that you dare not take credit for any of these six factors. You have won the ovarian lottery. Change any one or two of these factors, and your life would be dramatically different than what it is today. You could just as easily have been born in a rice paddy in Bangladesh, a mud hut in Tanzania, or a barrio in Brazil. He concluded by saying this: "Never look down your nose at a poor person. It could just as easily have been you."

Why do I share this story? Because many people think that they have earned all their wealth by their own efforts and that others should do the same, not realizing how blessed they actually are. As

Jesus reminds us, from the one to whom much has been given, much will also be required. So I often closed my stewardship sermons with this simple prayer: "Lord, you have given us so much. Now give us one thing more, a truly grateful and generous heart. Amen."

Duane: A Difference in Emphasis

The way I see it is that Paul and Roger each highlight differing but important aspects of stewardship in the church. Paul emphasizes the theological underpinnings and the overall meaning of an inclusive notion of stewardship. It's critical that we recall how all that we have is really a gift from God. Paul has stressed that not only in his writing above but also during his many years of ministry.

On the other hand, Roger places his emphasis on one important part of stewardship for the church, namely, the financial aspect of stewardship. Without proper fundraising and money management, the church would be in bad shape. One of the critical roles that a senior pastor has is to responsibly manage the funds of the church.

Although Paul and Roger call attention to different things regarding stewardship, in the end, everyone who works behind the pulpit must be mindful of both of these aspects—no matter the size or shape of the church in which they are doing ministry.

Chapter 5

BUILDING PROGRAMS

Duane: Constantly Building Buildings

Much of the time I was on staff at St. Andrew's and Shepherd of the Valley (SOTV), each church was in the midst of one building program or another—sanctuaries, educational areas, fellowship areas, and more. The reason for all this building was the dynamic growth happening at each church. Each building program began with some kind of fundraising campaign. Often while that campaign was ongoing, architects and committees were working on plans for the new building. Then the actual building commenced. Anticipation was high. Finally, the new area was opened, often with some kind of celebratory event. Then, not long after that, the whole cycle would begin once again for another building project.

Roger was involved in five building programs in his years at St. Andrew's. Paul was involved in six building programs. A large portion of both of their ministries was devoted to all that was involved in those ventures. What was it like for them? What insights might they have after their vast experience in so many building programs?

Roger: Discovering the Future

One of the major challenges facing St. Andrew's in 1972 was the fact that the village of Mahtomedi was not the hub of any great activity. Actually, Mahtomedi, a village of 3,000 souls, was on the way to nowhere in particular. Situated on the eastern shores of crystal-clear White Bear Lake, Mahtomedi's heyday was back in the 1920s when it was a destination for Twin-Citians seeking a break from the summer heat of the city. Their desire to make the thirty-five-mile trip was aided by the Twin City Streetcar Company that had run a rail line from Minneapolis and St. Paul all the way to Mahtomedi. Not only had the streetcar company created a means of transportation to get the city folks to the lake, but it had built an amusement park on White Bear Lake, complete with a roller coaster, a Ferris wheel, and a huge dance hall that brought in nationally known performers and bands every weekend in the summer. Thousands would make the weekend trek to enjoy the lake throughout the summer.

But all of that died in the 1950s with the explosive growth of the automobile industry. No longer dependent upon a streetcar for transportation, Twin-Citians could now go wherever they wanted. The choice was theirs. Soon the roller coaster, the Ferris wheel, and the dance hall had lost so many customers that the amusement park ended up being demolished and the land sold to developers who built beautiful homes on the shoreline. Not much later, the streetcar track was also abandoned.

Roger: Setting St. Andrew's Apart from the Crowd

Since there was no huge population from which to draw, it became very apparent that if St. Andrew's was going to grow, we had to somehow set this congregation apart from all the rest. In 1972, there were something like four hundred Lutheran churches in the Twin Cities. They were a mixture of every Lutheran synod then in existence. Many Lutheran churches proudly put their denomination name on their outdoor signage. They boldly proclaimed that they were a member congregation of the American Lutheran Church (ALC), the Lutheran Church – Missouri Synod (LCMS), the Wisconsin Evangelical Lutheran Synod (WELS), or, at that time, the Lutheran Church in America (LCA)—an alphabet soup that allowed passersby to quickly determine by the outdoor signage whether this particular congregation was of their own synod background. This kind of outdoor signage caused many to not even give a congregation a try because it wasn't of their particular tribe.

I decided not to follow suit. My thinking was that I did not want someone to roll on by our congregation simply because we didn't fit into their Lutheran alphabet. So *LCA* and, later, *ELCA* never appeared on any signage or mailings that we sent out into the community. I just wanted people to give us a chance to prove ourselves as worthy of their attendance and participation. Come and visit, allow us the opportunity to share the gospel with you, and maybe, just maybe, you'll decide to become involved.

Roger: Setting the Bar

One of the things we established very early in my ministry at St. Andrew's was that unless whatever we attempted to do was done with high quality and excellence, we weren't going to be doing it at all. Excellence and quality in programming, in worship, in preaching simply had to be the expectation of those who came to St. Andrew's.

And why not? The Twin Cities was known throughout the world as a metropolitan region where excellence was a trademark the community proudly bore: The world-famous Minnesota Orchestra; 3M, with its knack for taking an idea and somehow coming up with a product that people around the world wanted to buy; the University of Minnesota, with its innovative research laboratories; Target Corporation, with its marketing plan that grew from a single store in Roseville, Minnesota, to a brand found in over 1,800 locations throughout the nation. Add to that the scores of Minnesota companies headquartered in Minneapolis and St. Paul that are members of the Fortune 400. And don't forget to include cultural icons such as the St. Olaf Choir and the National Lutheran Choir. Every endeavor had as its goal to succeed and become the best in their field. So why not St. Andrew's?

Roger: Why Not World Class?

One of the givens in church life is that the biggest yearly attendance of both members and visitors will take place on Christmas and Easter. So, if the church will be packed on Christmas Eve, then why not do something special? Fortunately, in October of my first year at St. Andrew's, I was at a small gathering that included the conductor of the Minnesota Orchestra. I approached him and asked if it would be possible to get a string quartet from the Minnesota Orchestra for Christmas Eve at St. Andrew's? He said he could not speak for the musicians but gave me the name of one of the members of the orchestra who could be of help. A few phone calls later, we had our string quartet. And thus began an expansion of the quality of music St. Andrew's was offering the congregation and community. In fact, because of something we called "Patron of the Arts" (funds donated beyond our regular giving), we began to accumulate money that allowed us to have other musical events throughout the year that included the likes of the St. Paul Chamber Orchestra and, to celebrate the opening of our new campus, Paul Stookey of "Peter, Paul and Mary" fame. Later, a thirty-piece orchestra that performed on the third Sunday of the month would be added to our worship schedule. The orchestra would also accompany nine Christmas Eve services attended by at least ten thousand people—an event drawing people from throughout the east-metro suburbs.

We were now becoming a place with quality musical excellence of a caliber that few churches were even thinking about including in their yearly plans. It was this kind of "thinking outside the box" that came into play when we were designing the new 1,800-seat sanctuary. It was the same kind of thinking that followed a dream of having enough space in the front of the sanctuary to accommodate no less than four hundred singers. It was bold thinking that created a sanctuary large enough to hold major concerts from visiting choirs and musical groups, including the likes of the Minnesota Orchestra. It was confidence that led the congregation to include in its new sanctuary a $2 million 108-rank pipe organ that, with its 7,301 pipes, is now one of the largest functioning pipe organs in the Upper Midwest and is known throughout the world for its excellent musical quality.

Roger: Think Big

The 1980s was a decade consumed by the idea of church growth. Opportunities to attend conferences dedicated to growing the local church were abundant, and a visit to most of them meant traveling to places that had actually seen their church grow—congregations from which others could garner lessons learned.

One of those places was Garden Grove Community Church—later to become the Crystal Cathedral—in Orange County, California, which, under the leadership of Robert Schuller, a pastor of the Reformed Church in America, began worship services at an outdoor theater, with Schuller preaching from the rooftop of the concession stand. The church began to grow. Later, he expanded his ministry to nationwide television with what he called the *Hour of Power*. His first actual sanctuary was built with huge windows that opened to the parking lot so that those who had become accustomed to worshipping from their cars could continue to do so.

Through his *Hour of Power*, Schuller began to promote a church growth conference to be held in January at Garden Grove Community Church. One member of the St. Andrew's church council who was a regular viewer of *Hour of Power* mentioned the event to me and thought it would be a good idea for me to attend—he was even willing to pay my expenses. California in January?! All expenses?! I would have been an idiot not to take him up on his offer.

The conference was attended by two hundred to three hundred pastors and lay leaders from all over the nation. Methodically, over the three days of the conference, Schuller and his staff inspired those in attendance with a can-do attitude that broke the mold for many of us. Instead of thinking of our churches in small and confined terms, like the little church on the corner of 5th and Main, the conference encouraged us to think much bigger—to consider what it would take to expand and grow our ministries. Again and again, we were told how important parking was to the growth of a church. Not one space for every four people in a pew but rather one parking space for every two. They also encouraged us to think in terms of special kinds of ministries targeted to specific audiences. For us, it meant the construction of the Youth and Sports Center—a space dedicated to reaching out to youths of all ages. And, of course, in order for that to happen, our congregation would need to buy as much land as available.

One idea that continued to rattle around in my brain after I left the conference was the thought that if Schuller could do it, if other pastors around the nation were experiencing newfound avenues of growth, then he and others had already proven it could be done. If it could be done, then why shouldn't St. Andrew's begin to think in bolder terms about the kind of ministry we would hopefully offer.

Roger: Build It—Because They're Coming!

Back in 1982, we knew we had to do something. Attendance was soaring, youth ministry was growing, and Sunday school was bursting at the seams. So, we leaned on greater minds to help us discover our path into the future and contracted with nationally known church consultant Lyle Schaller. Schaller came and looked over the landscape of our pattern of growth and gave us two choices. We could expand and build on our two-and-a-half-acre site, but that would mean spending at least $1 million buying up houses, pulling out utilities, and still ending up with a sanctuary that could accommodate no more than six hundred to seven hundred people at a time. So, what else could we do?

Well, luckily, the early 1980s was not a period of expansive growth in Mahtomedi. There was still plenty of land available within a mile of our current site. So, we began the search for land upon which to build. Eventually, two parcels became possible sites for the new St. Andrew's Lutheran Church campus.

The first was a farm about a block off the main highway where we could secure thirty-nine acres for $90,000. It was flat. It would be easy to build upon and offered plenty of room for parking and future building. The only drawback was that it was a block off the main highway and so the site was not easily seen by passersby.

The second was a farm located right next door to Mahtomedi High School and Middle School. In addition, it was land situated right along a main highway. The only problem was that we were having a difficult time coming to terms with the owners of the land. Eventually, the best we could do was agree on fifteen acres for

$150,000—the greatest per-acre cost anyone had bought land in Washington County at that time.

So, what to do? The only solution was to call a congregational meeting and present the two offers. Thirty-nine acres for $90,000 or fifteen acres for $150.000. The cheaper and larger site tucked away on a side road or the expensive and smaller site on the main drag.

On the day of the congregational meeting, the room was packed. The pros and cons of both sites were discussed. Some saw it as a matter of the most acres for the money. Their point was that the thirty-nine-acre site was not the best, but we could make do. Others thought visibility and proximity to the high school and middle school was so important that it was worth the extra dollars, even if it meant a smaller site. In the end, the congregation voted to buy the fifteen-acre site.

Roger: Location, Location, Location

In 1986, construction was started on the new St. Andrew's campus. As construction was underway, it became quickly apparent that fifteen acres would not be enough land. So, while the bulldozers were still preparing the site, we entered into an agreement to purchase an adjoining seventeen acres. We now had a thirty-two-acre campus with plenty of room to expand and grow. However, apparently, God was not through with us yet, because not long after our first buildings were in place, another forty acres adjoining our property became available. As someone noted, "God made just so much land, and so much right next to you." It was an opportunity we simply could not pass up. So, over a period of ten years, the St. Andrew's campus grew to become a seventy-two-acre parcel at a total cost, including all three purchases of $900,000. The future of St. Andrew's had become secure. We had not only given ourselves the ability to expand and grow but also bequeathed to future generations options that few congregations would ever hope to have.

Roger: Years of Construction and Fundraising

Over the course of fifteen years, St. Andrew's was constantly turning the shovel in the dirt and expanding its footprint on its seventy-two-acre campus. Aided by a series of successful fundraising campaigns, the congregation and community witnessed a steady period of over $34 million in land purchases and construction.

- 1984 — Purchase of the initial fifteen acres
- 1986 — Construction of the 600-seat Great Hall
- 1989 — Construction of adjoining Education Wing
- 1991 — Construction of the Youth and Sports Center
- 1998 — Construction of the St Andrew's Village, with Presbyterian Homes
- 1999 — Construction of the 1,800-seat sanctuary and 108-rank pipe organ

Roger: Campus Design Challenges

With four parking lots, four forty-five-minute worship services, and Sunday school taking place every Sunday morning, the challenge of getting to where you needed to go was a major problem for parents with young children. One day, I opened my mail and read a letter from a mother who described her frustration at getting around our campus. She described first finding a parking spot, then dropping her child off in the Education Building. From there, she took the three-minute walk from the Education Building to the Sanctuary, finally plunking herself down in a pew, only to repeat the entire process in reverse forty-five minutes later. I could feel her exhaustion as my eyes ran over the words she had written. Something, obviously, had to be fixed if we were to have any chance of attracting and keeping members.

As soon as we could, we changed our worship schedule from four services to three and expanded the time between services to allow for a member to grab a cup of coffee and a cookie and engage in a bit of conversation with another parishioner. We still had the issue of disconnected buildings but giving more time between services gave everyone a chance to catch their breath and hopefully enjoy their experience at St. Andrew's.

Roger: The "Plus" of Separate Buildings

One of the challenges St. Andrew's experienced was how to accommodate the thousands of people coming for worship on Christmas Eve and Easter Sunday. Christmas Eve sort of took care of itself by simply adding more worship services, eventually ending up with eleven on-the-hour celebrations beginning at 2:00 p.m. and running all the way to midnight. Over ten thousand people from all over the east-metro area would make their way into the 1,800-seat sanctuary to experience Christmas Eve worship complete with choirs and a thirty-piece orchestra.

Easter, however, was a different matter. If we were only going to hold worship in the sanctuary, we would be limited to six on-the-hour services, with the earliest starting at 7:00 a.m. and the latest beginning at noon. The answer was to run three additional services at 9:15, 10:15, and 11:15 a.m. in the gym of the Youth and Sports Center. And, to make sure that both venues provided a quality Easter worship experience, we had the orchestra perform in the gym while those gathered in the sanctuary were treated to the sounds of a brass quartet and the 108-rank pipe organ. It worked, and more than ten thousand people heard the Good News that, "He is risen! He is risen, indeed!"

Roger: Soli Deo Gloria

No one in their right mind builds just to build. And especially not churches. We have a mission to fulfill that is best described in the words, "Soli Deo Gloria"—to God be the glory! Every ounce of energy, every dollar spent, every word spoken, and every life encountered should be done with the sole purpose of expanding the kingdom of Jesus Christ and letting people experience and know the power of abundant living that Christ gives. Buildings are just tools to be used to spread that Good News of Jesus Christ.

Duane: My View of That First Building Program

I was at St. Andrew's during that first building program that Roger describes. It was an extremely exciting time. For the groundbreaking, there was a parade of people from the congregation who walked the mile or so from the old church to where the new church was to be built. Once there, rather than the usual symbolic shovels for groundbreaking, Roger wanted something different. So a hobby farmer from the congregation brought a team of horses hitched to a plow, and he plowed a row in the dirt for a unique type of groundbreaking.

Despite the excitement around the new Great Hall at the new location, it was only a partial fix for the space the congregation needed. All that was in the new building was worship space, a kitchen, offices, and a nursery. No room for education—like Sunday school. Luckily, the church still owned the old building a mile away. Although that old building was for sale, we still were able to use it for all the Sunday school kids.

Among other things, I oversaw Sunday school. For a few years, on Sunday mornings, we opted to bus all the children from the new building where people worshipped to the old building where kids could attend Sunday school. Weekly, I was at the old church overseeing the buses that rolled in, the kids, their teachers, and all other things at what was then called the Activity Center. Although a huge headache for me, it was actually a pretty good solution to a difficult dilemma. Throughout that time, everyone yearned for the day when all classes and activities, along with worship, would be at one new location.

Because of this two-site situation, immediately after the first building was completed, the cycle to build a new educational wing adjacent to the new Great Hall commenced. Meanwhile, there were not many folks willing or able to buy the Activity Center. However, after a couple of years, a buyer was found (another church). And then, amazingly, on the very day of the closing sale of the Activity Center, the new educational wing was completed. It seemed a miracle had occurred before our very eyes. No one celebrated this accomplishment more than me.

Paul: The First Building (1984)

Over the years, I have talked with fellow pastors who have said that they would never want to undertake any kind of building program unless it was absolutely necessary. There are horror stories aplenty about how many things can go wrong when a pastor tries to build. One needs to make a case for the expansion, secure the needed funding for the project, coordinate many aspects of the expansion with city and county officials, hire the right architects, hope for favorable weather, find the right general contractor and subcontractors, finish on time and under budget with the least amount of disruption to parish life, and do all that while hoping for no on-the-job injuries.

In March of 1982, months after we began as a church, we had no building. We temporarily moved into Greenleaf Elementary for Sunday worship services. In addition, we were given permission by a local church to use their building for other programs at no charge. These were the nicest people you would ever want to meet. We volunteered to pay some rent because we used their building a lot during those first three-plus years of our existence.

Soon we bought five acres of land on Johnny Cake Ridge Road across from the Minnesota Zoo. We looked long and hard for this land and got it for $82,000. Some wanted land with a steep hillside so that we could build an earth-sheltered church (they were popular then because of the energy crisis), but the ALC would not allow it. The ALC argued correctly that earth-sheltered churches are often hard to expand should the need arise. And, of course, we did expand—five times, as it turned out.

Then we looked for an architect. We first went with an architect out of Northfield but fired him two months later because he thought we had unlimited resources. We had a $423,000 loan, and he kept coming to us with million-dollar proposals. I get frustrated when architects don't listen to the building committee. Such a waste of time and money. They often want to make some grand statement, but it is always at our expense, not theirs. Thankfully, we later hired Roger Sjobeck of the Lonnie Adkins Group in St. Paul, and he was particularly good to work with. He listened closely and gave us a well-designed sanctuary.

The national church wanted us to first build a 3,500-square-foot building I told them that many of our families lived in homes bigger than that and that if they were really serious about a new ministry in Apple Valley, it had to be at least 6,000 square feet. Finally, they relented, saying only that they hoped our dreams weren't too unrealistic. So we hired the David C. Volkmann Construction Co. out of Circle Pines, and we were off to the races. Groundbreaking was in June 1984, and the building was completed in late December 1984.

Paul: Expansion (1989)

From 1984 to 1988, the congregation enjoyed solid, steady growth, which is exactly what we had hoped for. (It was a few years later that we had to deal with what I would call explosive growth).

But it soon became obvious that we needed much more room for worship, offices, educational programming, and fellowship. By 1987, we had a Saturday evening worship hour and three Sunday morning services. Our lobby area was so packed with people between services that it was dangerous to walk around with a hot cup of coffee in hand for fear of spillage. (And you never want to deprive a good Lutheran of their coffee!)

So once again, we enlisted the talents of Roger Sjobeck, who designed another angular worship space with six walls. It also included a gorgeous stained-glass cross with natural lighting. On sunny days, the whole room was awash with soft yet vibrant colors. The angular walls in all three of our sanctuaries disseminated sound around the room with an absolute minimum of echoing. In fact, all of our sanctuaries had excellent acoustics. This particular sanctuary would seat a maximum of five hundred people. On the first day of its opening, the worship services were packed with parishioners, and extra seating was brought in. I still recall seeing two leading members of the building committee looking at each other and almost simultaneously saying, "We built it too small!" But of course, we built what we could afford at the time. It was only a few years later that we were having four Sunday services on-the-hour, and even that schedule was still not adequate to our needs.

Duane: About that Cross

Paul mentioned the gorgeous stained-glass cross that was a part of the 1989 sanctuary. People loved it. It was beautiful. However, just a few years later, it became evident that a new sanctuary needed to be built. All of us on staff and those on the church council wondered how people would react to a proposed new sanctuary. Amazingly, there was only one question people had during that transition time. It was, "What about the stained-glass cross? Will that be moved to the new sanctuary?" It's surprising how people be-

come attached to certain elements of worship in such a short time. By the way, unfortunately, the answer to their question was, "No"—it could not be moved.

Paul: Chuck Doyle

However, it wasn't long before we were again looking at the very real need to expand again, only this time we had a serious problem. We were running out of land. Looking to the south, the only direction we could possibly expand, I began a long, humorous, and sometimes bizarre relationship with the owner of that land, a cantankerous old man named Chuck Doyle. The first time I met Chuck, he cursed at me very loudly for parking two wheels of my car on his lawn even though he had a very narrow driveway. When I introduced myself as Pastor Harrington, his new neighbor to the north, he settled down a little. I am happy to report that over time, we did become quite good friends, and, in fact, I officiated at his funeral years later.

In his younger years, Chuck was an honest to goodness barnstormer who did all kinds of aerobatics in biplanes left over from the First World War. In his later years, he was inducted into the Minnesota Aviation Hall of Fame. While Chuck was still in high school, he borrowed a plane from a friend one evening and proceeded to buzz a football game and a stadium full of spectators. For this stunt, he was summarily kicked out of the high school, to which he never returned. It was many years later that he was given a diploma from the same high school and recognized for his pioneering efforts in the field of aviation. I think Chuck really enjoyed sharing the irony of this story.

Chuck moved out to Apple Valley in 1951 and bought forty-four acres for $150 an acre. Here he built a home, a hangar, and an airstrip where he could fly any of his planes at will. He did banner towing and sky writing, and he still engaged in some stunt flying on occasion. But in time, progress caught up to him, and he learned that

County Road 38 was soon to bisect his property. He fought it all in court, but eventually, the southern twenty-eight acres of his land were purchased by the school district for Falcon Ridge School, five acres were taken by the state for the highway, and Shepherd of the Valley bought eleven acres on the north side of the highway.

As you might imagine, Chuck faced a major issue with capital gains taxes because of this sale. He would have saved a bundle had he either donated some of his land to us or at the least sold it to us at a reduced price. He loved French silk pie. So I spent many hours trying to "bribe" him with pie into making what would have been a very tax-favorable move on his part. But, for some reason, Chuck could not see the logic in this.

So we paid fair market value, which was about $40,000 an acre at the time. In his defense, he did not gouge us, and had he not sold us the land, Shepherd of the Valley would look very different today. There was some talk, had we not gotten these eleven acres, of selling the church building and moving to a different location.

Paul: Another New Sanctuary (1996)

After purchasing the Chuck Doyle land, the next step was planning our third sanctuary. This chapter of the story includes an example of an architect with overly grandiose ideas. Our architect's design for the roof of the 1996 sanctuary was completely impractical and expensive. Believe it or not, the design called for a roof that was half concave and half convex. Because of this odd design, I knew that every piece of steel in the roof would have to be fabricated and that each piece would be different. I told the architect that the bids on this project were going to come in way over budget. But time and again, this firm assured me they would not. So on the night of the "big reveal," when bids were opened from five different contractors, the lowest bid was one million dollars over the estimates we had been promised.

This major miscalculation cost us money and a lot of lost time. During this period, our worship space was packed every Sunday morning with four worship services on-the-hour starting at 8 a.m. We told the firm to redesign the roof as soon as possible and charge us nothing for their efforts—and if the next set of bids came in too high, there could be a lawsuit for malpractice. So there would be no "flying wings" for a roof. Later, we got a bid we could live with. But to get there, it was a real year-long hassle.

One other note, not long after the sanctuary was finished, we had a day-long rainstorm with lots of wind. Our new 950-seat sanctuary was leaking like a sieve. Rain was running down half the walls, so much so that we had paint blisters on the wall full of water. We called the architects and the contractor again, and the next week they applied twenty-six huge tubes of caulk to the building. (I counted them in case we ever needed such information for a lawsuit.) How could a builder "finish" a project like this and forget the caulking? Were they somehow hoping we just would not notice?

Paul: A Not-So-Good Neighbor

I shall long remember what a huge distraction one of our neighbors was in the midst of our many building projects. I would much rather have been serving my flock than fending off all the nonsense this man threw our way for the better part of a year. As it happened, we needed a northern exit from our large parking lot, and we also needed a dumpster to hold all the trash that our church generated each week. It was not unusual to have three to four thousand people a week utilizing our facility for a huge number of events and activities. We often had eight, ten, or twelve separate events a day at the church. And people, as we all know, can create a lot of trash in a very short amount of time. But not everyone was happy to witness a church with such vitality and potential for growth.

Bordering our property on the north side was a very tenacious and irascible man who was determined that we would not have the exit we needed, and that the dumpster be moved anywhere but the one logical place where we thought it absolutely had to be. Or, at the very least, he wanted a gate installed across the exit that would be closed to all traffic on Sundays in order to, in his words, "preserve the peace and quiet of the neighborhood." Keep in mind that this man and most of our neighbors moved in sometime after the church was well-established at this location, so no one should have been surprised by our presence. So, we worked closely with the city planner, who assured us that we had every right to access the street that literally ran into our north parking lot and that the city had no interest in putting a gate across this road. The city planner also informed us that the location we had selected for the dumpster was acceptable to the city with all its guidelines, ordinances, and building codes.

Nonetheless, our northern neighbor canvassed the neighborhood, spreading misinformation. He circulated petitions and handed out flyers. One Sunday morning, he even tried to dissuade worshippers from using the north exit by parking his car at an odd angle in the street. He insisted the dumpster would be a health hazard, have a foul order, be an eyesore, and attract rodents. He sent us threatening letters and finally called for the Apple Valley city council and their planning commission to address this matter. The city complied, we were placed on the agenda, and any concerned neighbors got to have their say—as did I, the church's senior pastor. In the end, the city ruled in our favor on all counts with a couple of caveats which we were intending to do all along. The dumpster was to be placed in an enclosure with four walls and a roof, matching our existing building. All trash (mostly dry and odorless anyway) was to be tightly bagged before being placed in the dumpster, with pick-up weekly or more often if needed. We were happy to comply with any stipulations the city required of us. Over time, this "tempest in a teapot" finally subsided, and a few years later, this neighbor moved away.

Paul: More Expansion (2006)

After building our third sanctuary in 1996, we added more education space in 1998 and a new kitchen in 2002. By the time 2005 rolled around, we were again needing more space for nearly everything except worship. We needed rooms for fellowship, classrooms, nursery, our preschool, and a long-hoped-for chapel. I should mention that it was comparatively easy to "sell" the congregation on all of our expansions because the needs were so evident. We were literally tripping over each other at times. And, if memory serves, the congregational vote to proceed with any of our expansions was always in the 80th or 90th percentile, if not higher. One reason for this was that over time, the congregation had come to trust the pastors and lay staff, and we had come to trust the congregation in return. We all seemed to be on the same page, and whatever differences we had, we somehow worked them out in an atmosphere of goodwill and mutual respect. Our pastors respected the lay leaders, and they returned the favor in spades. Council meetings were productive, efficient, and even joyful at times. We felt like we were truly making a difference for the sake of the church and the kingdom of God as it breaks in upon the world. That was a very good feeling indeed.

For this last major expansion, we finally ended up with Mortenson Construction Company. I wish to heaven that we had hired them on day one of our first building program. They were pure joy to work with. I have never met such professional people. All contractors and all architects are surely not created equal.

Duane: Parking Lots Matter Too

Although Roger and Paul barely mention the construction of parking lots, both had plenty of experience with parking-lot expansion. In fact, they both realized how important adequate parking space was for the growth of the church. Simply put, in suburbia, when a parking lot is full, people don't come. For years, no monthly church council meeting at either church was complete until Paul or Roger had told the church council, "Parking—please don't forget about adequate parking."

The very first capital campaign I witnessed was with Roger at St. Andrew's. Parking was desperately needed. Roger was one to give each capital campaign a very catchy slogan like "Making Mountains Move," "Alive and Growing," or "Challenged to Grow." He even had a slogan for this first parking-lot-expansion campaign. It was called "Pave the Way."

Roger has told me that "Pave the Way" actually ended up being the worst fund drive he ever did. The cost was only $75,000. The church had about $40,000 in hand, and the contractor was raring to go, so they went ahead and "paved the way." However, once that was done, people must have thought the project was funded and paid for because, although some money continued to trickle in, St. Andrew's ended up with a $10,000 deficit on the project. Roger calls it "a lesson well learned." In other words, wait until you have all the money before you begin construction . . . or at least until you have a plan to pay for it via loan.

Chapter 6

STAFFING

Duane: Second Fiddle

Leonard Bernstein, the late conductor of the New York Philharmonic Orchestra, was once asked to name the most difficult instrument to play. Without hesitation, he replied, "The second fiddle. I can get plenty of first violinists, but to find someone who can play the second fiddle with enthusiasm—that's a problem, and if we have no second fiddle, we have no harmony."

You might say that Roger and Paul were the conductors of their respective churches. They were successful at surrounding themselves with lots of very capable second fiddles, people who could play the fiddle in harmony with the overall vision of the church. How did Roger and Paul go about re-

cruiting and managing their staff, which is a key task for most senior pastors?

Paul: I Didn't Learn Much About Staffing in Seminary

There are so many things that you don't learn at the seminary. Never in my five years at the seminary did anyone ever teach anything about how to develop a healthy church staff. Perhaps the professors themselves did not know or had forgotten. Or maybe I was absent from class with the flu that week. Instead, I learned about staffing on the job.

One of the first things I learned is to discern when to grow a staff. That may seem obvious enough, but it isn't. Of all the needs there are in a growing church, which position do you create and then fund? It's a crucial decision. Layperson or clergy? Full-time or part-time? Focused on one specific area or something of a generalist? Will the church council approve it or not? Money is always an issue. It's a good time to pray a lot.

At Shepherd of the Valley (SOTV), I worked with Cris Ireland, who had an almost uncanny radar for developing staff. She herself was a full-time volunteer for almost three years before becoming salaried. She seemed to know whom to hire, when to hire, how much to pay staff, and just what that job description would look like. Over the years, we hired more than eighty-five people, and most of them turned out to be excellent additions to our staff. One method Cris often used was to ask certain people to volunteer for a job at the church. Then she would observe and evaluate their performances. In fact, we ended up hiring a lot of church members, something other pastors do not like to do in case things don't work out well with a particular employee.

Another method we used involved hiring people for just a few hours a week, and if we thought they really added to the overall ministry of the church, we could always increase their hours. Several staff members started at five or ten hours a week. Then, over time, they became full-time staff members. Some of this, of course, was driven by the obvious growth of the church. The more members, the more help we needed to stay on top of this ever-expanding ministry. I often told the staff and the congregation not to get too comfortable because what is true today may not be true a year or two from now, simply because of our continuing growth.

Another challenge was knowing if volunteerism would get the job done or whether we really needed to hire someone. That question was frequently asked, especially when it felt like we were going out on a limb about the budget. I always argued that volunteers were particularly important to the life of the church. They benefited and the congregation benefited. But there were some jobs that just exceeded the abilities of a volunteer. In time, we had to have a full-time music director, a full-time human-resources person, a full-time Christian education director, full-time custodians, a full-time finance person, a full-time office manager, and so on. I always said that a good employee would eventually "earn their keep," and most often, they did.

Duane: Learning from Paul

Paul was a mentor for me. His style of mentorship was to teach by his example. For instance, as a brand-new pastor, I learned about officiating at weddings by following him around one weekend for a rehearsal and wedding. Paul has told me that he accomplished his teaching in this manner: "First, I do, and you watch. Then, I do, and you help. Finally, you do, and I watch."

Just observing Paul on a Sunday morning between worship services was a learning experience for me. Despite a sea of people in the narthex, somehow, he was able to focus on each person he talked with and give them each his full attention. When you talked with Paul, you knew he was present in the moment. People always came first for him. There were many times

*when his assistant, Cris Ireland, had to "rescue" Paul from some conversa-
tion because Paul had lost track of time and worship was about to begin. Often, Paul came into the service well after worship had begun. We often kid-
ded Cris that what she really needed was a large shepherd's crook so she
could hook him and pull him away from people to keep him on schedule.*

Paul: Human Resources

Over time, as the church's membership expanded and our staff
grew larger, we soon realized that even our full-time human-
resources person needed some additional help. After seeking advice
from several other large congregations in our area, we made two important decisions. The first of them was the development of an employee handbook that contained over twenty pages of policies and
guidelines for the smooth, efficient, and lawful functioning of the
church. As my father used to say, the church is not a business, but it
should be run in a business-like manner. It happened that my father
was a successful businessman who closely observed many churches
and found them wanting in this area.

The second important decision we made was to form a blue-
ribbon human-resource committee that met once a month to discuss
all kinds of employee issues and to set new policies or guidelines as
needed. The committee had up to eight members, and most of them
were HR people who worked in corporate America in the Twin Cities. These folks were all very knowledgeable and aware of any and all
current county, state, and federal laws that might in some way apply
to the employees of our church. I well remember leaving those meetings being very thankful for their wisdom, expertise, and genuine
love for the wellbeing of their church and its staff.

Paul: Six Important Questions to Ask about a Staff Person

There were six important questions we always asked in hiring and evaluating staff:

1. What is their commitment to Christ and the church?
2. Do they have the background, knowledge, and/or credentials to do the job effectively?
3. Are they self-starters or would we need to "pump them up" much like a tire that is always losing air pressure?
4. Do they have good people skills?
5. Are they team players? If you found this kind of person, you were going to make a good "hire." If you didn't, you might come to regret it.
6. If the job requires it, can this person ably and professionally supervise others?

A few examples: We hired a woman to run our Christian education department, and for a time, she did a very fine job. But we were soon having to add staff to that department, and we found out that this person absolutely could not delegate in any meaningful way. Eventually, we had to let her go. It was painful. But because of her style, she was leaving her staff frustrated, and she herself was overwhelmed, as the job had expanded beyond her capabilities. We also hired a business manager who was very good with numbers, but later, we discovered that he was not a team player and that he did not work well with other staff members. However, with the exception of these few people, the vast majority of our employees were pure joy to work with. I don't want that truth to get lost.

I could not have been prouder of my staff. Most of the time, they functioned like a well-oiled machine. They very honestly cared for each other—yes, even loved each other. They were very supportive of one another too. I always told the staff to work out their differences (and there were few) behind closed doors with lots of Christian love and forgiveness. There was little conflict and little dissension. I well recall a woman who came to the church one Sunday from a neighboring church that was having a lot of staff issues. She asked me point blank, "Does your staff get along well in this church?" I assured her that they did. "Good," she said, "I want to join!" And she did. It is interesting that a person can walk into a church, and it doesn't take long before they sense whether or not it's a well-run, loving, and welcoming place.

Duane: "You Get Along So Well"

While I was a pastor at Shepherd of the Valley, one of the things people continually commented on was how well all the pastors got along. At one time, there were seven pastors on staff. You wouldn't think that that many pastors together could get along. After all, Martin Luther once said, "Pastors are a lot like manure. Get them too close together and things begin to stink. But spread them out and good things happen." That wasn't the case for the pastors I worked with at Shepherd of the Valley. We got along. Not perfectly. But we did respect and care for each other.

For years, I wondered why people so often mentioned in amazement that we seemed to like each other. Then it dawned on me. The fact that we got along made them feel secure and safe at the church because they witnessed the respect we had for each other. In addition, it helped them to trust the message we that preached, which, of course, was the gospel of Jesus Christ and how to live together in harmony. In other words, the mere fact that we "got along" was one way to proclaim the gospel. And, no doubt, it strengthened the church as a result.

Pastor Randy Brandt, one of my pastoral colleagues at SOTV, tells the story of his first staff meeting at the church in 2002. With Randy, we had six pastors on staff at the time. He came to the meeting at which Chris spoke, then Mary spoke, then Bonnie spoke, while Paul, other staff members, and I chimed in. Afterward, Randy left the meeting and wondered to himself, "Who was in charge of that meeting anyway?" There was simply a feeling of camaraderie that was fostered by Paul and that caught on with the whole staff.

Duane: What About Staff Retreats?

Roger and Paul have a lot in common in their staff management style and philosophy. But I certainly noticed one sharp difference.

Roger was a huge advocate of staff retreats. Key staff people would go on a retreat together at least two times a year. These retreats were overnights, away from the rest of the world for two or three days and nights. I think Roger would say that he did those retreats for two reasons. First, to do some intense planning together so all were on the same page. And secondly, in order to build camaraderie. I certainly have lots of stories about those camaraderie-building experiences, including the nightly snoring of one staff person that literally rattled the windows of the retreat center.

Often, I felt like those retreats were a type of mountaintop experience. Great brainstorming, great relationship-building, lots of fun, and lots of work. But just like every trek up a mountain, you also need to get back to the valley. And that's where the really hard work occurred, back at church the following morning. I remember often thinking the day after a retreat, "Uh oh, what do I do now?"

On the other hand, Paul had a very different philosophy regarding retreats. In all the years I worked with Paul, we, as a staff, never had an overnight staff retreat. We had planning days, maybe one or two a year. But never overnight. To this day, I don't know if Paul snores or not.

Roger: You Need to Begin Somewhere

For three years, my ministry at St. Andrew's was that of a solo pastor. Other than a full-time secretary, my staff included a very part-time financial secretary who worked a couple of hours each week, an equally very part-time custodian, and a less than part-time organist. It was like that for my first three years. But apparently, we were doing some things right because our membership and worship attendance was beginning to grow. Of course, with increased attendance came increased financial support, which allowed us to begin to think about expanding the staff. The $50,000 budget I inherited in 1972 had grown in three years to $67,000 and though not a huge increase, it provided just enough money to fill some important holes in our ministry.

One of the blessings of ministry in the Twin Cities is the presence of Luther Seminary with, at that time, its eight hundred students preparing for the ministry. In September 1975, I put a notice on a bulletin board at the seminary advertising a twenty-hour-per-week job in youth ministry. I sugar-coated it a bit, saying that we were looking for an energetic seminarian willing to help create an exciting youth ministry program that would beat Young Life at its own game. One of the things I discovered in those first few years was that Young Life had become the youth ministry program for Mahtomedi. Instead of becoming involved in the weekly youth groups and summer experiences that St Andrew's had created, our high school students were boarding buses to head off to Young Life camp. It didn't make much sense to me that young people who had been baptized and confirmed and who had grown up at St. Andrew's needed to find another outlet to have their Christian batteries charged. My goal, as I stated in that little 3x5 ad at the seminary, was to build a youth program so powerful and exciting that there would be no need to go anywhere else for youth fellowship.

A first-year seminarian by the name of John Carlson was drawn to the advertisement. The next week, John and I sat down for an interview. I asked him why he would want to come and work at St. Andrew's? With a little glint in his eye, he said it was because of the challenge of doing something great. And with a hint of a smile, he said, "And it would be fun to try and outdo Young Life at its own game."

Seminarians come cheap, and so it was also possible in that third year to add a part-time director of Christian education whose job was mainly to help build our Sunday school program. Linda Wilson was a product of the Lutheran Bible Institute and came with some good solid background in Christian education. Under her leadership, Sunday school began to have some good structure and appeal that caused it to begin to see an increase in attendance. We were beginning to get on a roll.

Over the rest of my time at St. Andrew's, we were constantly seeking out talented pastors and lay professionals to add to our staff. One of those who made an indelible mark on the life of St. Andrew's was Duane Paetznick, who joined our staff in 1978 as our first full-time director of Christian education. Incredibly talented and committed to the task of growing a strong and effective education ministry, Duane changed the landscape of Christian education at St. Andrew's from run-of-the-mill to creative and exciting. Under his leadership, elementary youth sang, danced, and bonded as a group as they performed in musicals. It was that kind of bonding at the elementary level that would go on to become the foundation of a strong middle school and high school youth program.

Duane: A Group Hug

During my tenures at St. Andrew's and Shepherd of the Valley, staff members at both churches were treated very well. And many of us cared deeply for each other.

To illustrate how well we liked and cared for each other at St. Andrew's, one day, at the end of a long summer when many of us were out and about doing camps, youth trips, and our own vacations, Roger, John Carlson, John Keller, Phil Volkman, and I realized that we were all back together for the first time in months. We looked at each other with relief, walked toward each other, and began to embrace in a group hug. But we didn't let go. Instead, someone started jumping up and down (probably Roger). Soon, all of us big lugs were hugging, hopping, and laughing in unison. We were glad to see each other once again. Yeah, we liked each other.

Duane: Mentoring a Staff Person

Being a senior pastor in a large church usually means not just hiring and firing but also managing and mentoring the staff. My first year at St. Andrew's, when I was a wet-behind-the-ears twenty-four-year-old, Roger had that opportunity with me.

I was working with a group of high-school-aged youth on a musical play, and I was having difficulties with one of the kids. From my point of view, she was obstinate and self-centered. We didn't get along. One morning after a particularly difficult rehearsal with this young girl, I went into Roger's office and told him how I was feeling about the behavior of this fifteen-year-old. He patiently listened to my rant and then gave me some advice. He said, "Duane, you're the adult here. You're the one who needs to initiate making this right." Good advice. I tried to put it into practice. Eventually, the young woman and I came to understand each other. Best of all, though, I never forgot what he said—that I needed to take the initiative to make things right. It is also good advice for much of what happens in life. That's what good mentorship and management can do.

Roger: Was It Worth It?

When I was in seminary, I worked in several churches in the Twin Cities. A pastor in one of those churches was having some difficulty with his marriage. In fact, the unraveling of his marriage and his home life was beginning to affect his ministry. Wisely, he sought help and ended up in the office of the synod bishop. One afternoon, he shared with me something he had learned from one of those counseling sessions. The bishop had asked him how many hours he had worked each week. He had proudly said that it was around seventy to eighty hours. The bishop then asked if he had been taking his day off. Shrugging his shoulders, he answered, "Not that often." The bishop then asked why in the world he was putting in that much time in his church work. The pastor said that there was no one else to do all the things that needed to get done.

He said that the bishop just shook his head and said, "Let me tell you something! You can work yourself to the point of exhaustion. You can put all of your time and energy into building up your church. You can do that. It may mean the end of your marriage or, God forbid, a heart attack, but let me tell you this. You can work yourself to death, and I promise you, we'll give you a great funeral. Everybody will talk about how busy a pastor you were. And once you're in that grave, we'll put together a call committee, call a new pastor, and the congregation will pick up and move on. But what you need to know is that there will be a family left behind that will come and visit your grave and ask, "Was all of this worth it?"

One of the facts surrounding parish ministry is that the only person who can take care of the pastor is the pastor. It helps if there are some caring and concerned leaders who can help keep the pastor from getting too close to the cliff of personal self-destruction. Thankfully, in my ministry at St. Andrew's, there were many people who fulfilled that role for me and who verbally expressed to the church council and congregation the need for more staff. It was this kind of thinking and action that allowed St. Andrew's to begin to strategically hire more staff and call additional pastors to meet the needs of a congregation that intentionally wanted to grow.

Roger: Staffing for the Church You Want to Become

For years, church-growth experts who have studied congregational staffing levels have concluded that in order for a church to grow, there needs to be one full-time program staff person, or its equivalent, for every 150 people in weekend attendance. Go below that level and the congregation is staffed for decline. Stay at that level and the congregation is staffed for maintenance and not growth. Go above that level and the congregation will begin to experience a new sense of energy, growth, and purpose. What this simply means is that a congregation has greater control of its future than it might sometimes think. In other words, the congregation has a choice. It can either grow or die—and sadly, many churches have unconsciously decided to shrink and die.

One of the stumbling blocks toward adding more staff is money. In reality, it becomes a matter of seeing the congregation's budget as a glass that is either half full or half empty. The half-empty people see the financial resources of the congregation as having peaked. "We'd like to add staff, but where will the money come from?" is often the phrase that is spoken by pessimistic congregational leaders and members. It's a proper question to ask, but so often, the answer leads to the conclusion that the congregation has already contributed as much as possible and that there is simply no more money to be had. Thinking like that will put the congregation on a trajectory that will lead to its own demise. As it's true that mission follows vision, it's also true that once the vision is articulated, the dollars needed to fulfill that vision will begin to be contributed.

Part of the problem with many congregations is that they don't know where they want to go, so they never get to the point of letting their needs be known. A better way forward is to actually have a strategy for growth that the leadership and congregation can begin to embrace and fund. After all, what congregation doesn't want to see an exciting and meaningful education program for youth and adults? What congregation doesn't want to be a part of a vibrant ministry that includes exciting and uplifting worship? Congregations that actually hear the gospel's plea to feed the hungry and clothe the poor and want to act on it will discover willing givers who want to see their congregation make a difference in a hurting world.

Duane: Yeah, But . . .

Roger was always a glass-is-half-full leader. As he mentions above, he would cast the vision for the church and had faith that financial backing would follow. But not everyone on the church council had the same kind of glass-is-half-full attitude.

Understandably, one council member in particular, the financial person on the council, sometimes saw things differently than Roger. On occasion, Roger would enthusiastically bring up an idea, program, or possible new staff position. It was then that the treasurer would speak up, always beginning by saying, "Yeah, but . . ." and then going on to give his financial reasons why Roger's proposal might not be feasible. Eventually, the treasurer, in a self-deprecating manner, simply began to identify himself as Mr. Yeahbut. He saw that as his proper role. Every glass-half-full person needs a "yeah-but" in their midst—just so things don't go off the rails.

By the way, I have a sneaking suspicion that Carolyn, Roger's wife, was Mrs. Yeah-but at home.

Roger: Hiring and Calling the Right Candidate

Getting the right staff person is no easy task. The old cliché about wanting a pastor who is thirty-five years old with twenty years of experience, who is always out making calls yet always in the office—and who, in addition, can leap tall buildings in a single bound—is actually not that far from the truth. The only problem is that there is no such person. The sooner we come to grips with that reality, the closer we will be to getting the person we need.

Over the years, there are a few things I've picked up from leaders much smarter than myself. Here are those gems of wisdom.

The right candidate will pay for themself in the year in which they are hired.

A talented candidate who is energized, enthusiastic, and willing to contribute to the program growth of the congregation will bring about increased participation and the kind of support that will cause members to want to financially contribute to its continued success.

Vet the candidate before you hire or call them.

Getting the right person on board is more than just reading over a resume. Proper vetting of the candidate is essential for any success-ful hire. Experts have figured that getting the wrong person on staff and then having to let them go will cost the congregation at least $35,000 - $40,000.

The candidate needs to understand and fit into the culture of the congregation.

Every congregation and every area of the country has a certain kind of climate that controls the life of the congregation and contrib-utes toward its identity. Like it or not, different parts and regions of the country approach life and ministry in distinctive ways. Minnesota and the Upper Midwest gets cold and rainy . . . hardly a climate for someone used to basking in the sun and ocean surfing in January.

The right candidate might be closer than you think.

Congregations can sometimes fall into the mindset that a national search is needed for talent. But the person you want to add to your staff may just be closer than you think. One of the most talented business managers we hired during my tenure was right in the congregation. He was not only talented and skilled, but he also knew the culture of the congregation as well as its problems and potential.

It's better to hire people for their talent and not for their friendship. If you're going to be their boss, you can't let friendship get in the way. If friendships develop later, so be it, but let it be on the basis of knowing that you are their boss first and then their friend.

Hire from within your own denomination.

If someone is going to join your staff, that person needs to be able to embrace the theology and polity of your denomination. If the staff person is not of your denominational understanding of life and faith, they're going to go by the playbook of the denomination from which they came. They'll never be able to fully embrace a common theme and vision. The result can be a needless conflict between the senior pastor and the staff person. In addition, the kind of theology they bring to their task may even create confusion, which can lead to conflict amongst members who are forced to decide whose theology to follow.

Hire the person for what they like to do because that's what they're going to end up doing.

Square pegs never fit in round holes. Make sure the candidate wants to engage in the kind of ministry you're attempting to accomplish. The old cliché about the military putting the chef in charge of the motor pool not only robs the cook of the chance to prepare a great meal but also puts a wrench in the hand of someone who doesn't know squat about engines.

Give staff members the resources they need to succeed.

Lots of churches hire program people based on salary and benefits without taking into consideration the need for money in the budget to do the task at hand. Fund the budget line of staff people so they have some financial resources to use to do their jobs. Also, provide opportunities for continuing education with both time and money available in sufficient quantity to actually help them grow in their fields of endeavor.

Hire the best.

Hire leaders—because leading is what they are going to be doing. Hire the best you can find. Hire people who are capable of being team players. Hire staff who are capable of taking ministry to a new and higher level. Hire people with a good work ethic.

Allow current staff to grow.

One of the strengths of St. Andrew's was the longevity of members on staff. Many had been on staff for twenty or more years and were still contributing in new and exciting ways to the mission and ministry of the congregation. One feature that St. Andrew's offered its current staff was the ability to interview for new or vacant staff positions. The great part of this process was that it gave staff members the chance to rethink their current roles and decide whether they were still comfortable in those positions or wanted a change. It allowed a twenty-year veteran the chance for mobility without having to leave St. Andrew's to acquire it.

Duane: More on Roger's Point

I second Roger's advice to "allow current staff to grow." I was certainly able to do that during my stints at St. Andrew's and at Shepherd of the Val-

ley. I have told people, "Even though I'm still at this same church with the same title, every few years, I actually get a new job."

Perhaps this was most evident at Shepherd of the Valley. I began my ministry there as a director of Christian education, moved on to become a pastor in charge of educational ministry for all ages, followed later by focusing on adult education, and then ended my ministry overseeing care ministries. For one year, between senior pastors, I even was a co-lead interim senior pastor. In all, my position evolved into five or six different jobs. It is probably the main reason I stayed at the church for twenty-seven years. Allowing me to grow into multiple new positions was crucial to my longevity at both churches.

Roger: Two More Important Things about Staffing

Family comes first.

One time, a member came up to me and asked how my marriage was. The question sort of took me by surprise, and I wondered where in the world that question came from. After telling him it was fine, he said, "Well, that's good. Because you're no good to me if your family life and marriage is all a mess."

At St. Andrew's, family comes first. The reality of parish ministry is that our families put up with a lot of distractions and interruptions that are just a part of parish life. They sacrifice so that we can do our jobs, and the least we can do is to make sure that they know that family is important to us as pastors and staff. Take your vacation. Get out of town. For years, our family went to Canada for our vacations, going far enough out of town so that family time would not be interrupted. We also ate breakfast and dinner together as a family. In addition, we took the phone off the hook so that our meal would not be interrupted.

Know that you may have to let some staff people go.

Employment does not come with a lifetime guarantee. Sometimes the staff person you hired ends up being the staff person you need to let go. Coming to that decision is never easy. It's not easy for the person you need to let go, and it's not easy for the one who has the job of telling them . . . "It's over!"

My first firing was hard. I had mulled over the decision for quite some time. I consulted the council president, who said that the staff person was adequate but that he thought I never was satisfied with anyone who was just adequate. He agreed that I should go ahead and let him go. I sat down with the staff person and ran into some interference I hadn't expected. The interference was a strong defense as to why I shouldn't fire him. I wasn't prepared for this. I don't know what I had expected, but this was more than I was able to handle. It was lunch time, and I said, "We'll continue this discussion after lunch."

Now I was up against a wall. Wondering what to do, I called another council member. They said that I better let him go because if I didn't do it now, I was going to have to do it sometime soon and would have wasted time and money in the meantime. After that, I called a business owner who was a member. I laid out the issue, and the council member said that I'm actually doing the employee a favor. I said, "That's not what *he's* saying." Then I called my wife and told her of my dilemma. Within two seconds, she said, "Let me say this. You can't come home until you get it done!"

I got it done and was allowed to come home. In the end, it was the best decision that could have been made. His replacement excelled at the task and took the program to heights we had never anticipated.

Roger: Remember You Are Dust . . .

Ministry was never meant to be a solo experience. Try though we may, it's too big a job to be done alone. Even Moses tried it until one day, his father-in-law, Jethro, watched him working from morning to night doing the task of settling disputes among the people. Jethro noted that everyone else was just standing around watching Moses doing all the work to the point of exhaustion. So, with fatherly-in-law compassion, he sat Moses down and told him that this was not the best way to do it. "Keep this up," Jethro said, "and you'll just wear yourself out and wear out all the people who are watching you. The task is too heavy—you can't do it by yourself. You need to delegate! You need to let others do some of the work. Find some good, capable people out there and let them help you. And if you do this, God will give you strength, and you will be able to go on" (Exodus 18:14-23).

"Remember you are dust . . . and to dust you shall return"—words spoken on Ash Wednesday with the mark of the cross imposed on our forehead as a visual reminder of our humanity and the Savior to whom we belong. We are simply mortals with feet made of clay. We are mortals given the task of proclaiming the Good News of Jesus Christ to those who are willing to hear. Empowered by the Holy Spirit, we go from strength to strength, knowing that we have been chosen to participate in sharing the gift of Jesus Christ, who bids us to come and experience life in all its abundance. And the best part is that we do not have to do it alone!

Chapter 7

PREACHING

Duane: Two Different Styles of Preaching

One of the biggest fears many people have is speaking in public. Yet, *regularly speaking in public is a huge part of what it means to be a preacher. How do pastors do it? What kinds of things does a pastor need to be aware of while preaching? What skills are needed?*

As you might expect, Roger and Paul are both excellent preachers. Yet, they also are very different types of preachers. I've learned about good preaching from both of them.

They are particularly good storytellers. Both put a lot of work into their preaching. Each, in his own way, is invigorating, exciting, engaging, and challenging. People often say that they feel like Paul and Roger are speaking directly to them as they listen to their respective sermons.

Roger's style is inspirational, while Paul's style is more educational. Paul has a rich, folksy, informal, and low-key demeanor (à la Garrison Keillor). He tends to slowly reel you in with his stories, comments, illustrations, and key points. Roger, on the other hand, is more proclamatory. He tends to get to his point, make it with insights and illustrations, and end with a flourish that makes you feel like you've heard something important. Roger's sermons are relatively short—usually ten to fifteen minutes. Because of Paul's teaching style, his sermons tend to be longer—about twenty to twenty-five minutes in length. The fact that they are not the same yet are both equally engaging shows how there is no one exact formula for good preaching. You just know it when you hear it.

Roger: Preaching

Back around 2001, just prior to the beginning of a service, I walked up and down the aisle of our new sanctuary, greeting those who had come for Sunday worship. This was a practice I adopted early in my ministry. I always felt that it not only gave me the chance to welcome back a member we had not seen in a while or show a word of concern for someone who was struggling with a health or personal issue but also gave me the opportunity to greet newcomers to let them know how delighted we were to have them worshipping with us.

Well, on one Sunday morning, I got more than I bargained for. I was making my trek up the aisle greeting people when I happened to grab the hand of New Testament Professor Roy Harrisville of Luther Seminary. Roy was legendary for his frank and open opinion about most anything, and on that Sunday morning, he was in great form. As I grabbed his hand, telling him how happy I was to see him and thanking him for coming, he got up out of the pew, grabbed me by the front of my robe, and with a glint in his eye bordering on serious-ness and humor, said, "And this better be good!" To say that Roy took me by surprise is an understatement. Walking back to my seat, I kind of shook my head and wondered if, indeed, I would be able to meet his expectations.

Preaching, for me, has always been at the heart of what Christian ministry and being a pastor is all about. In fact, should St. An-drew's—or any church for that matter—shrink in size such that all of the added areas of ministry disappeared, it would still be the faithful gathering to hear the Word preached and the Sacraments adminis-tered. Pastor Harold Rasmussen once told me that the amount of time he spent preparing to preach was time well spent because it was in that hour of worship that he would be able to reach and speak to the greatest number of members he might see the entire week.

Roger: Preaching to Change Lives

It should go without saying that the life of Jesus Christ and the example he set through his teaching and preaching was fully intend-ed to make a difference in the lives of those who came to hear his words. For those who came to see Jesus as their Lord and Master, his words became a blueprint on how to live their lives. For them, there would be no going back to life as they used to live it. To know Christ's gift of forgiveness and another chance, to be able to put the past in the past, gave those who followed Jesus a new sense of free-dom and hope unlike anything they had ever known. The reality is that the story of the life, death, and resurrection of Jesus Christ is the most radical, life-changing story the world has ever known. The greatest privilege any preacher could hope to have is to be able to stand in front of hundreds and even thousands of people sharing what has come to be known as the Good News.

Someone has said that it is a sin to bore a kid. Well, it's just as much or maybe even a greater sin to bore an entire congregation of expectant worshippers who have come hoping to hear some words of inspiration and proclamation that can give clarity to the struggles and opportunities they are dealing with. What they don't want to sit through is a poorly prepared and sloppily preached sermon. I'll never forget Dr. Melvin Hammarberg, President of the Minnesota Synod, on the day of my installation at St. Andrew's, who let me and the rest of the congregation know that the pulpit can be a slippery slope if the preacher has not adequately prepared. He talked about taking the time to read, to study, and to pray before getting into the pulpit. He was, in a sense, putting me and the congregation on notice that one of the most important tasks a pastor is called to perform is that of preaching the Word honestly, with clarity and commitment. He also said that the preacher needs to prepare with the Bible in one hand and the newspaper in the other. In other words, to be biblically relevant to the contemporary needs and concerns of those who have come to hear.

Roger: Go for the Close!

One of the things a sermon should produce is action. To put it another way, the words that the preacher shares should be something more than empty words intended to fill a fifteen- or twenty-minute slot in the service. The sermon needs to motivate people to want to take up the cause of Jesus Christ in such a way that they will experience a change in direction, attitude, and commitment. What form that action might take will, of course, depend upon the listener. It could be the decision to make a complete change in the course in which their life was headed. It could also become a call to pause, slow down, and become more dependent upon the urgings of the Holy Spirit. It might also be the moment a person decides to seek forgiveness from someone they have offended or bring healing to bruised and ruptured family relations. Of course, to preach with the intent of changing people's lives means that preaching must be relevant and real. It means digging deep into the soil of what it means to be a human being and refocusing those struggles, opportunities, and disappointments through the lens of the grace and power of Jesus Christ. It means talking in a language that people today can relate to and understand.

Roger: What about Controversial Subjects?

I was once told by a parishioner that their impression of ministry was that the preacher in the pulpit was eight feet above criticism. What they were referring to is the fact that, barring a dialogue sermon, most all preaching ends up being a one-way conversation. Because it is a one-way opinion coming from the mouth of the preacher, tackling controversial subjects from the pulpit puts the member in the pew in an uncomfortable position of being unable to respond to what the preacher is saying. For example, there are cases in which good people on both sides of an issue disagree on how the situation should be remedied. To put the worshipper in the pew in a situation in which they have no chance of objecting to what the preacher is saying is, quite simply, unfair.

Now, there are occasions that demand the preacher puts both feet into the hot water of current and controversial issues . . . issues such as race relations or matters which clearly cross the line and are a flagrant disregard for justice and respect for the rights of others. And, as Jesus was not shy in shedding biblical light on questionable behavior or practices, neither should the preacher be.

There is, after all, an expectation that the preacher not run away from prophetic preaching that boldly declares the gospel. But, as in most things, there is a proper time and place for everything.

One thing I've learned along the way is that forums and scheduled conversations about controversial subjects that look at the matter at hand from a number of viewpoints not only become educational events but also offer the chance for reasonable people to hear and be heard. An event scheduled around a touchy subject offers the opportunity to bring in outside experts who can not only become avenues of information but also offer attendees the chance to verbalize their positions.

I remember one occasion during the Vietnam War when we created an event on a Saturday morning and afternoon where people on both sides of the war issue were invited to come and hear from protesters as well as members of the military. We even invited Lutheran representatives from Honeywell to talk about their personal struggle as Christians with building weapons of war in the face of Christ's admonition to seek peace. It was an event that not only included lunch and a time for conversation around a sandwich and a cup of coffee but also a prayer service at the end of the day pleading for an end to all wars. It was a challenging subject, but because people had the chance to hear and be heard, the potential for dividing the congregation was avoided and some new friendships were also created.

Roger: Preparing to Preach

With a houseful of kids and a congregation that was growing, finding the time for sermon preparation was paramount and challenging. As a father and husband, I never wanted to short-change my family. And as a pastor, I knew that if I wanted to avoid the pulpit becoming that slippery slope mentioned earlier, I had better well find the time to prepare.

There are pastors out there who have an entire season's worth of sermons "in the bag" and ready to be preached. Sadly, that is not me. I was a week-by-week preacher who, when my most recent sermon was preached, sat down to try and figure out what I was going to say the following Sunday. To help put together a sort of method that would work for me and not short-change the time I wanted to spend with my family, on Monday, I began reading and re-reading the text on which the sermon was going to be based. I also kept my eyes and ears open for illustrations and current events that could contribute to the message I wanted to convey. Tuesday and Wednesday were spent in a similar fashion. On Thursday, however, I stayed away from the office and headed off to the seminary, where the real preparation for the sermon would take place. Friday was my day off, and I made it a point to make Friday and Saturday time for my family. And then there was Saturday night.

When I was an associate at Richfield Lutheran Church, I learned that Harold Rasmussen made it a point never to schedule anything on Saturday night when he was going to preach the next morning. Rasmussen felt that he needed to be rested and prepared for the 1,500 people who would be coming to hear him preach at one of the three morning services. It was also known amongst those closest to him that Rasmussen would preach and re-preach his sermon in his basement using the ironing board as his pulpit. When he was through with that, he would take a baby aspirin and head off for bed, knowing that he was fully prepared for the next morning marathon.

For good or ill, I adopted the Rasmussen Saturday-night preaching plan. For fifty-four years, my wife and I have hardly ever done anything on Saturday night when I was scheduled to preach the next day. It just became a part of how we lived our lives. For me, the final sermon preparation took place after Saturday night supper. Leaving the kids and my wife at home, I would head off to my office at church. Locked in my office with no one around, I zeroed in on polishing up my final sermon draft. Once that was done (sometimes as late as midnight), I would head into the sanctuary, turn on the lights, fire up the sound system, get in the pulpit, and preach my sermon. Over and over, I would preach and re-preach that sermon until I was confident that I had it under control and could finally go home, get some sleep, and be ready for three—and eventually four—Sunday services.

Roger: Preaching Without Notes

There was a time when I would take the entire written text of my sermon into the pulpit. That all ended one Friday night in December 1979 when I was on a ski trip with our high school students at Welch Village in southern Minnesota. On the last run of the day, I fell, and the bindings didn't release. The result was three torn ligaments in my knee. Within three days, I was in surgery, and for months, I walked around with crutches and a cast. Since the pulpit involved going up a flight of stairs, the only option I had for preaching was to sit in the middle of the aisle on a bar stool.

Needless to say, sitting on a bar stool shuffling pages of sermon notes did not seem workable. So, the only solution was to preach while holding a single 3 x 5 notecard with a couple of bullet points to help me remember where I was in the sermon. It ended up being a blessing in disguise. Freed from being tied to pages of text, my preaching took on a new sense of freedom. Thus . . . ditch the pages and get it all on a 3 x 5 note card.

Duane: Preaching With Notes

I heard Roger preach both with a manuscript and with his 3 x 5 cards. Either way, he was a good preacher. I've heard plenty of preaching over the years and seen many different styles of delivery. Some preachers use manuscripts (word-for-word documents), some use note cards, some use no notes at all, and some memorize the sermon. In my experience, I have found that in preaching (as in all public speaking), the more eye contact, the better. But that does not necessarily mean that a preacher should not use a manuscript. If the preacher uses a manuscript, they need to be mindful of looking up regularly to make eye contact with the congregation.

I largely used a manuscript when I preached. The reason I did so was because my wife Phyllis, who has heard almost every sermon I've ever preached, said that there were times when being precise in what I had to say was very important. At some points in a sermon, I may need to actually read what I wrote. Using a manuscript was also helpful in that I felt I could focus on the message and not on whether I'd remember what I was trying to say. It was a kind of safety net.

Paul often used a manuscript at Shepherd of the Valley (SOTV), but he would stray from the manuscript from time to time. He seemed to use the manuscript as a road map. His eye contact during a sermon was superb. Sometimes you could tell that he was reading portions of his sermon, but that didn't seem to matter because his delivery was so smooth.

Once, I asked Paul if I could have a copy of his sermon, so he gave the manuscript to me. He had handwritten the whole sermon. Trouble was, I could hardly read his "chicken-scratching." I'm surprised he could even read his own writing. One time, he gave me one of his sermons, and I said to him, "I don't know how you can even read that."

To which he replied, "Everyone has their own hieroglyphics"—which was what his writing resembled.

Roger: Illustrate, Illustrate, Illustrate

One of the tasks that never ended for me was finding illustrations that I could use to give a sermon something people could hang their hats on and remember. In the old days, before computers and Google, that meant either subscribing to monthly newsletters or going through the stacks in the seminary library, hoping to find something that might be appropriate. I soon became quite adept at cutting out newspaper and magazine articles that I would file away for later use.

It was always amazing that when I found myself stuck on some sort of transition, there usually was an illustration or joke in that file folder that could come to my rescue. However, once the internet became a staple in every home, jokes and illustrations became harder to use since many people had already discovered and read them online.

Roger: "Pastor, We Want to See Jesus!"

There's an old story about a pastor who climbed into the pulpit for the first time in her new congregation. As she looked down at the pulpit, she saw a note with the words, "Pastor, we want to see Jesus!" It was a simple plea but a huge assignment for the new pastor. What kind of preaching should she be engaged in if she were to help them see Jesus? What kind of words would she use? What kind of attitude would she assume as she went about the business of preparing her weekly message?

That pastor, however, wasn't the first to be saddled with that task. In John 12:21, we meet a group of Greeks who come to Philip with the same request. They had heard about Jesus and now wanted to meet with him. They were on a journey they hoped would bring meaning and clarity to their lives, and now they wanted to meet the person they had heard could fulfill that longing. "Sir, we want to see Jesus!" A simple request—but one filled with more power and hope if granted.

"We want to see Jesus" is exactly where each and every person who walks through the door of any church is at. They are not looking for fluff. They are not expecting ten easy ways to get through life unscathed. They are wanting to meet the man—the God-man—Jesus, who rose from the dead and gave the promise of everlasting life to all who would believe. That is what they are looking for, and as preachers, we had better be ready and able to tell them about the one who has given hope to our lives and the lives of millions throughout the world.

Back in the 1800s, a powerful preacher by the name of Philips Brooks gave a definition of preaching. He said, "Preaching is the communication of truth by one person to another." Telling the truth about Jesus is what preachers are called to do. Sermons need to be bathed in prayer. A message that will change people's lives needs to be filled with the power and guidance of the Holy Spirit. It also means that the preacher needs to preach at the level of the people with whom they are trying to share the gospel, to humbly let people know that they too are human . . . a sinner in need of redemption. Or, simply put, that like the rest of the congregation, the preacher also pulls their pants on one leg at a time. You will know you're succeeding when someone comes up to you and says, "Pastor, you spoke directly to me this morning. How did you know what to say?"

Duane: Who Preaches When There Are Multiple Preachers on Staff?

People sometimes wonder how we figured out who would preach on any given weekend at SOTV when we had multiple possible preachers—at one point, seven pastors on staff. It wasn't always easy. Every person who becomes a pastor does so in part because they like to preach. So when there are only a limited number of times to preach, figuring out who preaches is very important to these preachers.

At SOTV, the senior pastor was the primary preacher. Usually, the senior pastor, which for much of my time at the church was Paul, would preach at about a third of the services. The remaining services would be divided equally between the remaining preachers. The schedule for preaching was put together by an objective third party well in advance—usually three to six months in advance. We often heard from people in the congregation that they really enjoyed hearing different voices by having a variety of preachers.

*For many years, we had worship services simultaneously in two loca-
tions—a band-led worship service in the Great Hall and an organ-led worship service in the sanctuary. Every weekend, there would be at least two
different preachers, one in each location. In addition, because there were
many worship services throughout the year aside from the regular weekend
services (for example, Ash Wednesday and Good Friday), there were probably close to 120 possible preaching events. Also, of course, each preacher was
able to preach at weddings and funerals. So I figure most years, I preached
about twice a month at regular worship services and once or twice a month
at a funeral or wedding. That comes out to about forty sermons a year. For
me, this was perfect. It meant I did not need to prepare a sermon every week,
which can become burdensome. In addition, it meant that I had some time
between sermons to do thorough, in-depth preparation.*

Paul: A High and Holy Calling

Many years ago, I took a class at the seminary on preaching. As I
entered the classroom, I noticed a small piece of paper tacked on a
bulletin board. What it said, I have never forgotten. It said, "There are
two kinds of speakers in the world, those who have something to say
and those who have to say something. The difference between them is
like a lightning bolt and a lightning bug!" Through almost fifty years
of ordained ministry, I have tried to make this a motto for my life—
especially as it applied to my preaching. Coupled with this thought is
something that Dr. David Preus once shared with a group of pastors.
He said that the greatest sin pastors ever commit is to make worship—and especially our preaching—dull, uninteresting, and uninvit-
ing.

Without a doubt, preaching is the most important responsibility
and privilege for any parish pastor. To stand before your flock week
after week and offer words of hope, direction, forgiveness, comfort,
encouragement, and conviction is a high and holy calling. In fact,

there is no other job in the world quite like it. And when it is done well, both the preacher and the congregation will greatly benefit from this experience. It is through the preaching of the word and the celebration of the Sacraments that the soul is fed and nourished. This is why our weekly pilgrimage to the church for worship is so very important. Even Jesus, on the Sabbath day, "went up to the synagogue as was his custom" (Luke 4:16). Without this regular "feeding," we become what T.S. Elliot called "The Hollow Men." And it is quite possible for us mortals to spiritually starve to death.

The admonition to do good preaching runs through the scriptures as well. Jesus came to his hometown one Sabbath day and was asked to read from the book of Isaiah. "The Spirit of the Lord is upon me because he has anointed me to bring good news to the poor . . . to proclaim release to the captives and recovery of sight to the blind, to let the oppressed go free, to proclaim the year of the Lord's favor" (Luke 4:18-19). St. Paul tells us to "proclaim the message; be persistent whether the time is favorable or unfavorable; convince, rebuke, and encourage, with the utmost patience in teaching" (II Timothy 4:2). And, of course, these memorable words from Romans 10: "And how are they to believe in one of whom they have never heard? And how are they to hear without someone to proclaim him? And how are they to proclaim him unless they are sent? As it is written, 'How beautiful are the feet of those who bring good news!' So, faith comes by what is heard, and what is heard comes through the word of Christ" (Romans 10:14-15 & 17). And again, in Acts 5:20, an angel tells the apostles to "go, stand in the temple and tell the whole message about this life." Peter preaches on Pentecost, and three thousand souls are brought to faith in Jesus.

In the earliest days of my ministry, when, I am sure, my preaching was quite lame at times, I would often ask myself: What keeps these good people coming back Sunday after Sunday? Their presence is totally voluntary. And every pastor knows that there are Sundays when the sermon is notoriously lacking in inspiration. Still, the people come. What is more, most pastors have had the joyful experience of the grace of God when, standing repentant after delivering a sermon that could only be called lousy, a sincere parishioner approaches and says, "Thank you, Pastor, those words really spoke to my heart this morning." There is an old joke about a pastor who preaches on Pentecost Sunday and then comes home to ask her husband if she had enough "fire" in her sermon that morning. Her husband replies, "There wasn't enough of your sermon in the fire!"

The privilege of preaching comes from knowing that people come to the church wanting to hear a word from God that also applies meaningfully to their daily lives. Of course, there are other reasons for coming to church, but each person is seeking some kind of revelation from God, no matter how small that bit of revelation may be. The preacher is privileged to set aside some serious time each week to plumb the depths of the Bible. Who else is granted the time and the tools to "mine" those biblical texts for nuggets of wisdom, truth, and meaning? Who else is asked to study and reflect on the human condition in order to translate these sacred texts and make them applicable to particular people at a particular place and time? Who else is asked to sojourn with a group of believing people for several years in order to be able to preach to them as a wise, compassionate, and faithful shepherd? Who else has a standing invitation to preach both the law and the gospel to a congregation that may be struggling to keep body and soul together? Thank God for all those humble souls who keep showing up for worship despite our sometimes-lackluster preaching. And, most of all, thank God for the Word that gives preachers something to say that is worth hearing.

Paul: Five Factors for a Good Sermon

Many years ago, a Rabbi friend of mine named Israel Halpern gave me his advice for preaching: "If you haven't struck oil after twenty minutes, stop boring." George Burns once remarked that the secret of a good sermon is to have a good beginning and a good ending and for these two things to be as close together as possible. So, what constitutes a good sermon? For me, there are five factors that greatly determine the value of a sermon.

The Text for the Sermon

I often did textual preaching, but I was not afraid of doing topical preaching as well. Good examples were the Sundays after the Martin Luther King Jr. assassination, the Challenger blowing up seconds after liftoff, the Columbine massacre, the events of 9/11/01, or the I-94 bridge collapse in Minneapolis. These events were so tragic, so powerful, and so timely that they needed be addressed from the pulpit. (We had a guest preacher at the seminary the morning after Martin Luther King Jr. was shot in April of 1968, and he never once mentioned the assassination. This was an unforgivable oversight.) Each of these events evokes all kinds of questions. Where is God in all of this? Who, if anyone, should be blamed? Why does God allow bad things to happen to good people? These are real opportunities to address such tragic events in the light of the scriptures and to help people make some sense out of our flawed, broken, and sinful world. When the preacher does this well, the audience will be grateful indeed.

Further, I have noticed that we almost seem afraid to highlight national holidays in our preaching. This is a huge mistake. Mother's Day or Father's Day are the perfect times to highlight the attributes of the Christian home and family. On July 4th weekend, talk about Christian freedom, which is the exact opposite of how the world often defines freedom. On Memorial Day, celebrate all the saints who have gone before us and especially those who have spilled their blood in service to our nation. Thanksgiving is a no-brainer. This theme runs through the whole of scripture. And how about a sermon on Labor Day entitled "God Looks at My Job"? These are secular holidays for the most part, but the preacher should always be closely attuned to where people are on any given Sunday.

Just to illustrate, one Memorial Day weekend during worship, we paused and paid tribute to all the past and current military personnel who were with us that morning. This can be done without glorifying war. I had all of the military members stand to be recognized. We saluted them with my words, ended this part of the service with a heartfelt prayer, and then asked for a round of applause. Later, as I was standing by the door greeting folks as they left the building, a middle-aged veteran came up to me with tears streaming down his face. He hugged me for the longest time and told me that as a Vietnam War veteran, this was the first time that he had ever received any public recognition for his service to our nation. He thanked me profusely. I learned that day that the church can do real ministry even on secular national holidays.

Preparation

There is no substitute for doing your homework and doing it well. I always said that preaching was a joy when you were prepared, and it was real work when you weren't. In the seminary, we were told to spend one hour of study for each minute in the pulpit. It is crucial to prepare well, and especially these days when those sitting in the pews have advanced degrees in just about every field under the sun. They are not going to tolerate a fool or shallow thinking in the pulpit.

Pastors today need to read from three libraries: the library of the Bible; the library of books, magazines, and periodicals; and, perhaps most important of all, the library of life. I used to put the preaching texts for the coming week in my left shirt pocket (over my heart) each Monday morning and refer to them many times over the course of that week. Then, when I got down to actually writing the sermon on Friday or Saturday, those texts were very familiar to me. The preacher has to connect these two- or three-thousand-year-old texts with people now living in the twenty-first century. It can be done and done well but not without lots of study, prayer, research, and due diligence.

Delivery

I used to practice my sermons four to six times each week using words and phrases that flowed smoothly off my lips. I also tried to use words that would leave no one feeling like I was talking "over their heads." Practice may not always make perfect, but it is vital to the effective delivery of a sermon. I would sometimes even preach the sermon to my wife for her honest comments and criticisms.

The Room

One of the real challenges of preaching has always been whether the preacher is telling the listeners what they *want* to hear or what they *need* to hear. To put it another way, is the preacher just a thermometer measuring the temperature of the room, or is the preacher's calling to be a thermostat that seeks to literally change the temperature in the room?

Also, it's good to take the literal temperature of the room. There is a need to consider the ambiance in which you are preaching. Too hot or too cold? Good acoustics or echo canyon? Crying babies or stone silence? Excellent sound system or the cheapest system money could buy? Cushioned seats or hard benches? Hanging from the rafters or sparsely attended? Any or all of these factors can affect how well your sermon is received.

It's God's Work

The most important thing of all is that the Holy Spirit shows up when you are preaching. In the end, this is God's work. There is an old saying: work like it all depends on you, and pray like it all depends on God. My mother used to tell me to preach like some people were hearing the gospel for the first time ever and some were hearing it for the last time ever. If you do this, she would say, you will be a good preacher. Another old friend told me that you don't have to hit a home run every Sunday, but you should at least get to first or second base. God chooses to use us mortals with all our foibles to bring about God's kingdom here on earth.

Duane: I Saved This Note from Paul

As a budding preacher myself, Paul would occasionally give me some sound advice about my preaching. The way he did this was through written notes. In fact, for good or ill, often when Paul was offering a critique of something, he would write it down and pass it along to me in my mailbox at church rather than delivering it verbally.

I saved some of those notes. Here's one of them that he gave me after I preached a sermon where I used the term "Jesus" quite often:

> Duane, you have had some great sermons late-
> ly. Keep up the good work. Let me add one word of
> comment. Actually, it came to me from an old
> preaching prof. He said that since we are almost
> constantly using the name of Jesus (a good name, by
> the way!) in our sermons, we should also try to find
> variations on the name to avoid repetition. I struggle

*with this myself but offer a few good substitutes: Je-
sus, the person of Christ, the Messiah, our Lord, the
Savior, the Man from Nazareth, Rabbi, our eternal
king, etc. Not all of these would fit in one particular
sermon, but it is kind of fun to think about variation
since, as I said, we are constantly using the name.
Food for thought. I also appreciate feedback on my
sermons, so don't hesitate to speak your mind if you
feel like it. Always good working with you, Duane!
It's a good partnership. Blessings, Paul H.*

Paul: Tell Me, Show Me, and Move Me

An old pastor friend of mine once told me that he judges the value of a sermon by how much he "silently dialogues" with the preacher. What he meant by this is he engaged with the preacher in a kind of
inner conversation, sometimes agreeing, sometimes disagreeing,
sometimes adding his own ideas. This is a very helpful insight about
the type of engagement that preachers should seek with their listeners.

There are three things that must happen if a sermon is to be
judged worthwhile. First, *tell* me what you want me to know and to
believe. Most preachers do well in this regard. State your case and
state it well.

Secondly, *show* me what you want me to know and to believe.
Here, many preachers fail miserably. A good sermon should always
include at least three illustrations that are so memorable people will
have a hard time forgetting them. These illustrations should not need
further explanation. The illustration should explain itself. If you have
to explain it in any detail, then it's not a good story. Finding these
priceless examples may be some of the hardest work a preacher ever
does. Examples and stories paint pictures in people's minds that
should be hard to erase. Whenever I started to share a good illustra-

tion in my preaching, I could literally see faces raised to a greater level of attention and engagement. I have over one hundred files in my office with hundreds of illustrations that illuminate many biblical texts. Jesus, after all, was a consummate storyteller, and we still remember these stories twenty centuries later. Also, in preaching, it's good to shoot just one or maybe two "bullets" rather than a "shotgun blast" that hits no one. Be focused.

Thirdly, *move* me. When the sermon is over, instead of people saying, "Ho-hum, so what," they should be willing to rise to the challenge and follow wherever the preacher may wish to take them. If all three of these things align themselves, it will have been a very good sermon indeed.

Paul: Some Preaching Hints

A few more thoughts come to mind. One, preach to people's possibilities. You don't get beans to grow by pounding them into the ground. You water, cultivate, nurture, and even fertilize plants to get them to grow. So too with people. You don't have to spend much time reminding them of their failures and shortcomings. They are often all too aware of such things.

Two, don't shed light on the Bible. Rather, let the light of the Bible shed light on life. Tell the biblical story but then move quickly to the practical application of life. What in God's name (spoken with all reverence) does this text have to do with my life? Answer that question satisfactorily, and you will know that you are a good preacher.

Three, be genuine. Sometimes preachers think that they have to put on some different persona to be effective in the pulpit. Actually, it's quite the opposite. Alvin Rogness once suggested that "preachers should talk about the gospel the way a farmer talks about his favorite Holstein cow." People smell phoniness a mile away, and there are already enough "snake oil" preachers and performers on television.

Just be yourself and people will come to embrace you as a fellow traveler on the road of life.

And four, when the sermon concludes, the people should want to pray, and the preacher should lead them in prayer, asking God to effect in their lives just what the sermon has promised and proclaimed. A good sermon should always put the believer into a closer proximity to God.

Paul: A Personal Note

When I was in high school speech classes and later in college and seminary, I was given opportunities to do a fair amount of public speaking and preaching. In addition, I spent several summers working at church Bible camps where some preaching was required. Also, while in college, I did a lot of "pulpit supply" at a number of smaller rural churches in northern Minnesota and eastern North Dakota where there were pastoral vacancies. My point is that I discovered that declaring the Good News of the Gospel from a variety of pulpits was very much to my liking. In fact, it was downright fulfilling. Later, as I became more proficient at preaching, I simply fell in love with the whole process. If worship went well on any given Sunday, I would go home feeling totally exhilarated. Even after preaching seven or eight sermons on Christmas Eve or Easter weekend, I would go home physically tired but emotionally elated and spiritually fulfilled.

Never once in my life did I ever doubt my call to Christian ministry, and nearly every time I stepped into the pulpit, that sense of call was further validated. For this, I thank God. I will be forever grateful to each and every one of the souls that I was honored to minister to and who in any way benefited from my preaching. As my college motto reads: Soli Deo Gloria. To God Alone the Glory.

Duane: Law and Gospel

I hate to get too philosophical here, but I think it is important to under-stand something about "Lutheran preachers." Besides all the things that preachers try to do—the things that Roger and Paul have recounted in this chapter—there's another thing that Lutheran preachers, in particular, try to do. That is, we seek to preach in a fashion we call "law and gospel." This is a phrase that comes from Martin Luther. Although you could study this no-tion for years and still not understand it entirely, essentially, what it means is that God's Word, when preached correctly, does two things to the listener.

First, it convicts. That is, it helps us to hear that we are not all we think we're cracked up to be. It names the fact that there is a brokenness we all ex-perience. We simply aren't able to measure up by using our own devices. The law reminds us of that. You might even say that when we really hear about that brokenness, it leads to despair, or, as preachers say, "the law kills us."

But, for Lutherans, good preaching doesn't stop with the law. The law is balanced out by the "gospel." Hearing the gospel helps us understand the message that even though we aren't what we think we're cracked up to be and that we are broken, God still loves us anyway—unconditionally. Preach-ers like to say that while the law leads to despair—and even kills you—the gospel gives hope and raises you up.

That may sound simple, but it is not, because different people hear things differently. Someone may hear something as "law," but the person they are sitting next to may hear those same words differently. This kind of preaching is always contextual, which means that how the listener hears the law and the gospel depends on their own situation. For example, when told the words "you are forgiven," one person might hear it as gospel and think, "Yes, I feel so relieved!" But a second person might not hear it as gospel at all because they are thinking, "Why do I need to be forgiven? I've done noth-ing wrong." People hear things through their own filters. Lutheran preachers try to be mindful of this dynamic in the listener, but it can be challenging.

Duane: Preaching at Funerals and Weddings

Most preachers would rather preach at a funeral than at a wedding. I liked preaching at both. As you might expect, the type of preaching that happens at funerals is vastly different from preaching at weddings.

At weddings, typically, the focus isn't on the preacher or what the preacher is saying. It's on the couple getting married. Yet, the sermon at a wedding can be done in such a way that it's both true to the gospel and honors the couple getting married.

Typically, the funeral sermon is much more impactful on the hearer. They wonder about death. They are listening for any word of hope and comfort. Thus, often those in attendance at a funeral are very open to what is being said by the preacher. One of my professors at seminary said that the one time that a preacher doesn't need to preach the "law" is at a funeral because "the law" is lying in the casket in the front of the sanctuary. People are already feeling the weight of human brokenness. They don't need to be reminded of it at a funeral. Rather, this is the place to proclaim the gospel because people are begging for that kind of hope at the time of death.

Duane: The Medium Is the Message

Like almost every pastor, I, too, loved to preach. For me, it was a highlight of my career in ministry. I loved every aspect of the task—Bible study, research, imaginative thinking, thinking homiletically, looking for good illustrations (including visuals), outlining, writing, preparing the delivery, delivering the sermon to the congregation, and, as my wife likes to say, being in front of a "captive" audience. Every part of that process was rewarding for me. When I did it right, delivering the sermon was probably the easiest part of the whole process.

There was one thing I noticed throughout the years in my preaching that struck me as odd. Over time, more and more people would say to me, "Pastor, your preaching is getting better all the time." Now, it was probably true that my preaching was actually getting better. But I have a sneaking *suspicion that the underlying reason people said those words to me is because they were getting to know me as a person. You see, preaching is autobiographical. By that, I mean that when a person preaches, that person is not only telling about God, the Bible, and life, but revealing themself to others. In other words, the preacher himself is bound up in the message he is proclaiming. Often, the better the listener knows the preacher, the more the listener is open to the message. Even for preaching, Marshall McLuhan's dictum is true: the medium is the message—or at least a big part of it*

Chapter 8

WORSHIP & MUSIC

Duane: By the Numbers

People have occasionally asked me, "How big is the church where you work?" I could have cited the number of members, the number of family units, or the yearly budget. The problem with each of these numbers is that different churches count each of those things differently. The best way to answer is to cite the number of people attending worship each weekend. From church to church, that number is quite objective and easily discernible. Using "worship attendance" gives a better perspective than any other measure.

It also is a crucial number because it can serve as a barometer of the vitality of a church. Worship is at the core of the church. So the number of people attending worship is a good indicator of how a church is doing. Is that number going up or down? The answer to that question may very well indicate the effectiveness of a church.

Roger was quite a stickler for tracking the worship numbers. Throughout his tenure at St. Andrew's, he kept his own chart of these week-to-week numbers posted on the inside of his office door. Every week, he wrote down the number and compared that number to the previous year. He always said, "In the church, people vote with their feet."

However important the number of people in worship is as an indicator of church size, growth, and vitality, worship is about much more than just numbers. Below, Roger and Paul both discuss some critical aspects of worship.

Paul: Gathering and Scattering

There is some humor connected with this matter of worship. One old gentleman complained that he only went to church three times in his life. First, they threw water on him, then they threw rice, and finally, they threw dirt. There is another saying that rather accurately describes a portion of our population. It declares that we worship our work, work at our play, and play at our worship.

I have always believed that regular worship of the Triune God is central to the Christian faith. It was Jesus himself who went "to the synagogue on the Sabbath day, as was his custom" (Luke 4:16). If it was that important for our Lord, how much more so for you and me? There is, after all, a commandment that reminds us that one day in seven has been designated for rest and, by implication, for worship. The world may make light of this admonition, but the commandment has surely stood the test of time.

I sometimes think of the story of "doubting Thomas." Actually, this title is something of a misnomer. He really was "absentee Thomas." Perhaps his real problem was that, for whatever reason, he was not with the other disciples when Jesus made his post-Easter appearance in the upper room. As a result, his doubts persisted. This great truth has never changed. When we come together for worship as God's people with some degree of regularity, we can be changed, and our faith can be deepened and expanded. Perhaps Oliver Wendell Holmes, the great Supreme Court justice said it best, "There is a little plant inside of me that needs watering at least once a week."

Do we find anything in the Bible that smacks of a private religious experience or teaches us that faith can be lived out in a vacuum? We are to be the gathered and scattered people of God who come together weekly around the Word and the Sacraments to be fed, nurtured, renewed, taught, inspired, and commissioned to go back out into the world with the light of the gospel. Some time ago, a woman told me why she came to worship each week. She said that the news was so good that after five or six days, she began to doubt it, and she just needed to hear it once again on the next Sabbath day. We were made for the human community. This is one valuable contribution that the church brings to the world.

Worship is the lifeblood of the church. But often, the world has a distorted understanding of worship. Well-meaning people say things like, "I don't go to church because I don't get anything out of it," or, "It's boring." The question is not how much do I get out of worship, but rather, how much do I put into worship? Worship is the "work" of God's people. The word "worship" and the word "work" have the same root derivation. Worship is not entertainment, though it can and should be both engaging and inspiring. I am giving to God my time, my voice, my attention, my thanks, my energy, my prayers, my praise, my wealth, and my confession—in short, my life!

In truth, worship is one of the most unique things we do in life that also rescues us from those powerful, innate tendencies toward self-centeredness. Worship calls us to break out of the cocoon of self and to offer ourselves totally and unconditionally to God and to others. In doing so, we discover exactly why God placed us on this planet.

Paul's Ground Rules about Worship

As many of you are aware, worship in the church in recent decades has changed dramatically—especially in the areas of liturgy and music. We hear such terms as contemporary, traditional, and blended. While the organ still has its place, we now use virtually every other instrument you can think of. I recall talking to a woman many years ago who introduced the guitar to her church while directing a children's choir, and for this, she received a huge amount of criticism. Only over a long period of time was this "new" instrument accepted at her church. At Shepherd of the Valley (SOTV), we made worship and music very high priorities. Besides good biblical preaching that addressed the real-life needs of worshippers and relevant, engaging liturgies, we also wanted inspiring, uplifting music, be it vocal or instrumental. We generously funded our music programs, hiring the most talented directors we could find. In short, we wanted the worship hour to speak to all people, regardless of their age, background, or previous church affiliations. Below are some things that we tried to do at SOTV over the years.

One, announcements need to be invitational and enthusiastic, have broad appeal, and, most of all, be brief! One to two minutes max. Some time ago, I worshipped at a church that had eleven minutes of announcements. If you want to "kill" a worship hour, this will do it every time.

Two, choose hymns that are melodic and user-friendly. In my judgment, about one-fifth of the hymns in any Lutheran hymnal are almost unsingable for the average worshipper. Remember that Martin Luther based some of his hymns on old German drinking songs, so the melodies he chose were familiar to his congregation. Even if the lyrics of the hymn fit the texts of the day, it may still be a very unsingable hymn. This is not to say that we should not learn new melodies. I was always thinking of the person in the back row who wanted very much to sing but had no special musical training. That person was often my target audience, someone I kept in mind when choosing hymns.

Three, I learned early on that there are two kinds of organists. Those that come to lead in worship and those who come to perform. The difference is like night and day. Organists can stifle congregational singing by drowning it out. I firmly believe that if the organist can't hear the congregation as they sing, then they are playing too loud. Their primary role is not to perform but to encourage robust congregational singing. Save the recitals for another venue. I know of one church where the organist insists on playing lengthy hymn introductions that are so convoluted and confusing that literally no one can find the pitch until they are about three or four bars into the hymn. Music must have genuine appeal to all worshippers and not just to an elite group of highly gifted or professionally trained musicians.

The organists I've worked with have often been finely tuned to the congregation. In fact, when the Minnesota Twins won the world series, our organist, who was an avid Twins fan, discarded her standard postlude piece. Instead, she played "Take me Out to the Ballgame." The congregation loved it and talked about it for weeks.

Four, effective preaching is essential. While on vacation some time ago, I attended a worship service in which the sermon did not include one story, one example, or one life illustration. The theological content was solid, but the delivery was that of a seminary lecture. Now, if Jesus was anything, he was truly a storyteller, and we do well to closely follow his lead.

Preaching need not be "fire and brimstone" to be effective. Though I do remember one Pentecost Sunday when we had a guest preacher who waxed eloquently about the "tongues of fire" that rested on the believers that first Pentecost. Just at that moment, some kid in another part of the building pulled the fire alarm. The alarm was so loud, it could easily have driven us all out of the building. Luckily it was a false alarm. But we had a good laugh at the coincidence of it.

Five, liturgy should be short, sweet, and simple. Liturgy is the glue that holds the other parts of the service together. Liturgy is not an end in itself but a means to an end. If it helps people to worship, use it. If not, change, modify, or even delete some of it. Liturgy can be uplifting, but it must be done well. Never let liturgy crowd out the sermon. Notice that growing churches today use a very simple and brief liturgy. They offer lots of good music and dynamic sermons but not much liturgy. St. Paul reminds us that people are converted by the preaching of the Word, not necessarily by some liturgy.

Finally, I think that there is a tendency today for churches to use Holy Communion as a tool for evangelism. It is not. This sacrament is for the faithful. When Jesus instituted the Lord's Supper, he did not invite the whole city to join him—only his closest followers. I think it is inappropriate to celebrate Holy Communion at a wedding or a funeral, for example. Because you have a wide variety of faiths in attendance as well as those with no faith at all, it becomes confusing for some and very uncomfortable for others.

I have been in churches that combine the common cup with individual glasses, kneeling with standing, wine with grape juice, and intinction with no intinction. Receiving the sacrament should not be complicated. Think of the first Lord's Supper in the upper room with a cup of wine and a piece of unleavened bread. When you spend more time thinking about how to commune rather than why you commune, you have missed the whole point of the sacrament.

Paul: The Importance of Music

Over the years, Shepherd of the Valley has developed an outstanding music program under the direction of a very gifted organist and choir director. We have an eighty-five-voice senior choir and multiple vocal, instrumental, and contemporary groups. In addition, we have a newly rebuilt $1.2 million Aeolian-Skinner pipe organ with three manuals, fifty-two ranks, and well over three thousand pipes. There are also three pianos in the building, including a nine-foot Steinway grand piano. Our sanctuary also has outstanding acoustics, which helps with musical programming. Over the years, we have hosted several the finest high school and college choirs in the Upper Midwest. Further, the St. Paul Chamber Orchestra uses our sanctuary four to five times a year, always drawing capacity crowds. In addition, we have invested heavily in the latest audio and video equipment. We have a full-time audio-visual person and several part-time people who handle all of our audio, video, and recording needs.

Psalm 122 begins with these words: "I was glad when they said unto me, let us go up to the house of the Lord." This invitation to worship has been the hallmark of the Judeo-Christian faith for centuries. And may it ever be so.

Duane: The Sanctuary and the Narthex

I grew up in a small church where once worship ended and you left the sanctuary, you immediately stepped outdoors. On a nice summer day after worship, people would congregate outside those doors for an important moment of socializing. But that didn't happen in the winter months nor on those all-too-frequent Sundays when there was inclement weather.

Certainly, a sanctuary is important for worship, but over the years, churches in the colder climates have discovered that having space where people can gather before or after worship is also an important part of building community. A time for conversation, coffee, and cookies does not replace worship, but it does serve as a critical part of the whole church experience. It enriches the worship experience.

Fortunately, while I was at St. Andrew's and Shepherd of the Valley, large spaces were built to accommodate this fellowship experience. This space, called the narthex, has proven to be crucial for the wellbeing and growth of the churches. Sanctuaries may be where we connect with God, but we connect with others in the narthex.

Roger: O for a Thousand Tongues to Sing

Growing up in Milwaukee as a teenager in the 1950s, there were a few places where I could go to experience the kind of "large church worship" I was seeking. One of those was Our Savior's Lutheran Church on Wisconsin Avenue. The sanctuary was large and impressive, and senior pastor Reuben Gornitzka preached the kind of message that even a seventeen-year-old high school student like me could absorb and understand. Gornitzka ended up becoming the senior pastor of Central Lutheran in Minneapolis while I was a student at a seminary close by, so I was able to get an added dose of his highly effective preaching through the eyes of a young man in my twenties. Central's huge sanctuary, capable of holding over 2,200 people and backed up by a large pipe organ that could seemingly rattle the rafters, was exactly what I was looking for.

It was this combination of exciting worship and powerful preaching that nestled itself in the back of my brain and became a sort of reservoir that fed my desire to create this same sort of experience in the congregations I would be fortunate enough to someday lead as pastor. That desire was there when I served as the mission developer of Christus Victor Lutheran Church in Apple Valley, even though this young congregation met in a school cafeteria and worshipped with less than one hundred people to the sound of an out-of-tune piano. The desire to be a part of something big was enhanced when I was called to Richfield Lutheran in Minneapolis and saw, Sunday after

Sunday, the over 1,500 folks jamming the pews for multiple services to hear the wonderful preaching of Harold Rasmussen and watched with awe as the endless stream of choir members made their way down the aisle to their places in the choir loft. I became even more certain when I served as an associate pastor at Holy Trinity Lutheran Church in Minneapolis and Edith Nordberg joined the staff as choir director. For decades, Edith had led the massive choir program at Mount Olivet in Minneapolis, so it was a strong sense of excellence that Edith brought to Holy Trinity. She was able to work her magic by turning average singers into a high-quality choir.

Decades later, there was that Sunday when I took my place in the front pew of the new 1,800-seat sanctuary of St. Andrew's. As the huge 108-rank pipe organ began to play and the congregation and choir joined in singing the hymn "O for a Thousand Tongues to Sing," I suddenly realized that it was more than one thousand voices I was hearing. I was actually in the midst of more than two thousand tongues singing and raising their voices in praise to Christ our Risen Lord and King. The dream of a Milwaukee teenager had become a reality—a reality few pastors ever have the chance to experience.

Roger: St. Andrew's in 1972

Palm Sunday was to be my last day at Holy Trinity. Soon, Edith Nordberg and her powerful choir along with the impressive Holy Trinity pipe organ leading the packed throng of worshippers would be just a memory. My next effort at leading worship would be Easter Sunday at St. Andrew's. Instead of numbering in the thousands, St Andrew's topped out at four hundred for this greatest of Christian celebrations. The stark contrast between the two congregations became most evident when I looked back at the choir loft and saw no one sitting there at the early service, just thirteen in the choir at the middle service, and, again, no one at the last service. In addition, instead of a pipe organ leading worship, there was a Hammond electronic organ emitting a sound more appropriately associated with what one might hear at a Minnesota Twins ballgame.

When the old, wooden-clapboard country church where St. Andrew's had been worshipping since 1925 was torn down to make room for this very modern-looking three-hundred-seat sanctuary in 1966, there were quite a few things that did not quite make it into the new building. The floors were bare concrete and lacked carpeting. There was no sound system in the new sanctuary. The architect had told them that the natural voice would carry just fine in their new structure. And he was right, as long as you shouted your entire sermon. To their credit, the congregation had built a structure that could accommodate a future pipe organ, but since money was tight, the old Hammond from the wooden country church would have to do. It strained to do the job, even though a few extra loudspeakers had been added in hopes of being able to fill a room far greater in size than this vintage vacuum-tube instrument was capable of addressing.

Roger: Progress Comes in Inches

One of the things a new pastor has to do is to walk very delicately into the future. When I arrived at St. Andrew's in 1972, the congregation had succeeded in erecting their new sanctuary, and they were rightfully proud of what they had accomplished. Still, there were some things that had to wait for better days.

Robert Schuller once said, "Make your needs known and sources of help will come from places least expected." Well, in ways both subtle and straightforward, I began to plan for the future by making some of those needs known. As Schuller said, help did come. Soon after I arrived, a couple decided that now was the time to put in carpet, and they stepped forward to make it happen. I made do without a sound system for about a year until the accumulated monies from the memorial fund made it possible to install a system appropriate for the size of the room. But the big one was the day a member called me up and said that it was probably time to put in a new organ. Like any good pastor, I asked when I could come to their home to discuss this possibility.

When I sat down and talked with this prospective donor, she admitted that she had a love for pipe organs and had recently donated an instrument in memory of her mother in her home congregation near Milwaukee. My eyes grew wide at the prospect of a new pipe organ suddenly becoming a reality in our future. She said that she was very aware of our need for a new instrument and that she would pay half of whatever the cost of it might be. The congregation would have to pick up the other half. She also included the caveats that it needed to be a pipe organ and that she would pay for the consultant who would lead us through the selection process.

Like someone who had just received news that they had the winning lottery ticket, I thanked her and immediately called a special meeting of the church council. As far as they were concerned, this was a slam dunk and an offer too good to let slip through our fingers. The congregation seemed to think so as well. In fact, it was probably the easiest money St. Andrew's ever raised. In just a matter of a couple of months, we were able to raise enough money to purchase a twenty-one-rank pipe organ that ended up changing our entire worship experience.

Roger: Music in the New Sanctuary

When St. Andrew's moved to the new campus in 1986, the twenty-one-rank pipe organ made the journey along with us. With a few modifications, the instrument was installed in the new 600-seat Great Hall. Until the new sanctuary was built in 1999, it served the congregation's worshipping needs for Sunday worship, funerals, weddings, and other gatherings.

But as we were making plans to build the new sanctuary, we had to decide what kind of worship experience we were going to offer the congregation in that new space. If it was going to be cathedral worship with huge choirs and traditional hymns, then we should begin making plans for installing a pipe organ. But, if we were going to follow the trend of the day by focusing on contemporary worship with drums, guitars, and other electronic instruments, then we had better start thinking about installing a massive speaker system.

The decision was important for several reasons. The first was the consideration of what kind of worship experience we wanted to carry over from the Great Hall. To suddenly go from a traditional format with organ and choir leading the congregation to electronic instruments might be too much change. Secondly, the kind of acoustics needed to accommodate a pipe organ were completely different than those associated with electronic instruments. With upwards of $12 million in construction design at stake, our decision was incredibly important.

What we eventually decided was to continue to enhance our traditional worship format by including a new pipe organ in our plans as well as including enough space in the front of the 1,800-seat sanctuary to accommodate no less than four hundred singers and a twenty to thirty piece orchestra. And, since we still had the Great Hall available for worship, we decided that contemporary worship could be held in that 600-seat place.

Roger: Taking Contemporary Worship to a New Level

One thing we needed to keep in mind was that there was a certain percentage of the congregation for whom contemporary worship was a style they enjoyed and had come to expect at St. Andrew's.

Frankly, we had no intention of eliminating that expression of Christian worship. Actually, with the addition of the new sanctuary, we now had the chance to focus our attention on holding contemporary worship in the Great Hall at the same time as traditional worship was taking place in the sanctuary. The acoustics of the 600-seat Great Hall were far better for contemporary worship than the new sanctuary.

One thing we set off to do from the very start was to make sure contemporary worship in the Great Hall would be of excellent quality. So, with the help of Bill Chouinard, who knew a whole raft of musicians in the Twin Cities, we assembled a band with singers who were excellent from the get-go. Now that we had the space, we also added a Saturday night worship service as well as a Sunday evening contemporary worship that we called "Good News at 6:00 p.m." None of this could have taken place were it not for the fact that we had eight full-time pastors on staff, most of whom were itching to have more chances to preach. Both the congregation and I were happy to satisfy their itch.

Roger: An Amazing Instrument

With the decision made in favor of a pipe organ in the new sanctuary, the architect and contractor began their work of coming up with plans. What kind of pipe organ? How large? And most importantly, how much would it cost?

One of the things St. Andrew's has been blessed with is extraordinary talent amongst its staff, and the music-department team, with Jan Gilbertson in charge of choirs and Bill Chouinard serving as organist, is a perfect example. Both of them were members of the building committee and were important contributors in deciding how to meet the music needs of the congregation.

One day, Bill showed up at a building committee meeting with news that he had just found the instrument that we should put into our new building. He smiled a bit and told us that it was a 1927 Casavant instrument with 108-ranks that had been taken out of its former home at Philips Academy in Andover, Massachusetts. That sounded interesting, but he added that it wasn't there right now. In fact, it was wallowing in an unheated barn in Traverse City, Michigan, for the past twelve years and we could get the whole thing for $50,000.

The chair of the building committee almost fell off his chair laughing. None of this made sense to him. In fact, the first words out of his mouth were to ask what would be wrong with a brand-new organ? Bill began to make his case that this instrument was from an era of organ building that included wooden pipes the likes of which you can no longer find and that it was the appropriate size for the new sanctuary with its seventy-foot-high ceiling, glass window walls, and large capacity.

The upshot was that word began to get out about the possibility of acquiring this historic instrument. Like Schuller said, "Make your needs known and help will come from places least expected," and indeed it did. One of our member families stepped up and paid the $50,000 to make the instrument our own.

Roger: An Historic Instrument Is Reborn

Bill's initial cost of acquiring the instrument for $50,000 was only the beginning. As it sat in that unheated barn in Traverse City, it was basically a pile of wooden and metal pipes that had succumbed to the snows of winter and the rains of summer. Now, someone had to put together the over 7,300 pipes that weighed over five tons. Our first thought was to send it back to Casavant. It made sense since they had built the instrument in the first place. So, back to Quebec, Canada, it went. When it got there, though, Casavant wanted to tear the instrument apart and create a new instrument with different tonal quality instead of restoring the instrument to its former greatness.

So, since Casavant wasn't interested in a restoration project, we contacted Schantz Organ Company in Orrville, Ohio, to see if they would be interested in bringing this historic instrument back to its former glory. They were more than excited to take on the project. After signing a contract, they sent four semi-trailer trucks up to Canada to retrieve the pile of pipes that, in just under two years (and $2 million later), would become one of the largest functioning instruments in the Upper Midwest. It would become an instrument that would magnificently lead St. Andrew's in Sunday worship, and its resurrection would go on to become celebrated throughout the world through multiple appearances on National Public Radio's program "Pipedreams." Obviously, with that kind of exposure, guest artists from around the globe were more than happy to be invited to entertain the Twin Cities community with magnificent organ concerts that would draw thousands to St. Andrew's.

Roger: Worship at St. Andrew's

When St. Andrew's went from two services in 1972 to on-the-hour multiple services on Sunday morning, the Lutheran liturgy needed to be looked at in earnest. Since we were limited to a service no longer than forty-five minutes in length, something had to give. So, we made a few cuts and eliminations to the liturgy while still maintaining its Lutheran integrity. Biblically, the service would include one lesson, a psalm, and the gospel. A new "Proclamation of Praise" would be written for each Sunday. Holy Communion would be celebrated every Sunday at 8:00 and 11:00 a.m. and at 9:00 and 10:00 a.m. on the first and third Sundays. Baptisms were celebrated at any service on the second and fourth Sundays, with sometimes as many as six children being baptized at the same service.

To one who has not experienced worship at St. Andrew's, that schedule might sound a bit too fast-paced to have any spiritual depth.

But again and again, we would hear from both visitor and member alike that they were amazed at how much we could pack into forty-five minutes and how they came away fulfilled without the feeling of being rushed.

Roger: The Drama of the Liturgy

When I was in seminary, we heard a lot about the drama of the liturgy. Basically, the professor was trying to emphasize that, like a good play or musical on Broadway, there has to be a good beginning, middle, and end. In other words, does what we are doing up in front of the congregation make any sense to those who sit back in the pews? Will they leave inspired and fed by the Word and Sacraments? Will the worship they just experienced make them want to follow Christ with greater energy, fervor, and devotion? And will they want to come back?

At St. Andrew's, worship begins and ends on time. Leaders know their roles and have been groomed not to be sloppy or stumbling in their performances. They know that they need to come prepared to share with those in the pews the greatest story the world has ever known in a way that will change people's lives. Like a good drama, the worship experience moves along and has times of pause and re-flection as well as moments of triumphant praise, worthy of celebrat-ing the Christ who has conquered death and the cross and rose again on Easter Sunday.

Roger: Worship Times the Same Year 'Round

One of the best things I learned from various church-growth con-ferences and seminars is that worship should be held at the same time all year long. Lots of churches in Minnesota decide to cut down on the number of worship services during the summer, thinking that since fewer people attend worship during the summer months, it makes sense to eliminate a service or two. The problem with that kind of thinking is that people are more creatures of habit than we sometimes realize. Take away the 8:00 a.m. service and you just lost those for whom Sunday morning is a chance to worship and then get on with the rest of their day. Eliminate the 11:00 a.m. hour and you just lost those who like to sleep late, have a relaxed breakfast, and then head off for worship. In other words, mess around with the worship schedule and you mess up more than you might think.

Roger: Christmas Eve and Easter

When you're planning on hosting ten thousand people for Christmas Eve and Easter Sunday worship, a little bit of planning needs to be put forth. In fact, when all is said and done, there are dozens of little things that can add up to big trouble if they are not thought through. There are all the elements of worship: the liturgy, preaching, and music. Then there are the logistics of moving people into and out of the sanctuary—and much more.

Easter Sunday and Christmas Eve are really two different animals when it comes to preparing to receive all these worshippers. Easter Sunday presented the challenge of having only six hours of worship available to receive the thousands who would flock onto our campus. But, thankfully, because of the number of worship spaces we had available, we were able to provide options for those who came to worship.

What we ended up doing was offering six services at 7:00, 8:00, 9:00, 10:00, 11:00, and 12:00 noon in the sanctuary, complete with orchestra and choirs. While we offered six services in the sanctuary, we also offered three worship services in the Great Hall with contemporary-style worship.

Roger: The Power of Choral Music

That first Easter Sunday at St. Andrew's in 1972 with only thirteen singers in the choir was only a temporary phenomenon. The next Sunday, it went down to eight! And, with the coming of summer, the choral program at St. Andrew's became non-existent. But truth be told, it was about as good as one could expect because other than a meager salary paid to the organist, the adult choir and the children's choir were led by volunteers who tried their best to raise interest in getting singers added to their rosters.

It became abundantly clear that limping along with a weak choral program was not going to cut it in a place like Minnesota known throughout the world for its great choral tradition. If we were going to have any chance of drawing new people to St. Andrew's, this was going to have to change—and change dramatically.

Change came in fits and starts and would not take root until 1979, when we hired our first experienced and talented organist and choir director. It was a half-time position with the expectation that the director develops and lead a middle school choir as well as an adult choir. On Sunday mornings, it was quite fascinating to watch him direct with one hand and with the other play the organ. To those who watched, it was a seemingly impossible task, but the director we hired pulled it off with musicality and a great sense of humor. He also created choirs for youth and adults where camaraderie was strong. The music they produced was greatly appreciated by the congregation. He would stay until 1986.

Hiring for a position that required the candidate to be both organist and choir director was difficult back in 1979, but it became a higher mountain to climb as the number of participants grew and the quality that the congregation expected rose to a new level. Painfully, the congregation was about to go through a number of organists who simply could not replicate what had already been established. One stayed six months and the other less than a year. It was becoming obvious that we had reached the point where we needed to hire two full-time musicians: one to serve as organist and the other to serve as choral director.

In 1988, God seemed to realize that we were in desperate need of some talented musicians to take us to the next level of music ministry, and God dropped into our lap not two but three of the finest musicians in the Twin Cities—musicians who to this day are still producing great music for those attending worship at St. Andrew's. The people God tapped on the shoulder and coaxed in our direction included Bill Chouinard, whose talents at the instrument are known throughout the organ world. Along with Bill, we ended up hiring his wife, Kristin, whose talents as a piano accompanist are such that visiting soloists and musicians need only to put a piece of sheet music in front of Kristin, and they are on their way toward producing wonderful sounds. Rounding off the Bill and Kristin Chouinard two-some is Jan Gilbertson, who serves as choral director and manages seven choirs and their directors.

What Jan, Bill, and Kristin have brought to St. Andrew's is beyond phenomenal. Annually they produce a musical extravaganza called "Christmas at St. Andrew's" that features over six hundred singers, bell ringers, and a twenty-five-piece orchestra under the direction of Charles Gray, a faculty member of St. Olaf College. Over six thousand gather from all over the Twin Cities to fill the pews for two performances that are based on the decades-old model that draws thousands to the campuses of St. Olaf, Gustavus Adolphus, Augsburg, and Luther College every December.

One time, I asked a new member why she had decided to join St. Andrew's. She reflected on the beauty of the sanctuary and spoke about how wonderful it was to have programs available for every member of her family. She went on and on, listing all of the great qualities she had discovered at St. Andrew's. All the while, I was hoping that she would say it was also the incredible preaching that she witnessed every Sunday. But preaching never made the list. In fact, after all was said and done, she said that the main reason they chose to join St. Andrew's was the music. In spite of the fact that she passed over mentioning preaching, I think Martin Luther would have been pleased. In fact, the music at St. Andrew's was probably part of the reason I stayed for thirty-three years.

Roger: A Destination Church

Over the years, St. Andrew's has grown from a congregation of 800 to a congregation that, with 9,000 members, is larger than Mahtomedi's population of 7,600 citizens. People come from all over the Twin Cities metro area to attend worship and become involved in the many ministries St. Andrew's offers. Many have pointed to the impressive music that St. Andrew's offers every Sunday. Others discover St. Andrew's through concerts, special speakers, and programs. Still others discover St. Andrew's because music groups such as Stillwater High School, the National Lutheran Choir, and White Bear Area Schools hold concerts in the sanctuary. Lutheran schools such as Luther and St. Olaf share their magnificent sounds to audiences that comprise not only St. Andrew's members but also alumni and friends of the college.

When I first came to St. Andrew's, I said that Mahtomedi is a place you can neither spell, find, nor pronounce. Well, that day is long gone. The reputation of St. Andrew's has grown to the point that it has found its place on the map. Music and worship have more than contributed to its success and growth.

It's been said that Luther and the Reformation expanded and grew on the strength of music. It was music that Luther used as an effective tool in sharing the gospel with peasants and princes alike. It is music that has also allowed St. Andrew's to flourish and grow.

Duane: Pipe Organs

Some people love pipe organs. In fact, there are those who love them so much that they say the church building is really only there to keep the rain off the organ. But then, there are others who see pipe organs as outdated.

Both Paul and Roger mention pipe organs. Both churches now have pipe organs that are used regularly for worship. Roger was intimately involved in the fundraising and purchase of two pipe organs at St. Andrew's. At Shepherd of the Valley, it wasn't until after Paul's departure that the church was able to purchase a pipe organ.

The road to getting a pipe organ was amazingly similar in these two churches. Both churches stumbled upon used pipe organs available for very reasonable prices that simply could not be passed up. Both churches purchased the organs rather quickly, but it took many months to refurbish and install the instruments. For both churches, the pipe organ has become one of the hallmarks of their ministries. And at both churches, the pipe organ continues to be used at worship alongside band-led worship.

Also for both churches, there was a bit of controversy surrounding the pipe organs. First, there was the cost. Because pipe organs are quite expensive, there was some resistance. St. Andrew's pipe organ cost $2 million. Shepherd of the Valley's pipe organ cost $1.2 million. In the midst of fundraising, some folks said that the funds should be used for other things—like feeding the poor. In other words, not all in the congregation were onboard with spending money on such an instrument.

Second, because music tastes are changing, some people wonder whether or not pipe organs will eventually become passé and even obsolete. In fact, it is indeed becoming harder and harder for churches to simply find a competent organist—even to the point where it's becoming a crisis in some churches.

Although both churches faced obstacles in getting their pipe organs, I think that both of them would now say that the instrument adds a wonderful richness and practicality to the church's ministry and that the purchase was worth it, despite the cost and controversy.

Chapter 9

EDUCATION & YOUTH MINISTRY

Duane: Ananias, Margaret, & Rich

When it comes to doing ministry, I sometimes think of the Bible story of Paul's conversion. Not so much because of Paul, but because of Ananias, who shows up briefly in this story. After Paul's encounter with Jesus on the road, Paul blindly wandered into Damascus. Simultaneously Ananias had a vision from God telling him to go and meet Paul and help him regain his sight. Ananias balks at doing this because he knows that Paul had been persecuting Christians. Yet, despite his reservations, he goes anyway, meets Paul, and heals him. Eventually, he even baptizes him. Ananias is a key figure in Paul's turnaround. Without Ananias, Paul may have never regained his sight. And Christianity as we know it would never have come about. Yet most people have never heard of Ananias. He is an obscure figure in the story of the Christian faith (Acts 9:10-19).

Many people who are involved in Christian ministry are more like Ananias than Paul. They work, serve, help, teach, and give in relative anonymity. *During much of my ministry, I worked closely with these types of folks who served behind the scenes. I helped recruit, train, and encourage many people who were Sunday school teachers, youth leaders, confirmation guides, and volunteers in Christian education, youth, and family ministries.*

Two kindergarten Sunday school teachers come to mind immediately when I think about these selfless, dedicated servants of Jesus. One is named Margaret. She taught kindergarten Sunday school the whole time I was at St. Andrew's. When classroom space was tight, she taught her kids in the hallway. When we bused kids for two years from the new worship building to the old Activity Center for Sunday school, grey-haired Margaret, who was retired and single, volunteered to ride the bus with the kids—as well as teach her class. Margaret made each child feel special because to Margaret, they were. Best of all, Margaret did all this (and more) without any fanfare. She simply wanted to serve.

Then there's Rich. He was an FBI agent who had just volunteered to teach Sunday school when I came to Shepherd of the Valley (SOTV). He did not have any specialty with kids. His specialty was catching bad guys. But in teaching Sunday school, he found a niche. He taught week after week the whole time I was at Shepherd of the Valley—twenty-seven years. Along the way, I wanted to tell his story in our church newsletter—an FBI Agent who teaches little kids about Jesus. But he declined. He didn't want to draw attention to what he did. He simply wanted to do his part—his Ananias-like part.

I tell these stories because people like Rich and Margaret display the essence of education, youth, and family ministries. These are ministries that are highly impactful, led by many folks who are often humble and unnamed.

Roger: Going Deeper . . . A Plan to Develop Leaders

Around 1975, it was becoming clear that just offering a smattering of adult forums and hit or miss presentations that came and went was not going to be adequate for the future of St. Andrew's. If we were ever to get to the point where we would have a congregation that had any real understanding of what it meant to be a Christian, we were going to have to come up with some kind of plan with a clear concept of what we wanted to see accomplished.

One spring morning in May 1975, I was going through my mail and picked up a brochure from Bethel Lutheran Church in Madison, Wisconsin, describing an adult-education program they had created called the "Bethel Series." It was not the first time I had come across their advertising. In fact, for a number of years, I had simply chucked it into the waste basket as yet another fundamentalist approach to Christian education that I would find impossible to embrace. That feeling was amplified by the fact that around this same time, the Lutheran Church in America was introducing a whole raft of new educational materials for children and adults that they wanted congregations to buy. Like the Bethel Series, they had been filling my mailbox for months with brochures showing off their latest efforts. Couple that with the word amongst pastors that the Bethel Series was, as many of us had been led to believe, a conservative approach to adult education, and the choice to go with the LCA material was a slam dunk.

But, for some reason, this time was different. Instead of simply throwing the Bethel Series literature into the wastebasket, I took another look at what they had to offer. The brochure talked about how the Bethel Series lifted up the commitment of those who became involved, how they would become the future leaders of the congregation. And it just so happens that a representative from the Bethel Series would be in the Twin Cities next week should we desire to hear more about the program. We were in such a mess regarding adult education that I felt we had nothing to lose, so I called and arranged for the representative to stop by.

When the representative showed up at the appointed hour, I was the only one in attendance. I scratched my head and admitted that I was extremely disappointed that others from the education committee weren't showing up. The Bethel Series representative had disgust written all over his face. He made it clear that without the support of the education committee, the Bethel Series would have no chance of succeeding. In fact, without their support, he wasn't the least interested in having us enroll. Enrollment in the Bethel Series meant that the pastor needed to spend two weeks in Madison under the tutelage of Harley Swiggum, the author of the Bethel Series, and that event was just three weeks away.

After about a half an hour, the representative admitted that with the lack of interest shown by the education committee, St. Andrew's was apparently not ready to undertake something like the Bethel Series, and he began to pack up his promotional materials—when everything started to change. One by one, within the span of about twenty minutes, members of the education committee entered the room. Each had their own excuse as to why they were late, but, no matter, they were now here. I could see the look on the face of the Bethel Series representative start to change. He leaned over to me and said, "Maybe St. Andrew's does have a chance at launching the Bethel Series."

He began his presentation. The eyes of our members began to light up as he talked about this program of educating twenty members of the congregation over a two-year period who would then become the teachers of the Bethel Series at the congregational level. With a smile on his face, he described how after teaching the teacher, our parking lot would be filled every Wednesday night with adults who have committed themselves to a two-year program of adult education based on a thorough trip through the Old and New Testaments. Part of what he said sounded like a snake oil salesman at a county fair, but he did have statistics proving what the Bethel Series had accomplished in other congregations throughout the United States and the world.

Eventually, as in all things, it came down to money. If St. Andrew's was going to be a part of the Bethel Series Training in Madison, he would need a check for $200 that night to reserve a place for St. Andrew's. Two hundred dollars?! That was like asking for a million. And the $200 was just a down payment. There would be the added cost of sending me to Madison for two weeks. We just looked at each other, shrugged our shoulders, and said, "I guess we're going to have to think about it."

It was then that one of the old stalwart members of St. Andrew's who had been born and raised in Mahtomedi stood up and said, "We've been thinking about this kind of a program for years, and the time is now." With that, Warren Marshall took out his checkbook and wrote a check for $200 that would, in reality, become a down payment on the future growth of St. Andrew's. It meant that I was headed off to Madison, Wisconsin, for two weeks and that St. Andrew's was going to be embarking on a trip into the future that would forever change the shape and direction of our ministry.

Roger: Promises Fulfilled

One of the things the Bethel Series representative told us was that not only would our parking lot be filled on Wednesday evenings, but those who participate would become our pool of future leaders. He was right. But it was a lot of work.

When we began the Bethel Series in September 1975, I was still the only pastor on staff. After attending the training session in Madison, I embarked upon talking twenty of our members into becoming involved for the next two years in a two-hour session every Wednesday evening, with one year spent going through the entire Old Testament and the next year taking on the New Testament. Included was a commitment on their part to attend every week and to memorize various passages from scripture. Eighteen of those in that initial cadre completed the two years and then began spending the next two years teaching the rest of the congregation the Bethel Series.

The result was beyond our fondest expectations. On Wednesday nights, our parking lot did, indeed, become full. For two years, every nook and cranny of our old Mahtomedi Avenue building was filled with more than two hundred members being taught the Bible from Genesis to Revelation in classes of ten to twelve adults.

Over a period of four years, the entire complexion of St. Andrew's began to change. Because our people were becoming biblically literate, they began to understand and recognize the power of the Holy Spirit upon their lives. Prayer became an important part of our life together, with twenty-four-hour prayer vigils that began at the end of our Maundy Thursday evening worship and ran until the beginning of Good Friday services. People who had never given the practice of tithing a second thought began to understand the biblical imperative, "To whom much is given, much is required." Folks who never thought they could teach began to volunteer to become Sunday school and Vacation Bible School teachers. And members who were elected to positions of leadership such as the church council began to understand the role of faith and trust in God's ability to provide for our every need. In other words, the Bethel Series raised up a whole group of leaders, some of whom, to this day, are totally involved in helping St. Andrew's capture the future God has laid out for us.

Duane: Transformational Bible Studies . . . Bethel and Crossways

The Bethel Bible Series was, indeed, a key event in the life of St. Andrew's and in the growth of the congregation. Similarly, there was a Bible study at Shepherd of the Valley that was also transformational in the life of the congregation. It was called Crossways. And it, too, changed the congregation.

Although not as formulaic as Bethel in how to put together a comprehensive program for the whole church, Crossways can be every bit as life-changing for those who participate. At Shepherd of the Valley, the church was fortunate to have a former pastor as a member. This pastor, Tim Schaefer, had taught Crossways when he was still serving a parish. Because he was devoted to the theology and outlook of Crossways, he agreed to teach it at SOTV. So he taught the first group of about twelve people for two years, taking them all the way through the Bible. Then he taught another group for two years. Word about this amazing Bible study spread, and soon people were lining up to take one of the Crossways classes. Shortly, not only was Tim teaching, but others took up the mantle as well and began to teach Crossways. Just like the Bethel Bible Series, Crossways "graduates" would routinely tell me about the profound impact the class had on them. They said that it helped them become literate with the Bible and to understand their faith in a new, dynamic fashion.

Roger: Where Are the Youth?

Having come from serving two congregations as their youth pastor, with hundreds of youths in our programs, when I started at St. Andrew's, I was ready to jump in with both feet and get some youth ministry going. In 1972, when I got there, St. Andrew's was a fifty-year-old congregation of eight hundred members with a respectable number of children in Sunday school. It had a three-year confirmation program with about twenty youths in each grade, but beyond that, there was nothing. Youths literally looked at their confirmation day as a day of liberation and the last time they had to come to church . . . never to be seen or heard from again. Obviously, this had to change. But how?

The answer was obvious. For Lutherans, confirmation is something that every kid has to go through. Families who never darken the door of the church suddenly show up wanting their kid to be confirmed. For some, it is simply the thing to do. For others, it is family pressure from grandma, wondering when her grandchild is going to be confirmed. Whatever the reason, three years of confirmation could be fertile soil for turning a teenager from a kid who hated church to one for whom church was to become their second home.

Roger: Confirmation as a Core Ministry

In 1972, the staff at St. Andrew's consisted of a pastor, a secretary, and a very part-time financial assistant. The staff of this eight-hundred-member congregation could literally hold their meetings in a VW bug. So, if any youth ministry was going to take place, it had to rest on me. Yes, there were lay members who helped, but there was no clear vision for creating a youth ministry program that would be sustainable and successful.

As I began to think through the problem, I decided that the senior high youth ministry was just going to have to wait. In other words, we would intentionally put high school ministry on the back burner and look at it as a program we would develop in the future. In the meantime, we would dump all our efforts into the creation of an exciting and attractive confirmation program that would become the basis for any future high school ministry we would create.

So we created a confirmation program that offered students choices in the classes they wished to attend on Wednesday evenings. We also used a little-known Minnesota law concerning religious release time to create one full day a year when kids would come to church for confirmation activities. Beyond that, we created week-long summer experiences in places like Winnipeg, St. Louis, and Chicago.

In addition, there were Boundary Water canoe trips and drama and musical presentations that students shared with the congregation.

Because of increased programming opportunities for youths, a couple of things happened. Firstly, students realized that church can be fun. Secondly, they melded together and found friendships that were meaningful and deep. Thirdly, confirmation became an evangelism tool for other, non-churched students in the community who wanted to become a part of the confirmation program at St. Andrew's. In fact, the draw that the St. Andrew's confirmation program created was so strong that unchurched adults began to come to Sunday morning worship at the insistence of their children—many because they wanted to know what in the world was going on that had caused their children to want to come to St. Andrew's when previously they and their children had had no relationship with the church. The strong confirmation program combined with an exciting and dynamic Sunday worship experience caused many families to join St. Andrew's.

Duane: Different Styles of Youth Ministry

When I came to St. Andrew's in 1978, I met John Carlson, a young seminary student working at the church part-time. Later, John would be called to be one of the pastors at St. Andrew's. He was an energetic, humorous, and charismatic guy. The young people loved him. He and Roger helped shape the youth ministry of the congregation, along with some volunteers from the church. John's style was that of a pied piper. He led and the youth followed. Kids loved what he did. He created excitement. Kids were inspired. They flocked to the events and activities that John creatively put together. I know that over the years, this type of "pied piper" youth ministry has gotten a bad name. But still, from what I experienced, John and Roger had a huge impact on many, many young people over the years.

That was the only style of youth ministry that I knew, understood, and participated in as a church staff person—at least until I got to Shepherd of the Valley. At SOTV, I saw that successful youth ministry could be done in another way. At SOTV, Bob White, Jeff Sandgren, and Bonnie Wilcox were shaping a different kind of youth ministry. This one was not centered on the youth leader as much. This youth ministry was much more peer centered. The youths themselves had a role in leadership and decision-making about what was to happen in ministry. Bob, Jeff, and Bonnie facilitated that, for sure, but the youths themselves were encouraged to teach and lead others and develop leadership skills along the way.

What I came to learn is that, like all the ministries of the church, there is no one "formula" for doing youth ministry. Good ministry can vary from place to place, situation to situation, and person to person.

Paul: Why We Do Christian Education

One day while sitting in my office, I got to thinking about this whole business of Christian education. To my surprise, I began to ask myself the "why" question. Why do we do this? That particular year, we were recruiting over 165 teachers and aides for our church school. We purchased the best educational materials we could find. Our department of Christian education was well staffed. From Pre-K through 12th grade, we had well over 1,700 students enrolled. (Our highest year of enrollment was close to 1,900). We had a beautiful facility that allowed for multiple hours of education for all ages. And, of course, this all came with a pretty hefty price tag too.

So I began to ask myself, with all these wonderful resources, what are we trying to produce here? We don't make anything tangible like lawn mowers, snow blowers, or bicycles. In fact, what we make here is quite intangible, vitally important, but not always easy to quantify. We are, simply put, in the business of making and growing people. There is an old saying: "If your vision is for one year, plant corn. If your vision is for thirty years, plant trees. But if your vision is for a lifetime, plant people." Very honestly, this is the goal of parish education: to plant and grow people in the Christian faith who daily celebrate their relationship to God as revealed in the person of Jesus Christ. It is a high and holy calling.

It was our Lord, after all, who told us to "go, therefore, and make disciples of all nations ... teaching them to observe all that I have commanded you" (Matthew 28:19-20). Martin Luther wrote: "I am convinced that the neglect of Christian education will bring the greatest ruin to the cause of the gospel. This is the most important matter of all!"

Some years ago, we had the Dakota County Sheriff speak at a luncheon at our church. He told a story that I have never forgotten. He told how one day, he put out a simple questionnaire to all 168 inmates who happened to be in the jail in Hastings on that particular day. One of the questions asked was: Do you now or have you ever had any kind of significant relationship to some community of faith? To his surprise, 161 of the inmates said, "No." The sheriff then went on to speculate about how different the lives of these men and women could have been had they had at least gotten some religious training and some introduction to the New Testament gospel of love, grace, forgiveness, and guidance. He was not implying that all our problems go away if we join a church. But he was implying that faith in God can often be a powerful resource in our lives in times of temptation, hardship, loneliness, and despair. We teach because we desperately need to know the great truths of the Bible as they apply to our daily lives.

We also teach for another important reason. Teaching the Christian faith always involves the development of a relationship. Education generally refers to the conveyance of a certain body of knowledge: facts, formulas, statistics, theories, calculations, methods, probabilities, interpretations, and philosophies. These can all be worthwhile. But Christian education always comes with another especially important component. Learning in the church is not just cognitive, it is also experiential and relational. It is not just knowing about God. It is about knowing God as personally and intimately as is humanly possible.

Today, we live in a society where there is a need to feed the spirit. This part of our being needs to be fed in order for us to be whole and satisfied. But often, it is completely neglected. Suppose you had a son or daughter who stopped growing either physically or intellectually at, say, age seven. Would this cause you to be concerned? Of course. So why can we sometimes be so lax when it comes to feeding the souls of our young people (and adults) through the process of Christian education? Ironically, it is this part of our being that is designed for now and forever, for all time and eternity.

At one of our church summer camps, the counselors sit down each week individually with the campers in their cabin for a one-hour discussion. The counselors ask the campers to talk about "their walk with God" and what they have experienced at camp that week. For many campers, it is the most helpful and encouraging hour of the entire week. Think of all the "isms" our youth have to face today: secularism, hedonism, materialism, agnosticism, atheism, nihilism, mysticism, humanism, new ageism, egotism, and many more. We in the church owe it to our children (and adults) to teach in such a way as to stimulate a deep and growing faith in the Father and in the Son, our Lord.

Duane: Bible Stories and Questions

Pastor Paul makes a wonderful argument about the importance of Christian education. As someone who has spent almost all my career in church work dealing with Christian education, I would add two other points that I think are important in teaching the faith.

First, it is important to teach Bible stories. Knowing Bible stories is critical because they are the language of our faith. It is through the Bible that we meet people like Moses, Ruth, and David—as well as Jesus and Paul. It is through those Bible stories that we hear about the ups and downs of faith and how people handled those ups and downs. It is through the Bible that we begin to understand the great love that God has for humanity and how Jesus embodies that love. Just hearing and knowing the stories in the Bible, without moralizing them, is inspiring to people of all ages because we see ourselves in those stories.

Second, Christian education can help people think about and live with questions. There are very few places in the world where people ask the deep questions of life like, "Why am I here?" "What is my purpose?" or "Why is there suffering in the world?" Yet, those are the very questions the church wants us to ask. There may not always be an answer. But permission to simply ask the deep questions is a step in the right direction.

Paul: Starting a Christian Education Program from Scratch

Starting a church from scratch can be a daunting task and especially when there are other churches in the area that already have all their education, fellowship, youth, and music programs up and running like a well-oiled machine. I have to admit that in the early years of SOTV, there were times when it seemed like we were "competing" on a very uneven playing field. We didn't even have a building to call our own for nearly four years.

However, there were two factors that soon put my concerns to rest. First was the explosive growth of northern Dakota County. The county was growing by double digits year after year. No pastor needed to feel competitive in any way. There were plenty of new "move-ins" looking for a church home. Demographically, SOTV had all the indicators in our favor: very few funerals, one to three births a week (most years we grew well over one hundred members just by births), lots of new families moving into our area, and somewhat surprisingly, corporate America stopped transferring its employees elsewhere (too costly), so our membership was both stable and growing.

The second factor in our favor was the amazing group of folks who signed up to help develop a new congregation and get it off the ground. They were really quite extraordinary people. They were willing to go the extra mile and do whatever it takes to get the job done. Having seen a vision of the future, they were more than willing to work to make it a reality. Not everyone was willing to sign up for such a challenge.

So, after just three weeks of worship in the Rosemount Elementary School gymnasium, I announced that we wanted to start our Sunday school program as soon as possible. I asked all those willing to help out to see me after the service. To my surprise and delight, we had all kinds of volunteers. Within another week or two, we had a fully functioning church school, albeit with only about thirty-five students covering a range of ages. It was a good start, and we built upon this foundation. Over time, we added new students, recruited more teachers, and acquired the best teaching materials we could afford. A few weeks later, we added an adult Bible class.

As is typical of most Lutheran churches, soon after that, we started our confirmation program. The first year, I had only one student. The next year, there were two students. Then four students. Then seven. I did not know it at the time, but this kind of multiplication soon became the standard for our church. At its peak, we had annual confirmation classes of about two hundred students. The first classes met in my office in my home, but as we grew, it became apparent that a bigger space was needed. So I began searching and was most pleasantly surprised to find that a church less than a mile away would happily accommodate us. It was a Reorganized Church of Jesus Christ of Latter-day Saints (RLDS) congregation. They were most gracious. I was also impressed that as I looked around their building, I noticed that all their educational materials came from Augsburg Publishing House, the publishing arm of the American Lutheran Church. So I figured these had to be good people.

In addition to weekly classes, we also strongly encouraged a week of Bible camping during the summer months along with a service component of some kind, which might include Feed My Starving Children, Habitat for Humanity, and helping with one of our weeks of Vacation Bible School. Because our confirmation program spanned four years, 6th through 9th grades, we also offered many kinds of summer mission trips, many of them organized by a ministry called Youth Works.

Paul: Confirmation

Confirmation classes at SOTV have always been a work in progress. During my youth I had many positive experiences with confirmation. I was anxious to offer a similar experience to the marvelous young people at our church. Once again, we purchased the best materials we could find, recruited and trained the best teachers who so willingly volunteered to teach, and put together a curriculum that we thought our youth would find to their liking. Confirmation was a place and a time when they could grapple with their faith.

Our lesson plans changed from time to time, but we used the 6th-grade year to study the Old Testament, 7th grade focused on the New Testament, 8th grade on Luther's Catechism, and during the 9th grade year, we did something called "faith application." In other words, now that you have learned some of these major doctrines, concepts, and principles of the faith, how does all this apply to your life in some very basic and meaningful ways? A key feature of the program was to enlist the help of older teens who had already been confirmed as a way of showing the younger students the value in all this teaching.

All of this faith training culminated in a very celebrative service of worship during which the youth were confirmed. Of course, we always wanted to stress that the rite of confirmation was not graduation—even though it looked like it with robes, open houses, gifts, and certificates. Well, it was a commencement of sorts, in which each student graduated into another level of growth, maturity, and responsibility in the life of the church. It was always pure joy to place my hands on the head or the shoulders of our kneeling youth and pray this prayer: "Father in heaven, for Jesus's sake, stir up in this young person the gift of your Holy Spirit, confirm her faith, guide her life, empower her in her serving, give her patience in suffering, and bring her to everlasting life. Amen."

Paul: Camping Ministry

Another important dimension of ministry for our church, early on, was that of camping. One of the first things I did in founding our church was to find a camp that we could relate to and that would become an extension of our ministry. After looking at several camps in our area, we chose Camp Wapogasset near Amery, Wisconsin. At the time, this camp did not have great facilities, but it always had a marvelous summer staff of college and seminary students who shared their faith with our kids in a truly engaging, evangelical manner. I often said that when our youth went to camp, some of them cried the first day from homesickness, but they often cried on the last day because they literally did not want to leave camp. Camp Wapo, as it was affectionately called, was a place where our youth celebrated their renewed faith but were also challenged to take that faith home with them and apply it to every area of their lives. I don't think in all my years of ministry that I ever had a kid tell me that he was sorry he had gone to camp. I also noted that over the years, a few of our youth went back some years later to become camp counselors themselves.

However, camping was not just for our youth. We had weekend campouts, retreats, and work bees for our adults as well. There is something almost magical when a group of people are around a campfire in the evening singing songs of the faith, telling stories, sharing their faith, and yes, eating s'mores.

Paul: One Generation Away from Extinction

Someone has noted that the church is always just one generation away from extinction if we "drop the ball." The Lutheran church was born on a university campus. So our long tradition of teaching goes back to the middle ages. Luther once wrote, "We must spare no diligence, time, or cost in educating and teaching our children, to the end that they may serve God and the world."

In the Bible, there is a verse that gives insight into the developmental years of our Lord. We are told that he "increased in wisdom and in stature, and in divine and human favor" (Luke 2:52). Is this not the wish we have for all our children and for all of humanity? We are called to sensitize our conscience to the voice and will of God and to grow daily in the grace and the knowledge of our Lord Jesus Christ.

Duane: More Than Just Sunday Mornings

Throughout my ministry, it has always annoyed me that some people think that church is all about what happens on Sunday morning. My father-in-law was a pastor, and sometimes someone would suggest that he only worked one hour a week, on Sunday morning. His humorous retort was always, "Yeah, but every minute up front for me on Sunday is like an eight-hour day for most people." Many folks have no idea how much ministry happens at the church on times other than Sunday morning. Education and youth ministry, as well as other ministries, take a lot of time and energy during the week. In fact, when I was at Shepherd of the Valley, I always told folks that until you come to the church building on a Wednesday evening when confirmation and other events are happening, you really don't know how active this congregation is. There was a joke that because the building was so busy every hour of the day, the only time available for the church to be robbed would be between 1:00 and 4:00 a.m.

Throughout my ministry at both St. Andrew's and Shepherd of the Valley, Wednesdays at church were always bustling times—confirmation classes, pizza suppers, choir rehearsals, music programs, children's educational programs, fellowship, and adult education. Literally hundreds of people would come through the doors on Wednesday evenings. Sunday worship is critical, yes—even primary. But much to my chagrin, sometimes other ministries that happen on other days of the week get overlooked.

Chapter 10

WELCOME, EVANGELISM, & COMMUNITY

Duane: Sales

I'm a golfer. Often when I play golf with others, if they know that I'm a pastor, they will say something like: "Well, you've got the connection to give us nice weather." My reply is almost always, "Actually, I'm not in management. I'm in sales."

Although said in jest, that rejoinder is true. Pastors are actually in sales. At least part of the job of a clergyperson (and of all Christians) is "evangelism," which is simply the Christian word for helping other people *understand and know Jesus Christ and the church. Or, when it comes down to secular terminology—sales.*

This chapter is designed to help give you a glimpse into that critical element in the lives of Roger at St. Andrew's and Paul at Shepherd of the Valley (SOTV). How was it that they led each church into tremendous growth during their pastorates? If you will, what sales techniques did they use? How did they buck the trend of declining church membership?

Roger: They're Coming, and We Don't Know Why

It was a cold Monday morning in January. Those arriving early for our regular Monday morning staff meeting were already on their second cup of coffee and would soon be joined by other staff members for whom this 9:00 a.m. meeting was a weekly rite of passage. Pleasantries and greetings were interspersed with laughter as one by one, they, too, grabbed their coffee and found a seat. We began, as usual, with a short devotion and a moment of prayer and then focused our attention on the written agenda. We had not gotten too far into the business at hand before someone looked out the window and said, "Hey, you have to come and take a look at this."

We got out of our seats, peered out the window, and saw a large group of high school students marching up the street heading toward the building. We figured that the group numbered somewhere around 150 students. Someone said, "It looks like they're intending to come into the building." Indeed, they were. Without missing a beat, they opened the doors, walked down the hall, entered the Great Hall, and sat down in rows as if they were there to attend an event. We looked at one another for a moment and then decided we had better go find out what in the world was going on.

What we discovered was that a group of Mahtomedi High School students had organized a protest march over the fact that Mahtomedi High School was completely ignoring Martin Luther King Jr.'s birthday—a legal holiday in Minnesota. School was in session, and nothing had been planned by the high school to honor Martin Luther King Jr. and the civil rights movement. So at about 8:00 a.m., they walked out, headed down to the middle school, and unsuccessfully attempted to encourage middle school students to join them. But it was cold, and so the group decided that their next move would be to come to St. Andrew's to warm up.

Once we learned the reason for their protest, we looked at one another and said, "Well, we better help them out." So, one of the pastors grabbed a guitar, the organist fired up the pipe organ, the choir director began to wave her arms, and in front of those 150 students began a chorus of "We Shall Overcome." The air was electric as the students stood up and joined in singing. It was the beginning of a day none of us will ever forget. This was no frivolous attempt to skip out of school. These were determined and sincere students who felt that segregation and racial inequities needed to be addressed by the high school. And their walk-out was an attempt to get the school district's attention. A number of students addressed their peers. Some shared stories of discrimination and taunts they had experienced as students. Seeing this as a teachable moment, we ended up grabbing some newsprint and magic markers and began listing their complaints and the remedies that they hoped might help bring attention to the issue of racial injustice.

While all of this was going on, I made a phone call to the high school principal and told him that if he was looking for his students, they were here in our Great Hall. Within five minutes, he walked through the door. I approached him and said that we had an opportunity here for a win-win situation—that these students were sincere and that we needed to hear them out. In the meantime, a local television station showed up and, with camera rolling, began to document the event.

What happened next was beyond amazing. The principal took the stage, and like the caring leader he was, he began to listen to what they were saying. He did say that they had to return back to school and was willing to give them time to organize their goals. The upshot of this day of protest was a Thursday evening gathering that week attended by hundreds of students and community members to address exactly what the students were calling attention to. Working with the high school staff, they put together an evening that even included speakers from 3M who were also involved in matters of racial equality. And, best of all, events focusing on the matter of race in Mahtomedi continued to take place in subsequent years.

Roger: It Wasn't the First Time

Around 1980, Mahtomedi teachers decided to go on strike. They staged the beginning of their strike to start at the end of the day on a Wednesday in October. On Thursday and Friday of that week was the Minnesota Education Association's annual convention, so students were already scheduled to be out of school. Hopes were that the teacher's union and the school district could do some heavy lifting on Thursday and Friday and start school on Monday as usual. However, that was not to be.

On Wednesday evening, one of the teachers came up to me and expressed hope that St. Andrew's could fill in the gap if the strike continued past the weekend. His hope was that we could provide some activities during the day for students so that parents could continue to go to their jobs. He didn't think that we would have to do it for very long—and we could be providing a very important service for the members of the community. He did puff us up a bit by saying that he had always been impressed at how St. Andrew's was involved in the community and hoped we could fill this particular void.

I gathered the staff, and together, we agreed that we could most certainly pull together some events to help the students and parents out. On Sunday, we let the congregation know that they could drop off their students at 7:30 a.m. and pick them up again at 2:30 in the afternoon. Lunch would also be provided.

Well, what we thought might be just a couple of days ended up stretching out to eight weeks. Every weekday from 7:30 to 2:30, we had over two hundred kids gathered in our Fellowship Hall. It was a far bigger job than any of us had ever anticipated. Quite frankly, we had no idea what we were going to do with them the next day, but invariably we did come up with something. Sometimes we provided movies and games. One day, we gave prizes to those who could solve a Rubik's Cube the fastest. Other times, we became a bit more adventurous and boarded all two hundred plus kids on buses to take them to the zoo, to a local television station, to the YMCA, or even on a tour of the Ford factory to watch them assemble cars. It was all-hands-on-deck as we solicited help from members of the congregation to help prepare lunch and act as chaperones when we took the students off-campus.

At the end of those eight weeks, no one was happier that the teachers had ended their strike than the staff at St. Andrew's. But we did gain the respect of the community for stepping up and offering some much-needed help when it was needed the most.

Roger: Multiple Entry Points

St. Andrew's, like most churches, opens its doors to community groups seeking a place to meet. It's just something churches do. Having groups such as Al-Anon, Alcoholics Anonymous, Boy Scouts, and Girl Scouts meeting in your building allows folks who would otherwise not even think of coming into a church to find themselves in your parking lot and walking through your halls. Preschool nursery is also one of those much-needed programs that St. Andrew's offered to the community with much success.

One of Robert Schuller's favorite phrases was, "Find a need and fill it!" He also said that if someone else is doing a good job at whatever the need might be, don't waste your time trying to compete with them. Instead, join them in their efforts or find some other need the community might have. To that end, St. Andrew's gave up hosting its own food shelf and instead cooperated with the local entity. They had the building and the staff capable of doing a much better job than we could ever hope to pull off. So, we simply joined hands and people got fed.

Roger: Evangelism, Evangelism, Evangelism

Telling the Good News is what church is all about. We have the best story the world could ever hope to know about in the life, death, and resurrection of Jesus Christ. So we need to do our absolute best at getting that word out. Many times, I would scratch my head and wonder how we could let people know that St. Andrew's was here and that they were invited to join us in this journey of faith. Lots of ideas ended up being abandoned. For example, we, along with many others, found out that putting an ad in the local telephone book was really a waste of money. With cell phones, people were getting faster and much better results by simply Googling the number they wanted to call. Likewise, with newspaper advertising. There was a time when we would purchase quarter-page ads every week, but eventually, we limited that sort of advertising to Christmas and Easter. Below are some ideas that worked for us:

Milk Cartons

One interesting avenue that I discovered, quite by accident, was placing an ad for St. Andrew's on the side of a milk carton. I came upon this idea quite innocently one day when I was picking up some milk at the local dairy. I noticed that an organization had placed an ad for their services on the carton, and I asked if it was possible to get St. Andrew's on one. The answer was *yes*, and the cost was *free*! So, for about a month, St. Andrew's stared at people while they ate breakfast with an ad that listed one hundred reasons why they should attend St. Andrew's. Coming up with one hundred reasons was easier than I thought, but when I was running out of ideas, I decided to include the fact that they could come and hear a "bearded, balding pastor." I knew that the advertising was working when people would come and say, "We're here because we want to see a bearded, balding pastor."

Cookies

I once asked a family why, out of the many churches they were visiting, they decided to join St. Andrew's. They gave multiple reasons for liking what they experienced, but when they had asked their kids where they wanted to go to church, they had said, "The one with the cookies." Who would have thought that the kingdom of God can grow on the strength of a chocolate chip cookie? With an average Sunday attendance of over three thousand, the cookie budget for St. Andrew's soared to something like $20,000 a year.

Visitor-Friendly Parking Lots

When visitors come to a church for the first time, it's like going to a city they've never visited before. How do you get in? Where do you park? Where's the front door? To the members, these are questions they no longer ask. They're familiar with the setting and routine that surrounds worship at their church. But for the visitor, it can be overwhelming.

At St. Andrew's, we attempted to provide adequate and informative signage for exits and entrances to the parking lots. Doors of the various buildings on campus were numbered so that visitors could be easily directed to where they needed to go. Also, we had vans roaming their way through the parking lots, offering rides to those for whom walking from their car to the sanctuary would be a struggle. The vans were also a welcome sight on Sundays when it was raining or extremely cold.

Frequent New Member Classes

A lot of churches offer new member classes only occasionally— maybe one in the fall and another in the spring. What I found over the years was that trying to get people's schedules to match the day and time when new member classes were offered was a losing battle. Instead, we offered membership classes between eight and twelve times a year. Our thought was that, hopefully, with that many opportunities, those desiring to join could find a time that fit into their schedule.

Direct Mail Campaigns

Most of us look forward to taking that daily journey to the mailbox. It's a ritual that will last as long as there is a mailbox at the end of our driveway. So, since the means are there, why not take advantage of that avenue of getting your message out to those who may not know much about your congregation?

Public Television Advertising

For a number of years, St. Andrew's bought a ten-second spot on Twin Cities Public Television. At that time, we had our choice of where we wanted our ad to show up, and as luck would have it, we were able to advertise at the beginning of *Sesame Street*. With multiple showings throughout the day, it ended up being an amazingly effective way of getting our name out there. The proof was shown to me one day by a mother who said that her three-year-old sat down to watch *Sesame Street* and when she saw our logo appear, she shouted, "Church! Church!"

Packets of Business Cards

Back in the 1960s, one of the Lutheran synods had an evangelism emphasis that included the phrase: "Each one-reach one." It was a simple invitation for a committed member to reach out and invite a friend, neighbor, or acquaintance to check out their church. Picking up on that phrase, we put together packets of ten business cards for St. Andrew's, including our address, phone number, and the times of worship, and mailed them to each of our members. The idea was for them to put a couple of those business cards in their wallet or purse, and then, when the opportunity arose to invite a friend to St. Andrew's, they could put in that friend's hand all the information needed to make the visit.

Hymns in the Bulletin

For someone not acquainted with Lutheran worship, one of the hardest things to do is to figure out where the congregation is at during worship. Hymnals are sometimes awkward to try to find your way through, and by the time you do find the page, the congregation is already five steps ahead of you. So, early on, we decided to print a bulletin complete with liturgy and hymns. Not only did it make it easy for a worshipper to figure out where we were in the service, but it allowed St. Andrew's to write its own liturgy, giving it some freshness.

Follow up, Follow up, Follow up

At St. Andrew's, we put a card in every bulletin that offered a visitor the chance to leave a name, address, and phone number. On Monday morning, one of the first things a staff member did was to flip through those cards and pull out those who had identified themselves as visitors. By that afternoon, I had those names on my desk and was able to print out a letter thanking them for worshipping and letting them know that we were there to offer any help they might need in their spiritual journeys. The intent was to have the letter come from me and, hopefully, for the letter to be in their mailbox by Wednesday of that week. I also let them know that I would be happy to visit them in their home if they so desired to share any information that might help them decide if St. Andrew's was the church for them.

Duane: Word of Mouth

I'm a little surprised that Roger only peripherally mentioned "word of mouth" as an evangelism strategy because while I was working with him, it was something he often talked about. The most common way that someone hears about a church is through word of mouth from a neighbor, friend, or family member. In fact, I think that is one reason why there was such a focus on the quality of ministry at St. Andrew's. If people experience something extraordinary, they are bound to tell others about it. That is grassroots evangelism.

Paul: The "Angel" in Evangelism

If you look closely at the word *evangelism*, in the middle, you will also find the word *angel*. Throughout the Bible, there are stories of angelic appearances, and almost always, they are bringing some wondrous Good News to someone who is about to play a key role in God's great plan of salvation for his world. In the Christmas story, Mary, Joseph, Zechariah, and the shepherds all were visited by angels who had messages for them. Ever since those ancient days, the task of evangelism has not changed. The people of God continue to proclaim the Good News of the Gospel of Jesus Christ as far and wide as possible to any and all who will listen and respond. The task of evangelism is wondrously simple and wondrously profound at the same time. The cross reminds us of our vertical relationship to God and our horizontal relationship to those around us who need to be welcomed into the Family of God.

Someone has noted, somewhat cynically, that the Lutheran Church has historically done a good job of obeying the "Great Commandment"—that is, love God with your whole heart and then show that same love to your neighbor. But when it comes to the "Great Commission" (to go into all the world and make disciples), Lutherans have not done such a good job. As we founded our little church, I wanted to change this perception. I was more than convinced that we could obey both of these commandments given by our Lord.

Now, to be honest, I don't think that we ever had some grand five-year or ten-year plan that included all kinds of goals and benchmarks. In fact, we were just too busy trying to get this infant congregation off the ground to do much long-range planning. I think that we all hoped we would just survive and grow, but there was so much to do in the present that we didn't look too far into the future.

Paul: Welcome

There were two guiding principles regarding evangelism that were always in the forefront of my mind. The first guiding principle for me was "be welcoming." A friend of mine moved to Minneapolis some years ago and began looking for a new church home. He told me about a church he had visited on three different Sunday mornings. He then told me that he was half tempted to show up the next Sunday buck naked to see if anyone would then notice him. Sadly, some churches can be rather indifferent to visitors and prospective members. This was not to be the case at Shepherd of the Valley. After all, it costs nothing to be welcoming, and it pays rich dividends. I always wanted to be as visible and as approachable as I could possibly be whenever people were in the building, and I asked the same of our staff. High-volume days like Wednesdays, Saturdays, and Sundays were no time to be hiding in our offices.

In each of my offices, I always had a big window looking out on the main entrance to the church. Whenever I saw anyone who looked lost, confused, hurting, seeking, or just in need of a hug or a warm word of welcome, I could see them coming into the church. I wanted to be there for them. I also encouraged our pastors to leave their office doors open unless they were having a confidential conversation. Just the appearance of an open door sent a positive message to the congregation.

Paul: Meet & Greet

My goal was simply to build this new church one member at a time and to make people feel as welcomed and as comfortable as possible. I didn't care if we had two hundred members or two thousand members. I just wanted them to know that I would be taking each new relationship very seriously. I would try to meet and greet as many people as possible on a Sunday morning, always trying to learn at least one unique or interesting thing about each one. It helped that I was something of an extrovert who genuinely enjoyed meeting people and getting to know them well. Frankly, any pastor who does not really enjoy working with people of all ages from all walks of life should perhaps think about a different vocation because this job is truly all about people!

We encouraged but never pressured folks to sign the guest book. We encouraged everyone to wear name tags for every Saturday and Sunday worship service. We began and ended all worship hours encouraging people to meet and greet those closest to them. We always had the coffee and donuts (the third Lutheran sacrament) available for people to gather and fellowship together.

Calling people by their first name while distributing Holy Communion was very meaningful to me and to those being communed. Every week, we added a few more names to our mailing list. We took photos of new members and posted their photos prominently around the church. We created something called Worship Partners, coupling individuals and families that might choose to sit together at any given worship hour. We sent out thank you letters to all visitors who signed the guest book.

I made follow-up phone calls to all visitors on Monday or Tuesday. For a time, we had gift bags for all visitors or potential new members. We promoted and distributed at least six or seven photo directories over the years that I would religiously (pardon the pun) study each Friday or Saturday so as to refresh my memory of people's names. I can tell you for a fact that when people walk into a church and the pastor calls them by name, their whole face can, and most often does, light up.

Duane: Calling People by Their Names

Paul mentions that it was important to him to call each person by his or her name. But he's too modest about how well he did that. It was legendary how well he could remember the names of people.

Over the years, I heard countless stories from people who told me that the reason they decided to get involved at Shepherd of the Valley was because early in their experience at the church, Paul had called them by name. Usually, the story goes something like this: a visitor came to the church and met Paul, often after worship when Paul took his "Paul Position" near the exit of the building. There he greeted everyone he could possibly greet. If someone was new, he'd ask for their name. Often, that person would come back for worship a second week. Again, they would go to greet Paul at the exit door. When Paul invariably remembered and spoke their name, the visitor's jaws would drop in astonishment.

It seemed like an uncanny ability that Paul had. Perhaps he did have some kind of special memory ability, but I know that he also worked at it because he saw the profound effects of this simple task of saying someone's name aloud.

Paul: The Power of Visits

I also learned early on that people are not just joining a church. They are also joining you, their pastor . . . your dreams, your visions, and your hopes for the future of the congregation. One of the most important things a pastor should do in building up a congregation is to make home visits. I know pastors who think that this is a waste of time or some relic of the past. Not true at all. In all my years of ministry, I never had one person tell me not to come after I offered to come to their home. I had a very set schedule. Two and sometimes three nights a week, I would visit their homes, one at 7:00 p.m. and one at 8:15 p.m. One hour each. I always wanted to do a home visit before a visitor was officially welcomed into the church. Those were some of the best and most productive hours of ministry any pastor can have. I met the family, the children, other family members, and even pets. In these visits, I asked them where they grew up, how they met their spouses, where they worked, and how they happened to show up at our church for worship. I had about six or eight leading questions that usually yielded a ton of good information. Sometimes I asked for a family photo and was often given one. I did that in order to make my own personal scrapbook of prospective members. There often was time to share my story, my hopes for the church, and how happy I was to welcome them into our fellowship should that be their desire. As soon as I left a house, I drove down the street, stopped my car, and made as many notations as I could recall on some 4x6 file cards. Then a letter was sent to the home a few days later thanking them for their warm hospitality. Pastors must bond with their members just as shepherds have to bond with their sheep. If this does not happen, the church will not succeed.

I wanted to take people seriously and meet them where they were—not always on my turf. I could certainly see people at the church. There is real staying power in seeing them elsewhere. One time, a young man named Dave, who was a very new member, called me with the very sad news that his brother had just taken his own life. Those are the kind of phone calls you never quite forget. We talked and prayed over the phone. Several days later, I saw the obituary in the newspaper. I did not know any of the family, and I barely knew Dave. But I decided to attend the funeral later that morning in Stillwater—about a forty-five-minute drive for me—despite a rather severe snowstorm. Driving down I-494, I thought about turning around as the weather got worse, but for some reason, I just kept going, keeping my tires in the proper ruts on the road. When I arrived at the church in Stillwater, there were no more than fifteen people there including me, the pastor, the organist, and a soloist. When I saw Dave, he came up and gave me a hug like few I have ever had in my life. My being there that day meant more to him than I could ever have imagined. Later, whenever I met Dave on the street, the first thing he would say to me is "Thank you for coming to my brother's funeral."

One other story. One morning, someone went through the church parking lot during the worship hour and smashed a couple of car windows, stealing whatever they could. The police came, but I don't think the thief was ever apprehended. One thing stolen was a small purse belonging to a little girl that had no more than a dollar or two in it. The little girl was heartbroken. A few days later, I went out and bought another purse based on the description the family had given to the police. I slipped a few bucks in the purse and mailed it to the little girl. The next Sunday, the family approached me, and I got another hug that I will never forget, this time from that little girl. Once again, this is how you do ministry and how a church grows. You can never put a price tag on that kind of goodwill. And sometimes, it's the littlest things that make the biggest difference in people's lives.

Recall Jesus's own words that when a cup of cool water is offered to a thirsty person, there is his kingdom. Both of these families were rock solid in the church for years and years to come. Take people seriously, meet them where they are, find out where they hurt, address that hurt, and you will be the kind of pastor to your flock that is so in keeping with the mind and manner of our Lord and Savior.

Duane: A Memorable Hug

One time, I witnessed an unusual hug that someone gave Paul. It came at the very end of a worship service. Paul was about to give the closing benediction in front of nine hundred people when suddenly a little girl, about four years old, came up the center aisle, walked right up to Paul, and gave him a big hug around his legs. Paul, who is six feet, six inches tall, stooped over and returned the hug.

Who knows what motivated the little girl to do that in front of the whole church? I like to think that she simply understood, at some level, the warmth and love that Paul exuded.

Paul: Evangelism and Community

A second guiding principle for me regarding evangelism is *community*. Part of evangelism is reminding people that we belong to three families. First, the human family, as we are all homo sapiens. Second, a family of origin, as we all have a mother and father, whether they are living or deceased. And third, the Family of God, which we join when we are baptized. It is this simple yet profound act that confers on us our eternal identity as Children of God, which comes with all the rights and privileges that our Heavenly Father wishes to grant us.

I often think of all the identities I carry or have carried through this world: son, brother, father, grandfather, husband, pastor, friend, citizen, graduate, Minnesotan, and many others. These are all important identities, but none are as important as "Child of God." Why? Because this identity has implications for now and forever, for time and for eternity. Nothing is more fundamental, more profound, and more life-giving than this identity.

The story of the Prodigal Son from Luke, chapter 15 is the story of a young man who forsakes his true identity, runs off to a faraway country, squanders his wealth in "loose living," and ends up in a pigsty. But one day, he "comes to himself" (vs. 17). He remembers his true identity. And though he no longer feels worthy to claim that identity, nevertheless, his loving and forgiving father fully restores his son with a ring, a robe, and shoes—all symbols of sonship in the ancient world. This is evangelism at its best. Lost and confused souls being reminded of their true baptismal identity and then finding their way back into the fellowship of God's Family. Helping and assisting in this process is really the primary calling of the church. We need constant reminders of both *who* we are and *whose* we are.

I know of a young man named Glenn Oscar Davidson who joined the army some years ago when new recruits were told to put their initials on just about everything they owned. Imagine the razzing this young man received when his duffle bag carried the letters G.O.D. Yet it was also a daily reminder to Glenn of his true identity: a Child of God.

Paul: Evangelism Takes Many Forms

Over time, evangelism at Shepherd of the Valley took on many forms. Stimulating worship and preaching, high-quality educational opportunities for all ages, small group ministries, a great music program (both vocal and instrumental, which welcomed any and all persons regardless of how much or how little talent they might have), outstanding youth programming, service, mission, and outreach events by the dozens, benevolence giving to well over two dozen various ministries to the tune of about $300,000 a year. Good ministry often creates better ministry. Even weddings, funerals, and baptismal services were opportunities to reach some people perhaps for the first time with the Good News.

And lest I forget, some of our best evangelists were our own members! I would often ask how someone found out about our church. The answer usually was some friend, neighbor, or work associate who was singing the praises of SOTV.

One piece of the story of evangelism at SOTV did catch me rather by surprise. As the church grew, sometimes almost explosively (we once had a new member class of over 180 people, and we offered the classes five times a year), there was some pushback from a few members of the congregation. I was told that the church had gotten too large and that we had lost something in the process. We are a church, I argued, and not a country club that has every right to limit its membership. Further, I mentioned that I had been in some small churches that were as cold as ice and some large churches that were warm and welcoming.

We tried very hard to make SOTV "feel" like a small church through the use of many small group ministries, including Bible studies, quilting groups, men's and women's groups, committees, ushers, choirs, ensembles, our Tanzanian ministry, the Mothers of Preschoolers (MOPS) group, and single's ministries. In every group, we sought to make it feel personal.

It should also be noted that for a time, some of our growth came from a neighboring church that was imploding because of some very poor pastoral leadership. This was not how I wanted to grow our church. At the same time, there was no way that we were going to turn away a group of people who were so hurt from the painful loss of their former congregation that some mornings they stood in our narthex literally sobbing. These folks proved to be valuable assets in the life of our church. This rather sudden influx of new members did put some stress on our staff and our facility for a short time, but in the end, we saw them as nothing less than a gift from God. We gave thanks for all the ways in which they came to enrich the overall life of our congregation. To this day, they continue to bless SOTV with their presence.

One time we calculated the fallout from that neighboring church. Turns out that there were about one hundred families that left and came to Shepherd of the Valley — so many families that we sometimes referred to that time period as the "Great Exodus." The people who came to Shepherd of the Valley were often hurting, even traumatized, by what they termed a "takeover" of the church by the new pastor. Many came to SOTV because they found a place that they realized was safe, that would accept them, and where they might begin to heal.

Paul: A Favorite Story

Frank and Henry were next-door neighbors and good friends. One Sunday morning, both came out of their houses at the same time. Frank called out to Henry. "Henry, why don't you come golfing with me this morning?"

"Thanks," said Henry, "but I am off to my church this morning." The next Sunday, the same scenario played out, an invitation by Frank to golf and Henry respectfully declining. This went on for several more Sundays. Finally, one morning Frank said to Henry, "You know, Henry, I have invited you to come and golf with me five Sundays in a row. What interests me is that you have never once invited me to go with you to your church. Why is that?"

Paul: Beggar to Beggar

Pastors should always be attuned to the news of the day. Some events in the news shake the very souls of people, like the events of 9-11-2001. You knew the pews would be packed the Sunday after that event. When something like that happens, it can be an excellent opportunity to do evangelism because people are begging for words of hope, comfort, direction, and explanation. The preacher had better be fully prepared that Sunday because this will not be a typical Sunday. Evangelism has been described as one beggar telling another beggar where to find the bread. There is a lot of cynicism about the church these days, but churches that are genuinely welcoming and are truly interested in promoting Christian community will both survive and thrive. May God grant that it be so.

Duane: Can an Introvert Become an Extrovert?

The importance of the pastor in evangelism is very apparent to me, having worked with both Roger and Paul. They are too modest to say it, but for many people, Roger and Paul were the reason that they got involved in the church. Both men possessed a kind of magnetism that was attractive to people. In the church, you can have all the "sales" techniques and methods you want, but the leader also needs to have at least enough charisma to draw people into the fold. In other words, a leader needs to be a bit of an extrovert.

My father-in-law, who was a pastor, asserted that he was not a natural extrovert. However, he also said that over the years, he was somehow able to become an extrovert in public because being a pastor simply called for him to show that hidden side of his personality. He learned to be an extrovert because that is what he needed to do in his job.

I think he was correct. In fact, surveys have shown that many pastors begin their ministry as introverts, but over time they tend toward more extroversion. Like my father-in-law, they have learned to be extroverts for the sake of the proclamation of the gospel message and in order to be effective leaders in the church.

Roger: Evangelism Is Job One!

When I was a young pastor at age thirty-one with a wife, five kids, two dogs, and three goldfish, it was necessary for me to take a paper route to help make financial ends meet. It didn't take long for me to realize that if I was going to make anything out of my ministry at St. Andrew's and afford to stay there as their pastor, I had to somehow get the turnstiles moving and get more people coming through the doors to come and see what we had to offer. I realize that some people may take offense at the perception that the church is a business and that if it is going to stay in business, it needs to have a product people need and want, with enough cash flow to support programs and staff. Call it whatever you want, even cloak it in all kinds of ecclesiastical language, but when it gets down to the nuts and bolts of growing a church, it's no different than the merchant down on the corner who needs people coming through his doors to buy whatever he has to offer if he's going to stay in business.

As I look at the church of the future, I think it needs to regain the energy and excitement that comes from following Jesus's marching orders to "Go into all the world and make disciples, baptizing them in the name of the Father, and of the Son, and of the Holy Spirit." That takes work! That takes commitment! But, other than hard work, there is no way to build the church if you want to help it grow. And it starts with the senior pastor! Unless the senior pastor has enough passion to go and make disciples, to build the kind of internal structure that helps feed people's faith to model by their own example a willingness to put in the time and self-sacrifice it takes to create an atmosphere that will inspire people to want to follow Jesus Christ . . . nothing is going to happen.

Yes, Jesus said he will build his church! But he also said that the field is ripe unto harvest and that we need workers to go into the field and gather the crops. So, enough with the excuses—enough standing by watching the membership numbers decline year after year! It's time to get to work and turn the future of the church around. It has been done before! It can be done again!

Create worship that is exciting, relevant, and real. Preach a message that is intended to blow the socks off those in the pews and compel them to action. Nothing is worse than sitting through a boring sermon—and there is no reason a sermon should be boring given the amazing power of Jesus Christ to impact people's lives. Demand that the seminary prepare pastors to run the church like a business, with attention given to cash flow and strategic plans.

Phillips Brooks, the Episcopal bishop and priest whose ministry in the 1870s touched millions of lives and led to the building of the impressive Trinity Church in Boston (which, to this day, continues to have a meaningful and powerful ministry), said this about the ministry:

"Do not pray for easy lives; pray to be stronger people. Do not pray for tasks equal to your powers; pray for powers equal to your tasks. Then the doing of your work shall be no miracle, but you shall be the miracle."

Chapter 11

CARE MINISTRY

Duane: Congregational Care and Pastoral Care

Before we get into this chapter on care ministry, it needs to be said that pastors only do a portion of the care ministry in any church. Regular congregational members often give lots of care to others, both formally and informally. That certainly was the case at both St. Andrew's and Shepherd of the Valley (SOTV) when I was on staff at those churches.

I've witnessed acts of care by lots and lots of church folks toward others. Much of this kind of care happens naturally—conversations, sharing hot dishes, praying for others, and attendance at funerals and other important occasions. Some of this care for each other happens through structured programs like prayer chains, prayer groups, planned visitation, programmed

calling, and organized mentors. Although care in a congregation is done by
the whole congregation, below Paul and Roger discuss pastoral care, care
done by the pastors.

Roger: Care Ministry

"The moral test of government is how that government treats those who
are at the dawn of life, the children; those who are in the twilight of life, the
elderly; those who are in the shadows of life; the sick, the needy and the hand-
icapped." — Vice President Hubert H. Humphrey, November 1, 1977

Hubert Humphrey spoke those words about the treatment of the weakest members of society as a reflection of its government, but he could have said the same thing standing in a pulpit of any of our churches, addressing a congregation and inserting the word "church" in the place of "government." And, if he had been speaking to a gathering of Christian worshippers, he would have the added privilege of including the words of Jesus:

> "I was hungry and you gave me food, I was thirsty and you gave me something to drink, I was a stranger and you welcomed me, I was naked and you gave me clothing, I was sick and you took care of me, I was in prison and you visited me" (Matthew 25:35-36).

> "Let the little children come to me, and do not stop them; for it is to such as these that the kingdom of heaven belongs" (Matthew 19:14).

Caring is one of the hallmarks of any congregation worth its salt. That basic understanding of what it means to be a church was impressed upon me by one of our members who owned one of the largest auto dealerships in the Upper Midwest. I was visiting with him in his office, and I was reflecting upon the growth of St. Andrew's over the years with a certain sense of pride in what we had accomplished. Well, if it's true that pride cometh before the fall, my fall was about to happen. He leaned back in his chair and said, "Nobody cares how big you get. We're the largest dealership around, but in my business, all people care about is, 'Can you sell me a car at a fair price—and when it breaks, can you fix it?'"

Roger: When I Break, Can You Fix Me?

One of the sacred privileges of being a pastor is that of being invited into the inner sanctum of people's lives. The telephone rings, and what begins on the other end is a parishioner or a stranger whose life has somehow run itself off the rails and is wondering if you can somehow help them get things put back together again. It could be a marriage that has turned into a daily nightmare and is headed for divorce. It could be a frantic mother whose son or daughter's life is completely out of control. It could easily be almost anything, and in my fifty-two years of active ministry, I have found myself sitting down with people who are desperate for answers, with tear-stained cheeks, hoping you might show them some compassion and understanding.

A long time ago, a religion professor summed up the pastor's job as being that of a garbage can—a place where people can get rid of the junk in their lives, a person to whom people can come and tell the most sordid and painful things in hopes that the pastor can somehow help them lift that burden off their shoulders and show them a new way to live. He went on to say that a pastor should not be too surprised when after people spill the bad and the ugly to you, they disappear and are never seen again. In other words, in each of us, there is a certain sense of pride that is shattered once we reveal the bad choices we've made, even though the person we share them with might be a pastor who has taken a vow to never reveal to anyone the deepest confessions of those who seek his or her counsel.

But not everyone runs and hides. In fact, the vast number of parishioners who have sought my counsel have stuck around. For many, they have been able to get above and beyond whatever was causing their lives to fall apart. For others, it is still a constant struggle to overcome the demons that haunt and derail their lives. Yet they're here! They're in worship! They partake of the Sacrament of Holy Communion! They hear the words, "I declare to you the entire forgiveness of all your sins, in the name of the Father, and of the Son, and of the Holy Spirit." Maybe the day will come when they can actually absorb and believe those words. Hopefully, they will come to accept the fact that Christ himself has forgiven them of all of the rotten junk in their lives and that they can breathe the full, fresh air of life as God intended for it to be lived.

Roger: The Church in People's Homes

When I was in seminary, a professor said there are two ways in which to build and grow a church. One is to offer fantastic, dynamic worship with spellbinding sermons that will cause people to hardly be able to wait until the next Sunday when they can find their place in the pews and partake of the joy of Christian worship. The second is to visit people in their homes. At St. Andrew's, we attempted to do both. Indeed, there is something unique that happens when a congregation of two thousand voices gathered in worship raises the rafters in song and praise. In fact, it's one of the reasons visitors come back and many decide to join. But being a part of a huge gathering of worshippers does not allow for the individual to have a chance to let their own individual concerns and needs be known. That is where the home visit comes in. Quite frankly, once you sit in a person's living room, you will never forget their name. By the time you leave, you'll find yourself taking away a little bit of who and what that person is. It's a call that can happen because of a tragedy that has taken place, or it can be the result of a visitor who desires you to sit down and tell them more about the church. There are even those times when a family invites you over for a bite to eat just for the pleasure of being in the presence of their pastor on a more informal basis.

In the early days of my ministry at St. Andrew's, Advent, Lent, and Holy Week meant making dozens of home communion visits to shut-ins. As the congregation grew, so too did that list of members for whom a visit by the pastor with the intention of sharing the gifts of bread and wine needed to be made. If truth be told, I didn't always walk out of the office with a spring in my step knowing that I was going to be spending the entire afternoon driving around town visiting people in their homes. Not every call was going to be a personal inspirational high. One time, I knocked on the door of a supposed shut-in only to be told that she was off Christmas shopping at the local mall. But there are those times when you are personally ministered to by those you came to visit. Those times when people share how God has so richly blessed them when you know they are deep in pain. Those times when you listen to stories about how they managed to overcome huge adversities that only deepened and strengthened their faith. As one retired synod president once told me, "If you can't think of what to preach, go and make some calls on some members. They'll fill you up with inspiration and faith."

Roger: The Variety in Parish Life

One of the things I've always enjoyed about the parish ministry is the variety it offers. You can be at the graveside of a family grieving the death of a loved one in the morning and end up leading a confirmation class with a room full of energized teenagers in the afternoon. What I've found is that no day ends like you thought it would. A phone call can send you rushing out of the office on your way to the emergency room. An unscheduled knock on the door can find you enmeshed in an hour's long conversation with someone who needed some words of encouragement and hope. There isn't a pastor who hasn't been awakened in the middle of the night by a phone call from the sheriff telling them that one of their members has just been in a horrible car accident and they need help now. It's then when you grab your pants, put on your shoes, get in your car and say, "God, I don't know what I'm going to say, but please give me the words you want me to share."

Roger: But There's Also Joy in Them 'Thar' Hills! . . . Baptism

But parish life is more than people struggling under the umbrella of life's difficulties. There is that moment of birth and the anticipation of an impending baptism. Over the years, we evolved in our approach toward baptism. For instance, it was a standing tenet that we don't do private baptisms unless it's an emergency. My theology tells me that baptism is the entrance of the individual into the community of believers and that it's necessary for that community to be present to welcome and witness this new birth in Christ as the gift of the Holy Spirit is bestowed. We also expected those who wished to have their child (or themselves) baptized to attend a baptism class wherein the theology of baptism was explained, and information was offered about how the church was ready to witness to their child through Sunday school, confirmation, and youth activities.

When I was in seminary, the professor said that we should never baptize the child of a non-member . . . that the family should become members first. I mentioned that to Pastor Harold Rasmussen at Richfield Lutheran Church as I noticed that he went ahead and baptized anyone who requested the sacrament. His reasoning was that this was a family who needed the church at a particular time in the life of their child. Yes, they did not belong. But, he said, someday they just might join knowing that there was this church that welcomed them at the time of their need.

Roger: Marriage

Get a group of pastors together, and, lo and behold, there are stories told about weddings that many parishioners might find hard to believe. Like the time I was working on a sermon on Saturday night and a young couple knocked on my window wanting to know if I did weddings. I went to the door to tell them that I most certainly did. The only problem was that they wanted to get married right then and there. I did not marry them, and I never saw them again.

And then there was the time when an airline pilot wanted to get married before his divorce was legally finalized. He boldly asked me to alter the date on the marriage license to satisfy his illegal plan. When I refused, he became quite upset, to which I said, "As an airline pilot, isn't your log a legal document? Do you alter your log when it suits your fancy? Well, the marriage certificate is a legal document, and I can't falsify it!" His anger never quite left him as he and his intended stormed out of my office.

I do have one particular weekend that I'll never forget. Usually, a pastor might have a wedding or a funeral take place on a weekend. But, for some strange reason, I ended up, like the title of the movie, presiding over "Four Weddings and a Funeral." Needless to say, I had to be at my best to make sure I got the right grooms married to the right brides and avoided ending the wedding ceremony with the words, "Ashes to ashes, dust to dust!"

Duane: A Wedding Story

At one memorable wedding where I presided, the keyboardist simply wasn't up to the task. I saw the first indication of this at the rehearsal, when the pianist, a friend of the couple, didn't really want to play anything in front of people at the rehearsal. At the wedding, he played the processional adequately. But at the end of the wedding, right after I said, "You may kiss—" and the recessional music would usually have started up, there was nothing but silence. I looked over at the pianist, and he was just staring straight ahead. I nodded as if to say, "Go ahead and play." Still nothing. Eventually, after a few very awkward moments, I whispered to the couple that they should walk on down the aisle. Which they did—to murmurs from the congregation and silence from the keyboard. I felt so sorry for everyone involved. I guess the keyboardist simply froze.

Roger: St. Andrew's Village

Mahtomedi was and still is a small town. Many of its residents are new to the area and were attracted by the lakes and trees that give the area an up-north feel even though the town is only fifteen miles from downtown Minneapolis or St. Paul. Yet, mingled among them are folks who were born and raised in Mahtomedi, and for them, this is the only home they have ever known. So, where do they go when age catches up with them and they can no longer keep up with the maintenance and costs of that home that served them so well over those many years? At one time, the answer was someplace other than Mahtomedi. Instead of being able to stay in the community where their many friends and relatives lived, they were forced to pick up stakes and head off to places less familiar.

As time went by, we began to discuss this as a staff and church council. In fact, we pondered this issue for almost two decades, always with the thought that someday, it would be nice if we were able to build some senior housing so that the eldest of our community didn't have to head off to a new community. Then, once we had acquired seventy-two acres of land, it offered us a chance to come up with a possible plan—that since we had the land, maybe we could embark on this whole new ministry to our elderly. It ended up that our timing could not have been better. More and more people were beginning to ask the question, "What about that senior housing you and the council have always talked about?" Mahtomedi and St. Andrew's were growing, and if we were going to do it, the time was ripe.

In the fall of 1998, the matter came up at our staff-council retreat. It wasn't a part of our regular agenda. In fact, the main item on our agenda was presenting plans for a $12 million, 1,800-seat sanctuary that the congregation had responded affirmatively to a congregational survey with over 90 percent saying the need was there. To say that our plate was full was an understatement. It was then that someone on the council said, "What about the senior housing? We've talked about that for almost twenty years. Maybe we should be building that before we build the sanctuary."

It was a good question, and the answer came in a way none of us really expected. "Maybe we could do both?" someone said. It was here that wiser heads than me began to plot a course that would bring St. Andrew's into contact with Presbyterian Homes in a plan where St. Andrew's would put up the land as its stake in the project, and Presbyterian Homes would come up with money to allow us to build. What resulted was a 60-40 percent partnership with Presbyterian Homes with St. Andrew's holding 60 percent of the ownership and Presbyterian Homes responsible for staffing and managing the facility.

Finally, the dream of offering residents of Mahtomedi the opportunity to continue living in the community that they had called home for so many years was becoming a reality. In fact, the need for a facility that offered independent living, assisted living, and memory care in Mahtomedi was apparently so great that when it came time for people to sign up and become residents at St. Andrew's Village, the entire building was filled in just two months.

Roger: Infant and Preschool Child Care

One of the first things I noticed when I came to St. Andrew's in 1972 was the lack of a weekday, preschool nursery on site. It was probably the fact that we were parents of preschoolers who had been enrolled in a program in Minneapolis that drew my attention to that fact. So, I immediately began to lay the groundwork for St. Andrew's to run its own preschool nursery. What I thought was a need was not apparently embraced by the majority of the leadership of the congregation. Questions began to surface as to why such a program was needed. How was it going to be funded? Who was going to run it? And wasn't St. Andrew's going into competition with other preschool programs that were being offered in the area by private parties?

Eventually, we got through all of those stumbling blocks, and it ultimately fell to Duane Paetznick to oversee and manage what would become one of the shining stars in our ministry. What began in the 1970s as a program with a dozen preschoolers in a single classroom in a wing of the old St. Andrew's that dated back to the 1940s ended up becoming an entire ten-thousand-square-foot wing of the St. Andrew's Village.

When we were designing the St. Andrew's Village senior housing facility, someone began to talk about how interesting it would be for our preschool nursery to be housed in that same complex. It was a thought that had merit simply because of the fact that we had run out of room in our current building and could use some new space for a program that was continuing to grow. But what we had not really envisioned was how exciting it was going to be to have young children in the same building as the elderly. There is no price you could put on the looks of joy on the faces of the St. Andrew's Village residents whenever those preschoolers would gather to sing a song or to parade through the halls in their Halloween costumes. The young got to see lots of grandmas and grandpas, and the elderly had the chance to spin a memory or two of when their own children were that age.

The saying is true: "How a community treats its youngest and its oldest is the true test of what that community considers to be of most importance."

Duane: Your Presence Is Enough

Early in my tenure at St. Andrew's, John Carlson, one of the pastors, was called to make a hospital visit to a young man in his twenties who was critically ill with cancer. Unfortunately, John was not able to immediately go up to the hospital. So he came to me and asked me to go in his place. At the time, I had made no hospital visits. That was not my area of ministry. So I hesitated. Then I asked him, "If I decide to go, what would I say?" His response was one that has stuck with me throughout the rest of my ministry. "He likely won't remember what you say, but he will remember that you were there." With that, he convinced me to go.

John told me a truism that I whispered to myself many times as I was on my way to hospital visits throughout my ministry. Although it is important what we say in visits, it's not the most important thing. What's truly most important is our mere presence. I whispered John's advice to myself not only to calm my own nerves but also because it was true.

Paul: The Church's DNA

The Christian church, despite all its flaws, has done more good for humanity on this planet than any other organization. Looking back over the centuries, it was the church that very often created the programs and the institutions that were most helpful in serving those in need. These creations included orphanages, hospitals, colleges, mental health services, seminaries, half-way houses, and many more such ministries. These were all founded by faithful and godly people who were effective in serving a hurting world. Since its inception, the church has always tried to heed the admonition of our Lord, who told us that "as you have done it unto one of the least of these who are members of my family, you did it to me" (Matthew 25:40). Caring has been a part of the church's DNA from its very beginning.

Paul: The Church as "Family"

One of my favorite lines for parish ministry is, "They don't care how much you know until they know how much you care." There are a number of descriptive words that are applied to the church today such as ecclesiastical, hierarchical, corporate, institutional, contemporary, conservative, liberal, and even megachurch. But the one that has always resonated the most with me is the simple word: *family*. To me, the church is at its best when it is a caring and inclusive family. And if you think I overstate the case, consider these concepts: Families have reunions—ours is called weekly worship. Families celebrate births—ours is called baptism. Families have rules—ours are the Ten Commandments. Families have "trees"—ours are the genealogies of scripture. Families promote maturity—ours is called the rite of confirmation. Families have cherished beliefs—ours are the three great creeds. Families enjoy food—ours is the Lord's Supper. Families have a history—ours is the Bible. Families have vocations—ours is service to God and to one another. Families have fun—which we call fellowship. When the church conveys to its members the notion that they are important and valued members of a particular congregational "family," then they are well on their way to discovering all that it means to be part of a New Testament community of faith, love, forgiveness, acceptance, and healing.

One of the real joys of parish ministry is to be unconditionally invited into the lives of people who are observing some of the most significant moments in their lives. These include weddings, baptisms, funerals, graduations, anniversaries, open houses, and hospital or nursing home visitations. There is probably no other vocation in the world where a person has such unhindered access into the life of an individual or an entire family. I always felt honored that, as their pastor, people would share so much of their lives with me. I also realized how important it was to keep their confidences in a highly professional and, at the same time, pastoral manner.

Duane: Boundaries

In the church, just as in families, boundaries are critically important. This has become very apparent over the last forty years as instances of clergy abuse have come to the fore. I am embarrassed and disheartened whenever I hear of a clergyperson who has not kept good boundaries when it comes to their interaction with those in church. It hurts and betrays us all.

I remember early on, after I became a pastor and started my call at Shepherd of the Valley, there was an instance when I became very uncomfortable meeting with a woman. She had asked to meet with me. But during our conversation, I just had a strange feeling that there was more going on in her interaction with me than there should have been. Nothing overt. Just some comments. Later, I went to see Pastor Paul and told him about how unsettling this was for me. His good advice was that if it didn't feel right, it probably wasn't right—that I should steer away from interaction with this person, which I did. Later, she left the congregation.

These days, there are many things that the Lutheran church does to help pastors and others on staff to keep good boundaries in their relationships. First, there is good training which is renewed regularly. Second, there is no tolerance in the Lutheran church for boundary-breaking. Third, in the churches where I worked, when building a new building, they would strive to build it in such a way that there could be privacy but also accountability. For instance, in every room where people could gather, including offices, there was a door that had a window in it. This was done so that there could be privacy as needed, but people could also easily look in and see exactly what was happening.

Paul: Baptism

As I grew in my understanding of parish ministry, it became obvious to me that there are certain "points of entry" into the life of the church and that baptism is surely one of them. Families that had had little contact with the church still wanted their children to be baptized, and this presented an opportunity for some genuine caring ministry. Our "process," like many churches, began with a class or two designed to help people better understand what baptism was really all about. The act of baptism itself is deceptively simple: some words, some water, and some prayers. A cynic may sit back and ask, what was that all about? Why is baptism so important?" So, the class was designed to help parents understand their role, in partnership with the church, to the end that this child might grow in the "grace and knowledge of our Lord Jesus Christ."

Over time, our church developed an entire program called Celebration of Baptism through which we planned several events each year for all our youth and their families, reminding them of their baptisms until they were finally confirmed in their faith at the start of their 10th grade in high school. Martin Luther once compared baptism with the grafting of a shoot onto an existing plant. He noted that if the grafting is to be successful, it will take time, attention, and real diligence. There is no magic in baptism. No one gets sprinkled with stardust. We believe that in this simple yet profound act, God welcomes us unconditionally while also signing and sealing us for all eternity as one of God's very own children. It is this amazing promise that our Lord makes to us that gives us the hope, faith, and courage to endure whatever life may throw our way, knowing that we are never alone and that the last chapter of our lives will be the best chapter of all.

A baptism story: one Sunday morning in the early 1980s, a young girl came up to me and asked, very sincerely, if I would baptize her Cabbage Patch doll. At that time, these dolls were all the rage. I told her as gently as I could that the church does not baptize dolls but that I would gladly give both her and her doll a blessing. So we sat down on some chairs, and I offered a rather lengthy prayer and blessing for Sarah and her doll, whose name I have long since forgotten. Sarah seemed quite pleased with the blessing, and her parents, standing not far away, were also quite taken with the whole scene.

Paul: Holy Communion

Holy Communion, like baptism, is one of those deceptively simple things that we do in the life of the church that also can be profoundly meaningful in the life of the believer. This is as our Lord intended. It will always be something of a mystery how God comes to us, as Luther wrote, "in, with, and under" these common elements of bread and wine. Surely, God knew that we mortals live in a world in which we value tangible things as much as we value spiritual things. So, in God's divine wisdom, we were given water, bread, wine, and even a book of books to enhance and increase our faith. It's not a lot, but it's as much as we need to sustain our journey on the road of life. I know firsthand just how meaningful the Lord's Supper can be for the faithful. I have seen people come forward with smiles on their faces and some with tears running down their cheeks. This family meal has a way of uniting us with other believers of every race and tribe as well as with our Lord. It is a meal of inclusivity, not exclusivity, though the church has sometimes wrongly made it exclusive. Our

Lord is always the gracious host who says to us, come and partake, be forgiven, be renewed, and let the relationships of your life be restored. Taste and see that the Lord is good. When God's Word is rightly proclaimed and the Sacraments are rightly administered, there is the church. What a blessing Holy Communion can then be for us and for the world.

Duane: Two Communion Stories

Once, when I was at St. Andrew's, I was serving communion wine to those coming forward. I would give each person a small plastic glass filled with wine and say, "The blood of Christ, shed for you." Each person would take a glass of wine, drink it, and return to his or her seat. However, on this particular day, there was a little hiccup. As I took the wine glass out of the tray of glasses, the glass caught the edge of the tray and flipped out of my hand into the air. It rotated once and landed smack dab in the cleavage of the elderly woman in front of me. Luckily, I knew her well. In my panic, I put my hand forward as though I was about to pick up the glass from where it rested. She quickly said, "No, Duane, I can get it myself."

One time at SOTV, I was visiting an elderly woman with dementia in the nursing home where she resided. We sat down at a table together. I said the words of institution, and we prayed. First, I offered her the bread, which she ate. Then when I offered her the small glass of wine, she looked at me, took the wine, raised the thimble-sized glass and said, "Here's to ya."

Paul: Funerals

Another care ministry comes at the time of death. You see, death has a way of forcing us all to think more seriously about our mortality. Truth be told, we do tend to get pretty comfortable with this life, and when it concludes, sometimes abruptly, we find ourselves needing and wanting the comfort and the ministry of the church. As a general rule, the pastors of our church were willing to officiate at the funeral of anyone whose family sincerely requested our services. Sometimes, this would be at the local funeral home or at the church. Always, the surviving family members were grateful for the work we did. Planning a funeral is not something a person does every day (thank goodness), and sometimes families come to the church knowing almost nothing of the wishes of the deceased. So, we would caringly and carefully walk the family through the whole process, beginning with the wake, then the funeral itself, followed by a luncheon and fellowship time, and finally the committal at the cemetery. There were many details to attend to, and most often, the families would abide by our recommendations and our policies. If done well, a funeral, almost by default, became an opportunity to do some quiet evangelism for the whole community. Death has a way of touching everyone, and when they sit in the pews looking at the urn or the casket, they cannot help but embrace something of their own mortality.

I recall especially three funerals of teenagers during which the sanctuary was almost filled to overflowing with high school students. I can tell you from experience that proclaiming the Good News of the Gospel in the face of death is one of the most fulfilling moments any preacher can ever experience. I have often said that people who attend weddings and funerals always seem to be a bit more receptive to the sermon than on a typical Sunday morning. The uniqueness of the hour seems to cause us all to think more seriously about our life, our faith, and our relationship to our Lord and Savior.

Every pastor has stories to tell about funerals. On one occasion, I was riding in a hearse as we pulled into the Fort Snelling National Cemetery, with its 220,000 graves. About two blocks from the gravesite, the hearse died (kind of fitting, I suppose). So, we carried the casket down the street to the gravesite and completed the committal.

On another occasion, we all arrived at Fort Snelling, got out of our cars, and walked to the gravesite just as the funeral director (a young woman who was a real rookie to the business) announced that she had forgotten the cremains back at the church! Have you ever seen a hearse lay rubber? I have.

At another funeral, one of the morticians slipped and fell into the open grave just as we were about to start the graveside service. I call him the mortified mortician. His face was as red as a beet as we pulled him out of the hole. Something like a resurrection, I suppose. But most folks don't realize how unstable the dirt can be around a freshly dug grave, especially in the winter months.

Duane: Funerals

Throughout my years as a pastor, I would sometimes mention to my colleagues in jest that they needed to remember that the first three letters in the word funeral are F-U-N. Just like the last three letters in Wisconsin are S-I-N, these little spelling quirks really have no bearing in the real world. They're just jokes. However, I must say that I really did enjoy officiating at funerals. It was a privilege to get to know the families of those who had died as we planned the arrangements together. It was a poignant time to be able to show that I, the church, and God cared. It was often amazing to hear the life stories of those who had died. I would think about how much I had missed by not knowing the deceased person better. Often, their life stories were rich and full. As Garrison Keillor has said, "They say such nice things about people at their funerals that it makes me sad to realize that I'm going to miss mine by just a few days."

Paul: Weddings

Another important caring ministry is marriage. Most pastors will tell you that planning a church wedding is a bit tricky because there are so many expectations from so many different people: the bride and the groom, the parents of the bride and the groom, the musicians, the wedding planner (if there is one), the pastor—and even the children of the bride and groom, in the case of a later-in-life second marriage. SOTV pastors were generally free to accept whatever offers they may have received to do a wedding. However, as the church grew, wedding and worship schedules grew tighter, and it became necessary to limit a church wedding to members only, with a few rather rare exceptions. Offsite weddings were still an option for non-members. However, it became necessary to ask that all weddings be booked at least six months in advance to allow ample time for the pastors and musicians to properly plan for and schedule such important events.

Further, time was needed for the couple to meet with the church's wedding coordinator and to take the "Prepare" readiness instrument, a tool used by us pastors as we helped couples prepare for marriage. Usually, after taking Prepare, the officiating pastor would want to meet with each couple at least two or three times before the wedding and the rehearsal. In addition to discussing what makes for a happy, healthy marriage, there were vows to choose or write, hymns and Bible texts to select, and determinations to be made about what kind of special music may or may not be appropriate for a church wedding. Again, if all of this planning was done carefully and respectfully, the families were usually very grateful. Parents especially were thrilled and delighted that the day had gone so smoothly for their son or daughter.

I would tell every couple that the wedding ceremony was the heart of the day and that all the rest were just trappings. Couples today sometimes get so consumed with those trappings (dresses, cakes, menus, flowers, rings, photos, limos, costs, honeymoon planning) that they tend to forget the essence of the day. I have even, on occasion, told couples as a kind of reality check that I am not really very interested in their wedding—but that I am very interested in their marriage. The wedding lasts one day. The marriage will hopefully last a lifetime. In my counseling, I also told couples to get help if they need it. There is no shame in acknowledging troubles in a marriage. It's the smart thing to do. And there are plenty of competent counselors (and pastors) around to offer direction and advice that could prove helpful, especially in those early months and years of marriage when two people are perhaps seeing each other as they really are for the first time (warts and all) and learning to adjust to this new relationship. Help can be found.

When I think of wedding mishaps, I need only think about my own wedding. When Margaret's home pastor died in his sleep just two weeks before our wedding, I asked one of my seminary professors to officiate. He was happy to do so, but he misjudged just where Dunnell, Minnesota, was located, and as a result, he was about forty-five minutes late for the start of the wedding. Luckily, it was just ten days before Christmas, and the church was beautifully decorated with candles, holly, pine roping, and a gorgeous Christmas tree that came from the family farm grove. When the prelude started, I told our organist (a fellow seminarian) to just keep playing every piece of Advent, Christmas, and post-Christmas music in the hymn book. If necessary, play them twice. This he did, and the guests just sat there and enjoyed the organ recital. The professor finally showed up, and the wedding commenced as planned.

Another mishap happened while doing a wedding on the beach in Key West, Florida. The bride, who had put herself on a starvation diet three days before the wedding, fell into a dead faint twice during the ceremony. She was understandably famished. Luckily, the groom caught her in the nick of time, and we stopped the service to get her some chocolate brownies courtesy of the Hilton Hotel. The wedding was paused for a third time when the photographer said, "We better get those sunset photos right now—otherwise, we won't get any at all." I am glad to report that they are still happily married.

Duane: Parish Nurses

About fifteen years ago, SOTV sent a few people to a training program so that they could become volunteer nurses at our church. They were to be called "parish nurses." I was skeptical of this new ministry. I cynically wondered what they could possibly do to enhance our care of people. Well, I soon found out. These volunteers, who all were trained nurses, became essential in the care ministry of SOTV. Not only did they help pastors and other staff members when it came to health issues in the congregation, but they also got involved in teaching, wellness clinics, visitation, and safety. Most importantly, though, these parish nurses connected with people in a way that pastors and others could not. I soon became a big proponent of having these people involved in as many aspects of care ministry as possible.

Paul: Volunteerism

When we discuss care in the church, something also needs to be said about volunteerism. One of the most valued members of our staff for many years was Cris Ireland. Cris wore a number of hats but none so vital as director of volunteer ministries. Churches today have a wealth of talent and expertise that so often never gets tapped or utilized. The Baby Boomers are a good example. They usually have the time, the health, the wealth, the expertise, and the desire to make their later years count for something. But they sometimes need to be asked and seriously recruited. Cris Ireland had an incredible "radar system" for scoping out people, assessing their gifts, and then enlisting their services for a huge variety of tasks at the church. It was a win-win for everyone. I could never say too many good things about this gifted woman who also saw filling job opportunities at the church not as a task but as a privilege. This was the key to her success on our staff. I, for one, shall be forever grateful for the time she spent literally "building up the Body of Christ" at SOTV.

Cris's ability to recruit volunteers, like others who also worked with volunteers, became more and more important over the years as we grew as a congregation. As we grew, no longer could the pastors alone do care ministry. It became important for us to recruit and equip others to help out in areas of caring. Over the years, the ways that non-pastors did that included participation in our prayer chain, friendly visitors, Befrienders, transportation, prayer-shawl knitters, friendly phone callers, small group leaders, guides for confirmation, and teachers for Sunday school. All those volunteers were crucial as more and more people joined the church.

Paul: Visitation

Pastoral visitation at hospitals, nursing homes, and private residences is very important. Pastors who neglect such visits are missing great opportunities to really get to know "their flock." It does take some time and some discipline, but it pays real dividends over the years. Pastors need to bond with their people, and one-to-one visits are a great way to do just that. We live in a very fast-paced, fractured, and frantic world, where we are now more isolated than ever. People long for a sense of community. Loneliness stalks the land for tens of thousands. Sometimes it is our time that is the best gift we can give to others. Pastoral visitation is a powerful dynamic in ministry.

I might add one word of levity. One morning, having just begun my time at the hospital, I entered a room to find a woman in a chair wrapped in a blanket. I began with a rather cheery word but soon realized that this conversation was going nowhere. Becoming a bit more observant, I realized that this lady was actually sitting on a commode. I asked her if she would like me to leave and come back later (talk about a dumb question), and she nodded her head in the affirmative. I did return later that day, and we both had a good laugh together. I learned that day to be much more observant when entering any hospital room.

Duane: A Memorable Visit

One of the retired pastors who was a member of our congregation was near death. I got a call from him. He asked if I would come over to see him. When I arrived, one of the very first things he said to me was, "Yes, I'm a pastor and I've spoken the gospel message to many people over the years. But right now, I need to hear it myself." So I spoke to him about the promise that we, as Christians, have from Jesus that there is resurrection and eternal life as we pass on from this life. That is the gospel message that he wanted and needed to hear.

That whole experience reminded me that all of us, even pastors, need to hear this message—not just once, but repeatedly. There is a healing power in hearing that message spoken aloud. When I'm near death, I hope someone comes and speaks those words to me.

Paul: Prayer Chain

I can't recall exactly when we started one, and it wasn't my idea originally, but prayer chains are a wonderful idea. Knowing that others (and in our church, it was *many* others) were actually praying for you daily—and even hourly—can be a great source of hope and comfort. Prayer chains sometimes carry rather intimate details concerning a person's health, life, marriage, children, and perhaps even finances. But I was always so grateful that our congregation did not indulge in gossip and that confidences were closely guarded and well respected.

Over the years, thousands have been prayed for, and this prayer chain has also brought so many people closer together. As a result, prayer shawls, devotional booklets, flowers, pans of brownies, Bibles, and Holy Communion all have been brought to homes and hospitals because people became aware of the needs of others through the prayer chain. It's just one more way by which the local congregation can carry on its caring ministry to a hurting and needy world—a ministry that is centuries old, yet ever new, and always needed.

Duane: A Prayer Story

I was humbled by one of my experiences of prayer and visitation. Near the end of my visits with people, I had the habit of asking them if they would like a prayer spoken on their behalf. If they said yes (and almost everyone did), then I'd follow up with "What should I pray for?" At the end of this hospital visit with Bill, who had a profoundly serious tumor, I asked my usual question, "What should I pray for?"

Bill quickly responded, "Well, if you don't know what to pray for, then we're both in trouble."

Chapter 12

MISSIONS

Duane: A Similarity in Their Mission Work

Both St. Andrew's and Shepherd of the Valley (SOTV) eventually became deeply involved in mission work. One common denominator in the two churches regarding their mission work is that both evolved into doing that kind of ministry. For both Roger and Paul, it took some time before these ministries took off at both of their churches.

I've wondered why the emphasis on mission lagged behind other ministries at these churches. It's probably because of that key thing in ministry — trust. Until Roger and Paul had built up a good amount of trust in their respective congregations, the mission endeavors really didn't gain any headway. It's related to what Mark Wickstrom, a pastor I worked with at St. An-

drew's, used to say. He said that service work and mission work were sort of like the roof of a house. There needs to be a solid, trustworthy building underneath before you can do roofing—or mission work. Maybe the time was just ripe for mission work at St. Andrew's and Shepherd of the Valley after years of building a good foundation.

Paul: The Old West-Centered Mission Work

As a young boy, I grew up in the old Augustana Synod of the Lutheran church. From its beginnings, this synod had deep roots in Swedish thought and theology. One of its true hallmarks was a genuine emphasis on missions and outreach to the whole world. I still recall something called the Junior Mission Band, which met in church basements once a month for the sole purpose of promoting mission awareness, even among the youngest members of the congregation. We would hear stories of missionaries in faraway lands, see photos or films of missionaries and their families, sing songs, study Bible stories about the mission work of the church, and finally take up an offering to support mission work at home and around the world. If we were fortunate, we might even get to meet a "real live" missionary who was home on furlough. They often had some really interesting stories to tell us.

It's fair to say that missionary outreach has been a major emphasis of the Christian Church since day one. Indeed, Jesus's parting words included a command to go into all the world and "make disciples of all nations, baptizing them in the name of the Father, and of the Son, and of the Holy Spirit, teaching them to obey everything that I have commanded you" (Matthew 28:19). Without this commandment, the church may well have died in its infancy. It is also worth noting that almost every nation in Europe and almost every church body in North America has done some serious missionary work. Margaret and I have made two major trips to Tanzania, and we were both surprised and delighted to learn that the Germans, the Swedes, and the Norwegians have done some excellent work in that part of the world.

But there is also a dark side to this story that should not be ignored. During the "Age of Exploration" when Europe was starting to wake up from the deep sleep of the "dark ages," men of great courage like Columbus, Drake, Cortez, Coronado, Magellan, and others from Europe boarded their tiny ships to explore the world and find a shorter trade route to the Orient. The goal, of course, was to obtain a number of commodities almost unknown to Europe at that time. Over time, it became clear that these intrepid explorers had discovered a whole new world and so their focus changed rather dramatically. What was found was gold, silver, copper, tobacco, fur pelts, and, tragically, even human slaves. Very often, missionaries accompanied these explorers in an attempt to "civilize" and "Christianize" these new lands and their inhabitants. It is now generally accepted by scholars that though missionaries had good intentions, their methods were very harmful to the native people.

One glaring mistake was that they not only brought the gospel of Jesus Christ, but they also felt obligated to bring along their European culture as well. It was this mindset that often proved disastrous to the newly converted. Sadly, it took many centuries before the Church realized its mistake. Christianity, yes, but culture, no. (The same thing was done to Native Americans in this country. When over 150,000 children were taken from their homes and placed in Indian schools.) There were exceptions, of course, like the work of Albert Schweitzer and those who helped to build hospitals for lepers and others who were seriously ill. But it is not hard to see why missionary work sometimes got a bad name when it was so closely aligned with colonialism, exploitation, and blatant profiteering by the so-called mother countries.

Paul: A Lesson Learned

I am now happy to report that the church has long since learned its lesson and that the missionary work of the church today is motivated by a vastly different mindset. Long gone are the days of arrogance and exploitation. If anything, the church now sees itself almost entirely in the role of the "foot-washing servant" who comes only to ask, "in the name of Jesus, how can we be of help to you?" This part of the story is truly worth celebrating. Today's missionaries meet people exactly where they are without any traces of colonial rule or dominance. Missionaries today often come as servant doctors, nurses, teachers, pastors, agronomists, dieticians, community health workers, midwives, carpenters—even computer programmers and technicians. Also, today's missionaries are sometimes working with poor yet healthy indigenous churches that only need some very specific assistance. Having been in Tanzania twice, I often comment that these people are materially poor but spiritually rich. In fact, I think they have a lot to teach us westerners who so often drown in our own love of materialism.

Paul: Shepherd of the Valley's Journey with Missions

In 1995, our church became acquainted with a program called YouthWorks, whereby teens, with adult supervision, travel to various ministry sites around the United States, Canada, and Mexico. Once there, they spent a week or more doing various service projects while also interfacing with people who often come from very different backgrounds and cultures. Youth Director Bob White took our first group to Pine Ridge, South Dakota, to work on a tribal reservation of the Lakota Sioux. Apparently, it was an amazing week of learning, growing, and service because what followed were many more such journeys to YouthWorks sites.

There were other trips involving Habitat for Humanity where Shepherd of the Valley members and friends traveled to places like Biloxi, Mississippi, to build new homes in the wake of Hurricane Katrina's devastation. In addition, more locally, we sent out teams every summer to work on Habitat for Humanity projects in the Twin Cities.

Paul: The Birth of Bega Kwa Bega

In 2001, the St. Paul Area Synod, to which SOTV belongs, made a rather bold move. It decided to "adopt" an area around the southern Tanzanian city of Iringa and to also assign a village from that area to every congregation in the St. Paul Area Synod. By every measure, this has been a successful endeavor. Shepherd of the Valley was to partner with Tungamalenga, a small village about ninety kilometers from Iringa. In 2002, Pastor Bonnie Wilcox, an able and inspiring member of our staff, decided to form a group of ten brave souls who all got their shots, updated their passports, did some research on a place none of them had ever been before, learned a few phrases in Swahili, and prepared for what they later called "the trip of a lifetime." Talk about culture shock and warm Christian fellowship all rolled into one! After a twenty-hour flight through Amsterdam and then on into Dar Salaam (the capital), you board a van or bus for another eleven-hour ride to Iringa on a road that at times does not feel much like a road at all. But in the end, it's all worth it. For eight or nine days, you are exposed to and integrated into an amazing group of people who live out their faith in poverty with an unshakable trust in God's goodwill and providential care. While there, you worship together, eat together, sing and dance together, visit a school for the deaf or perhaps an orphanage, and travel to various "preaching points" where itinerant pastors seek to minister to a widely dispersed group of people. There is also time to visit some Maasai villages whose inhabitants are mostly shepherds of sheep and goats. Some time, of course, is also left for a safari to the Ruaha big game preserve. To witness elephants, giraffes, zebras, lions, cape buffalo, ostrich, baboons, and rhinos up close and in the wild is truly unforgettable.

Over the last nineteen years, some remarkable things have happened to this ongoing relationship. Our congregation has built a health clinic in Tungamalenga and enlisted the help of someone named Barnabas Kahwage, who has become pretty much a self-made doctor. He studies when and where he is able, always seeking to improve his skills. He is also something of a miracle worker. We try hard to supply him with the best equipment and medications that we possibly can. In the early days of this ministry, our members would each bring along a suitcase full of vitamins, aspirin, bandages, gauze pads, thermometers, tape, and nearly every kind of over-the-counter medication you could name. Sometimes, it brought tears to Barnabas's eyes. He once took me aside and said, "With these gifts that you have brought today, I will be able to save lives." Health in Tanzania can be so precarious at times that even a simple vitamin a day can make a difference in someone's health and wellbeing. Malaria, AIDS, dysentery, respiratory issues, and malnutrition are conditions that he seems to treat most often. Broken bones and prenatal care are also high on his list.

Much of our focus as a church has been on building village wells with adequate pumps and PVC piping to provide clean drinking water, buying mosquito-repellent netting for sleeping (most people are bitten while asleep), distributing condoms and other forms of birth control to contain the spread of AIDS, and even funding for ample food supplies. Believe it or not, none of these "cures" costs a great deal of money.

In addition, our synod has founded Tumaini University in Iringa. Tumaini is the Swahili word for *hope*. When the school first opened, it enrolled fourteen students. Today, it has over one thousand students who are getting a good education. Our congregation contributes rather substantially each year toward paying the tuition for worthy young people to attend a prep school (something like our high schools) and hopefully to then go on to the university. I dare say that we have now supported hundreds of students in this manner. In addition, we have also supported a number of pastors with their seminary costs.

One other part of this amazing relationship is the Ilula Health Care Center, which is on the road between Iringa and our village of Tungamalenga. Many years ago, we joked about Ilula being the Mayo Clinic of East Africa. With God's help, it is no longer a joke. The last time I looked, there were over twenty different buildings there. Medical staff are doing all sorts of medical procedures that were totally unavailable to the population before the center was founded.

Dr. Randy Hurley, an oncologist from Shepherd of the Valley, is but one example of how fervently people have supported this ministry. Randy flies to Tanzania about twice a year on his own dime and offers his considerable services free of all costs. He has done this now for almost twenty years.

Another "pioneer" along with Pastor Bonnie is Kirsten Levorson, a woman who has worked tirelessly for over two decades to raise money, learn the language, and travel to Tanzania every year to help form a synod-wide ministry called "Bega Kwa Bega," which means "Shoulder to Shoulder." Bega Kwa Bega now oversees this vital and growing ministry.

It should also be noted that the Tanzanian government, not having any great wealth of its own to work with, always seems grateful that the Christian church shows up with financial backing to make good things happen. This is all done with no hidden agenda and no ulterior motives. Missionary work as it should always be.

From the beginning, Pastor Bonnie, Kirsten, and Randy all wanted this relationship to be reciprocal and anything but paternalistic. The world has had enough of that already. So, they and others working in this mission field made sure that the Tanzanians had an opportunity to share their gifts with us. For example, we were given hand-carved candle sticks, carved animals, various fabrics with beautiful animal designs, shorts and dresses, and even small stools with tripod legs (a bit tricky to get on the plane, but we did manage). I was given a Masai spear when Margaret and I were made honorary "parents" of the village. To date, I believe that our church has made no less than twenty trips over there. On three different occasions, we have arranged for some of these good people to come to Minnesota for a visit. I must confess that there is some cultural shock for those coming here and for those going there.

Paul: Giving to Mission Work

There is another aspect of mission work at Shepherd of the Valley that is all done monetarily. We have a $3 million annual budget from which we have pledged to tithe (10 percent), the result being that at one time, we had the joy of giving away about $300,000 a year to over dozens of different ministries and missions. In later years, we shortened this list, but I always argued that even modest gifts to some ministries acted like "seed money" that often encouraged others to at least match or exceed in their giving. Surely a great deal of good missionary work was done through these dollars year after year.

One more example of service and witness is found in our own church's food shelf. In 2019, our church gave away almost one hundred tons of food to people in our county. Yes, there is poverty even in a county that often looks quite upscale and trendy.

Paul: Mission Work Today

It seems to me that in some ways, today, we have lost our zeal for mission work. Gone are the days of the Junior Mission Band, the missionaries home on furlough, and all those stories from far-off lands. Things change over time, even mission work. We also live today in a world in which diversity and pluralism are greatly honored and the idea of converting someone from one faith to another somehow seems almost inappropriate, perhaps even offensive to some. Even the church-growth movement here in America from just a few years ago seems to have abated. At times, evangelism seems to happen more by accident than by intention. And yet, if we are listening, we can hear the voice of our Lord who still asks us to go, to teach, to baptize, to welcome, and to expand the Body of Christ on this earth. There are still millions who have little or no connection whatsoever with a healthy, vital, life-giving community of faith. If the church is really doing its job well, people will respond in a positive and supporting manner. Shepherd of the Valley began by knocking on doors and telling our story. But later on, this was not so necessary. The best missionaries that any church can have are its own members who, by word of mouth, share the Good News and offer gentle yet persuasive words of welcome and engagement.

Paul: Other Sheep

One thing that has changed over the years is how we as Christians have come to understand and even appreciate other religions that are often very different than our own. It is true that the other four great religions of the world (Hinduism, Judaism, Islam, and Buddhism) vary greatly from Christianity. So how do we make peace with these differing theologies? I find some comfort in the words of Jesus when he said, "I have other sheep that do not belong to this fold; I must bring them also" (John 10:16). Who might those "other sheep" have been? Christians should always be ready and willing to give witness to their faith in both word and deed. For me, the litmus test for all true religions is this: how well do they (and we) love one another? How dominant is this theme in their various theologies? If unconditional love is expressed in a person's life for all people regardless of their color, creed, ethnicity, gender, or national origin, then I don't worry too much about that person's eternal destiny. But if that theme of love is somehow sublimated by hate, bigotry, tradition, national pride, or arrogance, then I have a problem with that religion. I like to think that every religion of the world teaches its followers to love the neighbor. The question is, of course, how well do the adherents of that religion practice this command: to love God with all your heart, soul, mind, and strength and to love your neighbor as yourself.

Roger: A Cold January Morning

One cold January morning, I was sitting in my office sorting through the morning's mail. Included in that stack was a calendar from the ELCA Office of Global Missions. I flipped through it, and to my delight, I saw a photo of one of my seminary professors, Dr. Norman Bakken. Bakken had taken a call in Kingston, Jamaica, serving as the Lutheran religion professor at the United Theological College of the West Indies, an ecumenical seminary training male and female clergy in Kingston, Jamaica, for Protestant ministry. I called Norm and learned that he and the entire island were in the middle of trying to put their lives together after the ravages of a Category 5 hurricane named Gilbert that had hit the island in September of 1988. Roofs had been torn off; debris was everywhere. In other words, they needed help. With flash bulbs going off in my head, I knew that, if at all possible, Jamaica could be a mission project for us. Bakken agreed, saying that I should make plans to come down some time and that together we could see what kind of help we might provide. Faster than a speeding bullet, I said, "How about Thursday?"

He said, "That soon?"

"Norm, it's bitterly cold up here," I said. So, on Thursday of that week, I was on a plane heading to Jamaica to see what kind of project St. Andrew's could become involved with.

Roger: Mission Jamaica

When I arrived in Kingston, it became evident that there was so much devastation that there would be no end of possibilities for mission involvement. Norm and I spent the morning surveying what projects the seminary grounds might provide for us, but it became apparent that almost everything on that campus needed huge construction equipment and skilled workers, not to mention the kind of costs it might entail. Eventually, he led me over to Hope Valley Experimental School—a public elementary school with about one thousand students, many of them crippled or abandoned and some suffering from the life-long challenge of being Thalidomide babies.

Coming back home to St. Andrew's, I began to lay the groundwork for our involvement in Kingston. One of the basic tenets I put into place was that we would only become involved in a project the people themselves wanted. They needed to tell us how we could help. We weren't going to tell them what should be done. In addition, any project needed to be something we could pay for and accomplish in a week's time. In other words, we would not start a project that we could not complete. It was a principle that has served us well over the years.

Roger: Vacation with a Purpose

For Mission Jamaica to be successful, it needed people to guide the project who were skilled at construction and could teach a bunch of volunteers, some of whom had little experience. Two members of St. Andrew's, Kent Jefferson of Jefferson Homes and Denny Kiel, a private contractor, were just the people to send to Kingston to survey the situation. Both men had the kind of experience that would allow us to be realistic in our expectations and have a clear understanding of the kind of budget we would need to raise in order to accomplish our tasks. Eventually, Denny Kiel became the director of Mission Jamaica, spending the month of January in Jamaica preparing and arranging necessary supplies for week-long projects volunteers would tackle in February and March. During Kiel's years as director, Mission Jamaica expanded beyond Kingston to include other areas on the island. Montego Bay soon became a second base for Mission Jamaica with projects that included bringing help to orphanages that had been operating on a shoestring. In addition to construction volunteers, Mission Jamaica sought out members and friends who were doctors, nurses, and dentists to bring free health care to an island deep in poverty. The medical team was well-received. We were told that when the time approached for the medical team to arrive, word went through the community, "The Lutherans are coming! The Lutherans are coming!"

As time went on, word about Mission Jamaica began to spread among other pastors and congregations that were also looking to expand their mission projects. Eventually, thirty-five congregations in seven states joined Mission Jamaica in bringing over eight hundred volunteers per year who would spend a week at a time bringing help to those less fortunate. We also invited college campus pastors to present the challenge to students to participate in what we called "Spring Break with a Meaning." Over the years, various Lutheran colleges, including Augsburg, Luther, and Concordia Moorhead sent teams of students to Jamaica as part of our program.

And now, thirty-one years later, it's still going strong! From its beginnings in 1989 with Hope Valley Experimental School, Mission Jamaica now includes involvement in Penwood Medical Clinic, West Haven Children's Home, a Mobile Medical Clinic, a preschool, and Jamaica's equivalent of Habitat for Humanity.

Roger: Vision Slovakia

In 1995, we traveled back to Slovakia for the dedication of the church building we funded in Prievidza, which I mentioned in chapter 3. After the dedication ceremony, a member of the bishop's office in Bratislava mentioned that there was a church in a town called Martin in the northern part of Slovakia that was interested in creating a Bible school. It was not going to be just any kind of Bible school, but one where students would live together in a kind of dormitory setting. It was the brainchild of one of the sons of the pastor of the Lutheran Church in Martin. Bohdan Hrobon's dream was modeled after Finkenwalde, the seminary Dietrich Bonhoeffer had created as a biblical church community that included learning, worship, friendship, shared ministry and hospitality, all of this with the Bible as the centerpiece of their life together. It was just a dream, but St. Andrew's was eager to help flesh out that dream and make it a reality.

That fall, Bohdan made a trip to Mahtomedi. We sat for hours in a restaurant talking about his dream and how it could become a reality, sketching out on a paper napkin how a dilapidated old building could be transformed into a modern dormitory. Bohdan's goal was to re-awaken amongst the pastors and lay people of Martin a sincere desire to follow Christ. For decades, they had been listening to propaganda spewed out by the communist party, and Bohdan thought that now was the time to reach the population for Christ. St. Andrew's ear-marked $10,000 to get the project going.

Over the next couple of years, members of St. Andrew's would travel to Martin to help in the reconstruction of a parsonage and with repairs to the Martin Lutheran Church building. During the years of communist rule, many churches had fallen into disrepair, and the people of St. Andrew's were itching to do their part to make the Bible school a reality. For a number of years, our visits to Martin consisted mainly of construction and remodeling projects. Other churches from Minnesota, Illinois. and Arizona soon joined us in pounding nails and swinging paint brushes.

But all of this was about to change in 1998 when the St. Andrew's Choir decided to travel to Slovakia and share their gift of song with their fellow Lutherans in Eastern Europe. As good as the gift of music might be at stirring people's souls, Bohdan had another dream he hoped we might be willing to embrace. It was the dream of offering Vacation Bible School to the children of Martin.

The idea to create a week of Christian education complete with music and games was something the Lutherans in Martin, Slovakia, had never experienced. Bohdan shared his idea with Jan Gilbertson, the director of the St. Andrew's Choir, who immediately saw this as an opportunity to involve members of the choir in a project that could change children's lives. So now, when the St. Andrew's Choir makes its yearly trip in June to perform on a Sunday morning before the members and friends of Martin Lutheran Church, their gift of music is really only the beginning. Because when Monday comes, the gloves come off, and members of the choir take on the task of running four days of Vacation Bible School for the children of Martin, Slovakia. Over the years, this project has grown to the point where it now draws more than 250 children for what just might be the best four days of their summer.

Professor Paul Berge, a member of St. Andrew's and former religion professor at Luther Seminary, now leads Vision Slovakia. Under his guidance, many more congregations have become involved, including summer trips for high school youth who develop some strong friendships with teens from Martin. And what Bohdan thought of as a bold dream to establish a Bible school has now grown to include a campus that offers Christian education opportunities to lay adults and over five hundred children and youths, preschool through high school. The Bible school now goes under the name Center for Christian Education, and in January 2012, it established the Department of Religious Studies within the University of Zilina—something that would have been unheard of happening in a secular university when the communists were in control.

Truly God works in mysterious ways. What began with hammering nails and swinging paintbrushes in 1996 has become a huge Christian presence in a former communist country that is leading lives to be lived with Christ at the very center.

Duane: Contrast in Mission Styles

Although over time, both St. Andrew's and Shepherd of the Valley became quite mission-oriented, there is a difference in how they each developed those mission connections. At St. Andrew's, Roger and his team were quite independent in seeking out mission work. They alone initiated the work on Mission Jamaica and Vision Slovakia. Only after Mission Jamaica and Vision Slovakia were quite well-established did other partners join in on these endeavors.

At Shepherd of the Valley, the beginnings of various mission endeavors were different. There, mission work was not done independently. Rather, it was done in collaboration with other already-established entities. Yet, like St. Andrew's, over time, SOTV became a leader within many of these missions.

Two different senior pastors. Two different congregations. Two different ways of establishing and doing mission work.

Chapter 13

MEGACHURCHES

Duane: Both St. Andrew's & SOTV Were Megachurches

I*first came to St. Andrew's in 1978 when it was not yet a megachurch. I'm not sure when it became one. But according to the commonly accepted definition of a megachurch, which is a church that regularly has two thousand or more people in attendance at worship, at some point, St. Andrew's became one. The same is true of my time at Shepherd of the Valley (SOTV). When I started at SOTV, it was a medium-sized church, but soon, it too became a megachurch. This chapter includes the reflections of Roger and Paul on what it meant to be a senior pastor at a Lutheran church that grew to become a megachurch.*

Paul: Behold, the Megachurch

If you have been around the American Protestant church for any length of time, you may have noticed something of a change in the past three or four decades. It's called the rise of the megachurch in America. It is a relatively new development in the world of Protestantism. Most churches across America have perhaps no more than three to five hundred members. I once read that the majority of churches in America, many being rural, worship with fewer than one hundred on any given Sunday. But that size of congregation, while still quite common in many communities, now has a "challenger," so to speak. Say hello to the megachurch. Interestingly, for many churches today, membership seems to be of less value than worship attendance. As the saying goes, "Those who show up are most often the true believers."

It has been estimated that if all the people who worship at a megachurch were combined, they would comprise the third-largest religious group in America. There are approximately 1,250 megachurches in America. 80 percent of Americans live within ninety minutes of a megachurch. Some of these churches have now become so large and influential that their agendas sometimes supersede those of their own denominations.

There are some very good reasons why megachurches have flourished in recent years. People would sometimes complain to me that our church was "getting too big," but at the same time, people today, especially in urban areas, have become quite comfortable with "bigness." We go to big hospitals, schools, malls, factories, entertainment centers, and sports venues. Bigness does not seem to threaten people today as perhaps it did years ago when our nation was much more agrarian. It would appear that churches today are simply following suit.

Some contend that our very culture today has been conditioning us toward larger churches. We are now more comfortable reading signage, proceeding through a maze of hallways, waiting in lines, walking through vast parking spaces, registering online, and viewing large video screens. We have become accustomed to large crowds. The pace and character of church life has changed. In some cases, it has changed rather dramatically.

Paul: Why Are People Attracted to Megachurches?

So, we might ask, why have so many Americans adapted so willingly to these changes? One answer: *choices*. Americans today love choices. Larger churches, unlike smaller ones, can offer many options. These include multiple hours for worship and Christian education, forms of worship, avenues for musical expression, opportunities for youth ministry, options for service and mission projects, and methods for community outreach. Megachurches often feature their own bookstores, coffee shops, nurseries, preschools, health clinics, counseling services, wellness programs, Sunday breakfasts, support groups, and even gymnasiums for various athletic events. It is truly remarkable what megachurches can do when they are organized, focused, and structured for efficiency.

Paul: Built Around a Person

There's another characteristic of megachurches worth noting. Many are initially built around a single, highly motivated, visionary, charismatic person. The danger of this is that once any of these highly visible and charismatic preachers are no longer around due to reassignment, retirement, death, or disgrace, the ministry can easily flounder. One thing we tried to do at Shepherd of the Valley (SOTV) was to have all of the pastors involved in all aspects of parish ministry so that the congregation came to embrace the pastors equally. This is critical for healthy sustainability for any large congregation.

I should also add here that while SOTV became a megachurch over time, I was never intentional about this goal, and I never wanted for a moment to denigrate smaller churches. They all have an important role to play. Our growth was basically determined by three factors: 1) we had an excellent location; 2) northern Dakota County exploded with growth; and 3) we tried our level best to do engaging, invitational, Gospel-centered ministry. Apparently, a lot of people really came to appreciate all of this. Still, I am very thankful for any community that has churches of varying sizes because people need to find a community of faith that meets their level of comfort. From house churches to megachurches, the Holy Spirit will always find a way to motivate and empower the people of God.

Paul: Megachurch Myths and Realities

There are several myths surrounding megachurches that deserve a comment or two. One myth is that megachurches are often too big and almost out of control. Not really. On the contrary, they are highly organized because they absolutely have to be. At one time, our church had almost sixty full- and part-time salaried staff. It took that many people to make sure the place was running efficiently and at the level of professionalism we desired. I have been in some very warm and welcoming megachurches, and I have also been in some smaller churches that were close to being ice cold. It's not really the numbers that matter so much as how the pastors, staff, and other lay leaders deploy themselves and how they understand their respective ministries. Lyle Schaller contends that no matter the size of the congregation, every member needs a large group experience (usually worship) and a small-group experience. Members will never know everyone in a large church, but they need to know some members. These contacts could come from almost any small group setting, settings that are priceless in getting folks to be better connected and feel like they belong.

One of our church council members used to say that ours was a large church that somehow managed to feel small. I took that as a real compliment. For years, we had a program called ACTS—Adult Christians Together Socially—whereby four couples or individuals would gather once a month, rotating from house to house and sharing a meal together, often potluck style. For many, this was a real bonding experience. When you have been together in a group for two or three hours and dined together, you come away from that event much more connected to the life and ministry of your church. Some of these relationships are still going strong after nearly forty years.

A second megachurch myth is that megachurches tend to water down the faith. Large churches are accused of being one mile wide and one inch deep. Not so. This comment often comes from folks who have never had a good look at just how these churches function. (And perhaps some of the criticism may be motivated by just a touch of envy.) One friend of mine calls megachurches "circus churches." Perhaps there is a grain of truth in such a comment. But for the most part, megachurches seem very committed to evangelism, reaching the unchurched, discipleship, Bible study, responsible stewardship, service, and witness to the wider community.

Another myth is that megachurches hurt other churches. A number of credible studies show this not to be the case. In fact, one surprising find was that some unchurched folks are first drawn to a megachurch and find it not to their liking, so they slip out the "back door," often ending up joining another smaller church where finding fellowship is easier for them.

Megachurches are also accused of being kind of monolithic in that everyone who joins is close to the same age, race, class, income level, and even political orientation. Again, there could be a tad bit of truth here for some megachurches, but for the most part, there is a great deal of diversity in income level, racial makeup, religious backgrounds, and political convictions—depending, of course, on the community in which one resides. For any healthy congregation, the one real unity should be found in Christ Jesus and his redeeming love. With this as a starting point, Christians can agree to disagree on a great many issues while still remaining brothers and sisters in the Lord.

Duane: Were St. Andrew's and SOTV Built Around Roger and Paul?

Paul mentions above that often, megachurches are built around one key person. He's right about that. Both St. Andrew's and SOTV are examples of that notion. Roger and Paul were certainly key figures in the growth of their respective megachurches. I saw them function up close. And I can say that they were both absolutely instrumental in the phenomenal growth of those churches.

However, as time went on, both churches became aware of the "key charismatic leader" syndrome in megachurches. To some extent, both churches understood the problem that when a key leader leaves the church, a huge void is created, and people might possibly become disillusioned, leading to ministry that might suffer as a result.

I believe that both St. Andrew's and SOTV sought to mitigate that dynamic in their churches. One way they did that was by raising the status and standing of all the pastors and others on staff. Another thing they did was to focus on doing great, all-around ministry. If ministries were strong, then people would have many relationships within the congregation that weren't dependent on that one key leader—Roger or Paul. They would be more connected to others in the church and thus less susceptible to disenchantment when that key person leaves. A third thing that both churches did was to bring onboard good lay leadership who also had a vision for the future—a vision that would include a future without those key leaders, Roger and Paul.

Roger: So Now You're a Megachurch

The phenomenon of becoming a megachurch is a lot like watching your kids grow up. At one point, they're just babes in arms needing to be held and spoon-fed, totally dependent upon you for everything. Then comes the day when they are no longer satisfied with crawling on all fours, and they rise up to take those first baby steps. And soon, before you even know it, they are off spreading their wings, becoming more than you ever expected and nothing at all like what you may have had in mind.

To the outsider, a place like St. Andrew's, with its thousands of weekly worshippers and its seemingly unending array of programs, trips, and special events comes across as if it's always been this way. It hasn't. More than anything, the growth of St. Andrew's into a megachurch was actually a matter of pastors and members putting one foot in front of the other, sometimes blindly, as together we followed the urges of the Holy Spirit into a new and fascinating future. I've often said that there truly has to be a Holy Spirit because none of us are smart enough to have pulled off the transformation of St. Andrew's into a megachurch by ourselves.

Roger: There's No Training for Something Like This

One of the last classes we had in seminary was a fleeting introduction into leadership. But as newly minted pastors just weeks away from graduating from seminary, we actually didn't know very much. Our future in the parish to which we were called was dependent upon a very forgiving and compassionate congregation that understood better than we that this was going to be a journey of discovery and adventure. Hopefully, we wouldn't get shipwrecked along the way.

As St. Andrew's began to grow, it became very obvious that we—as pastors, congregational leaders, and staff—needed to grow as well. The fortunate part of all of this was that the megachurch phenomenon was new territory for most mainline congregations and that we, as senior pastors, were all new at trying to figure out how to run something that kept getting bigger with every passing year. Of course, there were those outliers like Mount Olivet Lutheran Church in Minneapolis that had already grasped what it meant to be a megachurch and had become quite good at moving their ship of faith through the rocks and shoals that would threaten lesser congregations with certain destruction. For the rest of us, however, we had to find church growth conferences and workshops that might give us some insight into how to run a large congregation that was quickly becoming huge. For the most part, in the 1980s and 1990s, there were plenty of conferences and church growth experts from which to choose.

One of the best was Fuller Theological Seminary in Pasadena, California. Not only did I and other staff persons make multiple trips to Fuller to soak up as much knowledge and experience as they were willing to share, but fortunately, we were able to secure the services of Carl George, who was, at that time, heading up Fuller's Church Growth Movement. Giving us additional insights into what we were undertaking was Lyle Schaller, who, on numerous occasions, helped guide St. Andrew's into the future. A more Lutheran approach was afforded us through a week-long conference held each year in May that was meant specifically as a gathering place for senior pastors of the largest ELCA congregations in the nation. Here, we were able to share ideas and best practices and make connections with pastors who were experiencing similar issues. It was a conference put on by senior pastors for senior pastors, and to be eligible to attend, the average weekly attendance of invited congregations needed to be eight hundred or more.

Roger: Faithful Growth

In the 1980s and 1990s, St. Andrew's was experiencing worship attendance alone that hovered close to three thousand. Add in Christmas and Easter worship with close to ten thousand in attendance, and it became quite evident that we needed a whole different type of leadership model if we were going to succeed in providing superior worship and educational experiences for our members and friends. Going from one pastor in 1972 to a staff of eight pastors and over 147 full- and part-time employees in 2005 meant committing ourselves to a very steep learning curve. There were program demands that kept pushing us into new territory. Music staff found themselves directing not just one choir but seven. Gone were the days with just a dozen or so kids in confirmation. Now the challenge was to create an inspiring and meaningful confirmation experience for over 175 students in each grade, 7th, 8th, and 9th. Add in retreats, Sunday school, women's ministry, men's ministry, a sports ministry, and the expansion of our mission projects in Jamaica and Slovakia, and St. Andrew's was becoming an extremely complicated place to oversee and run. Without realizing it, we had become a regional church—drawing worshippers from throughout the Twin Cities—which presented new expectations and demands.

The question that invariably faced us was, do we have what it takes to faithfully grow? Here again, we were forced to lean upon experts in staffing systems to help us create models that would help each staff person thrive. To be honest, we made a ton of mistakes along the way, but many of those mistakes were corrected through weekly staff meetings and multi-day program staff retreats where we could be honest about our expectations as well as our failures.

Roger: Create, Invent, Innovate, Experiment

In the 1990s, there were very few megachurches in the ELCA, and the thought of turning to synod and churchwide leadership for help was non-existent. So, in reality, we were left on our own to figure out what to do next. Places like Fuller Church Growth Institute were invaluable in offering us insights into what our next steps might be. Through church growth conferences such as those held at Fuller, we were able to rub shoulders with senior pastors of large congregations that had already experienced huge growth. Many of these pastors were from Baptist, non-denominational, and independent congregations. We may not have agreed on theological terms, but it was very apparent that these pastors were committed to fulfilling their role in the Great Commission of making disciples. Where, for example, in any ELCA conference did you hear of a pastor saying that they were going to claim their city for Christ? Well, these pastors did. These were pastors who had bold dreams of what their congregations could accomplish, and they were willing to step out and create programs and ministries to fulfill those objectives. Someone once said that no congregation will ever achieve anything greater than its leadership envisions. In other words, the responsibility of a leader is to cast a bold vision for the future, one so big and bold that it is God-sized and will require God to accomplish the task.

Roger: The Role of the Holy Spirit

In Luther's explanation of the Third Article of the Apostle's Creed regarding the role of the Holy Spirit, he includes some words that a follower of Jesus Christ needs to take seriously. Note Luther's emphasis on the fact that I cannot on my own, but when God equips me, I can. He writes:

"I believe that I cannot by my own reason or strength believe in Jesus Christ, my Lord, or come to him; but the Holy Spirit has called me by the gospel, enlightened me with his gift, sanctified and kept me in the true faith."

And here's the important part regarding the Holy Spirit's role in church growth:

"In the same way he calls, gathers, enlightens and sanctifies the whole Christian church on earth, and keeps it with Jesus Christ in the one true faith."

In other words, we, as pastors, leaders, members, and followers of Jesus Christ are totally and completely dependent upon the Holy Spirit to equip us for the task of growing the church. We can't do it by ourselves. That was never God's intention. In fact, we cannot even envision and dream of what God has in mind for our congregation. But God, through the Holy Spirit, can enlighten and lead us in the task of building up the kingdom of God where we are, with the people God has given us.

Roger: It's Risky Business

To follow the Holy Spirit is risky business because you don't really have any idea just how far the Spirit is going to take you. Following the Holy Spirit is not for the faint of heart. To do so means being willing to get out of your comfort zone and to risk taking a chance. It means getting out in front of your people and boldly declaring the amazing things God intends to do with us if we're willing to follow. Some may laugh! Some may call you crazy. Some might just leave and go to a church where the pastor is more normal. Basically, it means pushing aside all of the reasons why something can't be done and, in its place, proclaiming, "Why not?" It means putting an end to limiting the power and presence of God. It means getting on your knees and asking God to show you the way and to give you the power and strength to do whatever God has in mind.

Having said that, however, following Christ is not as much of a risk as we might think. It's not as big a risk because Jesus promises to equip those who are willing to follow him with whatever they might need to accomplish the task. In his own words, he tells his disciples: "Ask, and it will be given to you; search, and you will find; knock, and the door will be opened for you. For everyone who asks receives; and everyone who searches finds; and for everyone who knocks, the door will be opened" (Luke 11:9-10).

That's the task! Ask, seek, knock, and then discover just how wondrous life with Jesus Christ can be for those who are willing to follow his lead.

Roger: Competition Had Come to Town

As other churches were feeling the effect of St. Andrew's presence, so too, the time eventually came for St. Andrew's to be affected by the intensity and growth of the evangelical movement and the desire for many to shed the trappings of liturgical worship in favor of something more informal. The Holy Spirit movement, with its emphasis upon speaking in tongues, was filling the pews at nearby North Heights Lutheran Church. Its ministry emphasizing prayer and small groups became a calling card that caught the attention of some who later left St. Andrew's to join their ranks.

But the biggest competition that was going to affect St. Andrew's was happening right in our own backyard. First Baptist Church had experienced a change in leadership through the retirement of its senior pastor. Taking his place was an energetic young pastor by the name of Bob Merritt. Merritt was a man on a mission who surrounded himself with a cadre of young, like-minded professionals who shared his desire to see First Baptist reach its full potential.

He began by dropping the word "Baptist," changing the name of the congregation to Eagle Brook. He then marshaled the creativity of his young staff to produce music and video that would catch the attention and interest of a younger crowd. He encouraged his staff to produce programs for women, youth, and senior adults with the kind of quality and vitality that few churches could match. If some thought St. Andrew's had caught the Protestant work ethic, Merritt and his crew left us standing in the dust. We ended up losing members to Eagle Brook. The old First Baptist Church with 450 in attendance in 1995 has grown under the Eagle Brook name to something akin to a mini-denomination of twelve locations throughout the Twin Cities with more than 20,000 people worshipping weekly in these twelve metro-wide locations.

Roger: Who Are We?

When Eagle Brook was starting to make its presence felt in the community, one of our staff members said, "We have to become just like them if we intend to grow." What that staff person really had in mind, I'm not quite sure. If she meant adopting modern technology like the internet, video, social media, and dynamic programming, then she was right. We were woefully lacking in that area and could learn a lot from how they attracted a new and younger generation. However, if she meant adopting a Baptist theology of salvation that included decision theology where a person must come into a personal relationship with Jesus before they are saved, that was a line we would never, as traditional Lutherans, be able to cross.

St. Andrew's was really a congregation made up of people from lots of different religious backgrounds. A survey we once conducted in preparation for a building campaign uncovered the fact that one-third of St. Andrew's members were former Roman Catholic, one-third were life-long Lutherans, and one-third were made up of a mixture of all kinds of denominations as well as people with no religious background to speak of. It was an exciting mixture of folks from all kinds of backgrounds that brought to St. Andrew's religious insights and perspectives that gave us a unique color and flavor.

Roger: An Open Door

Back in 1995, St. Andrew's invited nationally known and respected church growth consultant Lyle Schaller to help us discover not only who we were but also what kind of future we might want to embrace. Schaller spent three or four days surveying and talking with members, both the newly minted and those who had been a part of St. Andrew's for decades. He even went to Eagle Brook to discover how we compared with them and what kind of ministry they were embarking upon.

His analysis of Eagle Brook was that it was like most other churches in the Baptist General Conference—a church that projected high expectations of those who seek to become members. One expectation, Schaller noted, was that its members would be present for two periods of time on a typical Sunday morning. In this respect, Schaller went on to say, Eagle Brook resembled a covenant community.

St. Andrew's, on the other hand, was described by Schaller as an "Open Door." St. Andrew's, he said, projected the message, "You are welcome here! The door is wide open. You are welcome to come in at your pace and on your terms. We recognize people are not all at the same stage in their personal religious pilgrimage."

Roger: Right or Wrong?

Who is to say which is the right way for a congregation to go about its business of proclaiming Christ? The old saying "different strokes for different folks" is absolutely true. The personal relationship each of us has with Jesus Christ is just that—personal. What is meaningful and important about one person's journey of faith might seem frivolous to another. I have a friend who said that someone with an evangelistic zeal once asked him on the street if he had a personal relationship with Jesus. He looked at the man and said, "I'm sorry, but that's a very personal question, and I don't go around sharing that part of my life with just anyone."

I did answer the staff person who said that we need to become just like Eagle Brook if we're going to succeed. My response to her was that instead of trying to copy and become something we are not, why not spend all our efforts in becoming the best at who we are. I remember a church growth consultant saying that the goal is not to adopt but to adapt. In other words, take the time to discover which churches are doing the best job at proclaiming Christ, and instead of adopting their theology and methodology, adapt it utilizing your own theology and understanding of who Christ is and what Jesus wants us to accomplish in his name.

Popeye the Sailor was famous for saying, "I yam what I yam and tha's all what I yam." St. Andrew's is what it is, and hopefully, through thoughtful prayer, dedication, and commitment, we will fulfill all that God has in mind for us as individuals and as a congregation.

Roger: None of Us Can Do It Alone

One of my favorite passages from scripture comes from 1 Corinthians 3:5-9, where the Apostle Paul writes:

"What then is Apollos? What is Paul? Servants through whom you came to believe, as the Lord assigned to each. I planted, Apollos watered, but God gave the growth. So neither the one who plants nor the one who waters is anything, but only God gives the growth. The one who plants and the one who waters have a common purpose, and each will receive wages according to the labor of each. For we are God's servants, working together: you are God's field, God's building."

Each of us stands on the shoulders of those who have gone before. The St. Andrew's of today is due, in part, to the faithful commitment of twenty Lutherans who, in 1922, gathered in a house along the shores of White Bear Lake with the intention of establishing a Lutheran congregation. To them belonged the task of bringing St. Andrew's into being. With each and every successive generation, God put in place a variety of pastors and leaders who would add their faith to the mix. Some planted and some watered, but in the end, it will be God who gives the growth.

So, how do you become a megachurch? Actually, I have no idea. All I know is that somehow, through trial and error and a bit of dumb luck, all the while trusting that God would show us the way, it happened. It happened, and it has been an incredible privilege to have been allowed to be a part of it. And in this, as in all things, "Soli Deo Gloria!"—to God alone be the glory!

Duane: What It Felt like to Be on Staff at a Megachurch

I have always felt that megachurches are misunderstood. Many people stereotype megachurches and the people in them. I chafed whenever I felt that the church I was a part of was being put in a box. I knew each church to be a people-oriented, gospel-oriented, helpful, healing, and spiritual entity. So when I would hear that megachurches were "snobbish" or "theologically empty" or "only conservative" or "authoritarian" or "rich," I knew that was not the situation I encountered at SOTV or St. Andrew's.

Of course, each church had its downsides. There were times when people got lost in the shuffle. There were times when not all voices were heard. I vividly remember my disappointment when a very talented staff person at SOTV with whom I worked rather closely resigned because, he said, the church was too big to be effective. He thought that the staff were doing all the work, not the people of the church. Like all churches, SOTV and St. Andrew's had their own share of problems.

Neither St. Andrew's nor SOTV felt like those stereotypical megachurches to me. They felt like large churches, yes, but not megachurches. What a megachurch is has evolved over the last forty years. Now, the typical caricature of a megachurch is one that has a television ministry, multi-site worshipping communities, and mall-like campuses. Neither St. Andrew's nor SOTV have done ministry in that fashion. Instead, over the years, both have stayed largely planted in classical Lutheran ministry (worship style, governance, structure, theology, and culture), albeit on a very large scale. I must say that I have always been proud to be on the staff of these two megachurches. Not because they were megachurches but because the ministry that happened at each church was good, solid, faithful ministry.

Chapter 14

SUCCESSION & ENDINGS

Duane: Everything Must Come to an End

Even though Roger and Paul had wonderful pastorates at St. Andrew's and Shepherd of the Valley, eventually those pastorates came to an end. As it is for most pastors, the end of their time at these two churches was not easy. In this chapter, Roger and Paul explore this period of time at St. Andrew's and Shepherd of the Valley.

Roger: Endings

Time, like an ever-rolling stream,
bears all our years away;
they fly forgotten, as a dream
dies at the opening day.

With those words, Isaac Watts in his hymn, "O God, Our Help in Ages Past," makes an observation that can only be understood from the vantage point of years already spent; years that have passed so swiftly that one can scarcely believe they were once here and now are gone. As one who has been privileged to watch, walk alongside, and be a part of the changes at St. Andrew's for thirty-three years, there are so many people whose faces come to mind as I recount how we got from where we were to where we ended up three decades later. Faces of staff members, fellow pastors, congregational leaders, and faithful parishioners who poured their energy, faith, and financial resources into making St. Andrew's what it is today. Faces of people who, along the way, made all the difference. Yet, as Isaac Watts observes, so much of what we have lived is forgotten like a dream that vanishes once you open your eyes to the morning sun.

The thought of ending my tenure as senior pastor of St. Andrew's was far from my mind as I approached that magic age of sixty-five in 2005. As far as I was concerned, there was much more that could be accomplished—we had done so much in the past that there seemed to be no limit to what we could do in the years that were before us. We were just gaining strength and speed, and with strong mission projects in Jamaica and Slovakia, we were even making a difference on the international scene. But there were others who were adding up the years I had served as senior pastor and were not shy about asking when I intended to retire. I had had a full head of black hair and beard when I arrived and was now sporting a shiny dome with a beard that had turned white. Apparently, it was a sign for some that the time had arrived for me to think about applying for Medicare and joining my wife Carolyn, who had already retired. When asked about retirement, I would simply push back with a smile, declare that I'm too young to retire, and let the subject drop.

But, as another song writer, Bob Dylan, has observed: "The times they are a-changing," and such was the case at St. Andrew's. The leadership with whom I had shared visions and dreams were no longer in place. Those valiant comrades with whom I had shared dream upon dream had faded into the background. Men and women with whom ideas on newsprint at a weekend retreat became buildings, foreign mission projects, exciting programs for youth and adults were now gone. Indeed, a new generation of leaders was emerging that saw St. Andrew's and its future through a different set of lenses.

New and different priorities began to emerge. One of those focused on the seventy-two acres of land that we had strategically acquired over the years for $900,000. It was now seen as a convenient source of cash to pay down debt. In the back of my mind, I had always thought of that land as a place for future generations to use as a springboard for new and creative ministry. It could be a school. It could be ball fields. In fact, everything we built at St. Andrew's was always done with the thought of giving future generations options. Yet dreams such as these vanished when leadership saw the opportunity to sell seventeen of those seventy-two acres for just over $3 million.

Maybe it was time! I remember my mentor, Pastor Harold Rasmussen—who had stayed for twenty-seven years and developed a remarkably successful ministry at Richfield Lutheran Church in Minneapolis—telling me not to do as he did but to do as he said: "Don't stay that long!" Well, I had already stayed six years longer than Rasmussen, and St. Andrew's was really the only place I could ever see myself as a pastor. But, as a former bishop once reminded a group of pastors, "All calls are interim. You're privileged to be there for a number of years, and then it's over and you're gone." Or as one parishioner commented, "Pastors are really wayfarers—nomads, wanderers, roamers, here for a while and then eventually gone."

Roger: Time to Move On

The decision for a pastor to leave a congregation is not an easy one. Over the years, friendships are formed—some more meaningful and fulfilling than others. There's a special kind of bond that happens between a pastor and members of the congregation. You're privileged to be with them at moments of elation, birth, and joy as well as times of disappointment, death, and despair. Yet when you leave a congregation, all of that comes to a screeching halt. You're no longer their pastor and soon, another member of the clergy will occupy the office once thought to be yours. All of this goes through your mind as you ponder what your next move should be. Do you stay or leave? Do you risk overstaying your welcome? I remember hearing a personality on the radio who surprised everyone when he decided to retire early. When asked why, he simply said, "I didn't want to stay beyond the 'sell by' date like you find on a loaf of bread. I wanted to leave before they asked me to leave."

The truth of the matter is that there is a terrible price in terms of lost relationships that is paid not only by the pastor but also their spouse. The church family that supported you is gone. The simple act of sharing a cup of coffee in Fellowship Hall is no longer available. Church hierarchy makes a point of telling pastors that when you leave a congregation, there's no going back except to attend a wedding or funeral as a guest. Quite simply, the decision to leave creates a huge empty hole that is difficult to fill.

Roger: I Resigned! I Did Not Retire!

In February 2005, I notified the congregation that in June, I would resign as senior pastor of St. Andrew's. In that letter, I tried to make it as clear as I could that I was not retiring—rather, I was resigning with the intent of making myself available for another call. I simply could not see myself hanging up my clerical collar at age sixty-five and calling it quits. I had a feeling inside that there was still more for me to do as a pastor and that there must be some other congregation that could benefit from my years of experience at St. Andrew's. In December, I applied for "On Leave from Call" status with the synod and began a three-year journey that I had not quite envisioned.

You see, it wasn't as easy getting another call as I had thought. There is supposedly no such thing as age discrimination in the church, but remnants of it can be found lurking in call committees that politely invite you to interview only to tell you that with your experience at St. Andrew's, you're obviously overqualified to serve as the pastor of their much smaller congregation. One congregation went so far as to say that they had no intention of becoming a large congregation like St. Andrew's and that I probably would not be a good fit for a congregation that wanted to remain small. Another told me that I failed to get the congregational vote to become their pastor because I talked too much about the importance of tithing. My response was that I would not want to be a pastor of a congregation that did not want to encourage the biblical example of tithing as a faithful response for all that God has given us.

Roger: The Rest of the Story

For three years, I interviewed at urban and rural congregations with no luck. However, in the spring of 2008, a wonderful opportunity was presented to serve as the senior pastor of the then two-thousand member St. Luke's Lutheran Church in Middleton, Wisconsin. Accepting the call meant pulling up stakes in Mahtomedi, buying a home in Madison, and becoming a part of a town shaped by the presence of the Wisconsin state capital and the flagship University of Wisconsin-Madison. In many ways, the call to St. Luke's gave Carolyn and me a new lease on life. The move proved to be one of the best decisions we could have made. Not a day goes by that we don't give thanks to God for offering us this opportunity.

St. Luke's had its own set of issues that had to be addressed. One of them was a $3.2 million debt. But in my ten years at St. Luke's, we shaved $1.2 million off the debt, witnessed the congregation growing to 2,900 members, and enjoyed weekly worship attendance blossoming from 400 to 900.

Eventually, however, there comes the time to retire. So, in May 2018, at the age of seventy-eight, I officially retired as an ELCA pastor, with St. Luke's as my last congregation. Having been ordained in 1966, it meant that I had had the high privilege of serving fifty-two years as a Lutheran pastor.

Roger: Succession

A well-thought-out succession plan that recognizes that the senior leader of a congregation will eventually leave through resignation, retirement, or death is important for its continued success. A smooth transition, handing the baton of leadership from the old to the new, can go a long way in providing the kind of confidence that members of a church need to have when the former pastor departs, and a new pastor arrives on the scene. Unfortunately, no well-thought-out succession plan for the departure of the senior pastor was in place at St. Andrew's when I announced my resignation.

Part of the reason no plan existed was, of course, my personal inability to accede to the wishes of some for a date when I was going to retire. When church council members asked the question, I honestly told them that I did not know. Not knowing a date, they, as I, were left in the dark. Their first real opportunity to begin to put succession plans into motion was when I submitted my letter of resignation to the congregation in February notifying them that I would end my tenure as senior pastor of St. Andrew's later that year on June 1, 2005. Once the St. Paul Area Synod was notified of my decision, conversations began between the bishop's office and the St. Andrew's Church Council to start the process of putting an interim senior pastor in place. Soon, a call committee would be created, and the search for a new senior pastor would be underway—a process that, under the best of conditions, would stretch out the calling of a new senior pastor one or two years.

One of the biggest frustrations that senior pastors of the largest ELCA congregations have is the incredibly long time it takes to put new leadership into place once someone decides to leave through resignation or retirement. All the good work a pastor has done in leading and guiding their congregation prior to their departure begins to unravel as months go by and no visible progress toward finding a new senior pastor is shown to the congregation. The departing pastor watches from afar as attendance and financial support begins to diminish. The creation of new programs is put on hold with the excuse that the congregation should wait until a new pastor arrives. Quite understandably, prospective members put their decision to join on hold, deciding, instead, to wait and see what the new senior pastor might be like.

In an attempt to smooth out the process of finding a successor, some congregations have decided to go it on their own. Some congregations begin national searches for their new pastor knowing that the synod model will simply take too long.

One other model involves the current senior pastor hand-picking their successor. A potential candidate could be a current pastor on staff or a friend of the departing senior pastor who might look like a good fit. Personally, I have never wanted to become involved in hand-picking my successor. Far be it from me to know who my successor should be. My feeling has always been that I need to keep my mitts out of that whole process and let the Holy Spirit have the room it needs to do its job. After all, if we honestly believe that the call to serve as a pastor of a congregation comes from God then we need to let God do what God does best.

The upshot is that each congregation is unique and that what works in one place might not be appropriate in another. The saving grace in all of this is that a congregation of the ELCA will never be left to figure it out by themselves. There are procedures in place that can be followed with guidance from the bishop's office. It may not move as fast as many would desire, but somehow, the work of the Holy Spirit does get done, and in more instances than not, the eventual choice of a new senior pastor has proven to be one that is good for the congregation and good for the new pastor.

Roger: Time to Pack Up and Go!

As the date to pull up stakes and leave got closer, I spent a good amount of time packing up books, shredding files, and piling my personal items into the station wagon for the journey home. Trying to decide what to keep and what to throw was quite the task. Since I was resigning with the full intention of receiving another call, there were sermon files I copied onto CDs that I felt might come in handy at some future time. There were photos of the various phases of campus construction, which brought back powerful memories of watching vacant land becoming buildings that almost appeared to rise from the earth—visions and dreams that had become real and would be there for decades to come. But it would soon be over, and the next chapter of my life was going to be written and lived with St. Andrew's Lutheran Church in my rearview mirror.

Roger: The Last Sunday

Eventually, there was that Sunday morning in mid-June which was filled with lots of lasts: the last sermon I would preach as the senior pastor of St. Andrew's; the last time I would preside at Holy Communion; the last time I would raise my hands over the congregation offering a blessing and benediction; and the final goodbyes to fellow pastors, staff, congregation leaders, and faithful members. In the afternoon, a special service was held with presentations by various staff members and Bishop Peter Rogness of the St. Paul Area Synod. Then, in good Lutheran fashion, it was time to eat. The people of St. Andrew's were gracious and kind in putting together a going away celebration that included filling one of the parking lots with a huge tent where a grand banquet was held for the hundreds of guests who showed up to wish Carolyn, me, and our family well.

Eventually, it was time to call it a day, but there was one last thing that I needed to do before I could call it quits. Leaving the banquet tent, I walked into the now empty sanctuary. I took a moment to look around, taking in the beauty of a space that had ultimately become a dream come true. The mighty organ was now silent. The sun was shining brightly through the seventy-foot wall of windows—a sun soon to set as it made its way toward the western horizon. My eyes welled up. It was truly over. That final task was to pick up my robe and stoles from the sacristy. These were the tools of my trade—robe and stoles—tools that would soon find a three-year resting place in a closet at home, tools that would eventually be given new life in August of 2008 as I began what would end up being a wonderful ten-year ministry as senior pastor of St. Luke's Lutheran Church in Middleton, Wisconsin. And who knows, even though I am officially retired, there are still so many more roads out there beckoning Carolyn and me to come and see what new adventures await.

"There's a trick to the graceful exit.' It begins with the vision to recognize when a job, a life stage, or a relationship is over—and let it go. It means leaving what's over without denying its validity or its past importance to our lives. It involves a sense of future, a belief that every exit line is an entry, that we are moving up, rather than out."
— Ellen Goodman

Duane: What Happened at St. Andrew's after Roger Left

After Roger left St. Andrew's, Del Jacobson served as an interim senior pastor for two years. In addition, they also had a consultant come to aid in the transition. As can be expected, worship attendance fell. In 2007, a new senior pastor, John Hogenson, was called.

Gradually, Hogenson reshaped some of the ministries at St. Andrew's. A few pastors left and some new pastors were called, including Mike Carlson as executive pastor. Attendance perked up. Then, in quick succession, Mike Carlson left for a new call at Shepherd of the Lake in Prior Lake on the other side of the Twin Cities. Shortly thereafter, John Hogenson took a call as the senior pastor at Mt. Olivet Lutheran Church, a renowned Lutheran church in Minneapolis. Almost immediately after that, St. Andrew's recalled Carlson, this time as their senior pastor.

At the time of this writing, Mike Carlson remains Senior Pastor at St. Andrew's. Worship attendance has been on the upswing—rising from 2,246 in 2008 to 2,643 in 2016.

Throughout these years of transition at St. Andrew's, ministries have ebbed and flowed but some of the ministries that Roger highlights in this book, notably Mission Jamaica, Vision Slovakia, and the music ministry at St. Andrew's have continued in high gear.

Duane: When a Pastor Leaves

What happens to the congregation after a key pastor leaves a church? Unfortunately, there's usually a drop off in participation by members of the congregation.

A few years after Pastor Paul left Shepherd of the Valley, I, along with a small group of others, embarked on a year-long task seeking to find out why people who were once highly active had become inactive. What we found was more complicated than the simple answer that "Pastor Paul is gone."

We called, emailed, and visited several people who at one time, had been very active in the church, but had, at some point, become inactive. We asked them what happened.

What we heard from many of them is that they had moved into a new phase in their lives. Because of this change in their lives, the old connections at the church no longer seemed relevant for them. As they negotiated this new phase in their lives, they often simply faded away from regular participation. For some, it was an overt decision to leave the church. But for many others, they simply drifted away.

A common example of this was when a couple had moved into the "empty nest" years. They had often been quite active at church when their kids were younger. But once the kids moved out of the house, they felt a void at church. Then either their participation would fade or there would be a precipitating event that would lead to their exit. For some whom we interviewed, that precipitating event was Pastor Paul's retirement. But the key event could also be any number of other things, like a perceived slight, a sermon with which they disagreed, a mistake by a staff person, or change in the culture at the church.

After making these findings, this task force recommended enhancing ministry for people during the transition periods of their lives. Those transition times might be when they get married, have their first child, move, experience a key death in their family, become empty nesters, or retire. Those are crucial times for doing ministry with people. If a key pastor leaves while *these members are experiencing one of those transition times, then they are quite vulnerable to becoming inactive.*

Paul: Thinking about Retirement

I was a graduate of Luther Theological Seminary in 1972 and began my pastorate in July of that year at Sylvan Lake Lutheran Church near Pontiac, Michigan. It was a wonderful place to start my ministry as the people were loving, forgiving, and even quite responsive to my sometimes-fledgling attempts at leadership. It was a great place for me to earn my "ministerial spurs."

Then, after almost eight great years in Michigan, we wanted to be back closer to parents, grandparents, siblings, extended family, and a host of close friends. So it was that I began my ministry at SOTV in January of 1981, where I served as founding and senior pastor for almost twenty-eight years. But after nearly four decades of ministry (I had also served two churches doing "pulpit supply" during my pre-ordination seminary years), I began to think seriously about slowing down if not retiring altogether. But just how does one go about doing this, especially in a large and complex organization like SOTV, where I had become so embedded in the life and ministry of the congregation?

Paul: Succession

When you think about it, there are several different ways for a congregation to do succession, which is just a fancy word for saying farewell to one pastor and replacing them with another. This process can go very smoothly, or it can be difficult, despite the best efforts of many caring and dedicated people. We all know the old saying, "The best-laid plans of mice and men often go astray."

Unlike the Roman Catholic Church tradition in which the bishop simply appoints a new priest to a parish with little or no consultation with the lay leadership, most Lutheran congregations use a call committee, appointed by the church council, to seek their next pastor. This call committee is charged with many tasks, including working with the local synod office, reviewing and revising the job description, conducting an "exit interview," soliciting names of potential candidates, prescreening candidates, doing in-person interviews, compiling a list of questions to be asked of each candidate, reporting progress to the church council and the congregation, conducting second interviews, selecting the candidate, and recommending this person to the congregation. Then, following a favorable vote by the council, the congregation, or both, an official "Letter of Call" is extended to the candidate with a detailed job description, a salary package, and a promise from the congregation to the pastor to be helpful and supportive during this entire time of transition. You can perhaps see now why the Roman Catholic Church's process is so much simpler. But again, if a congregation is going to support and "own" such a sometimes-messy call process, this system still seems to be the best way to go about it.

Paul: What Happened at SOTV

I have briefly described two common ways for churches to do succession: the traditional Roman Catholic model and the traditional Protestant model. In my case, I was interested in doing it differently. I had noted from time to time how difficult and disruptive it can be for a church to lose a long-tenured pastor and then to commence what could be a nationwide search for their replacement. This is a critically important decision for any community of faith but especially for some of our larger churches where an incoming pastor will have to work well from day one with other staff pastors, a large and diverse lay staff, a strong church council, a multiplicity of existing programs, a congregation numbering at least several thousand if not more, and, of course, the local synod bishop as well. It can be a daunting task, and frankly, there are not a lot of pastors in the ELCA who have been specifically trained to oversee and manage a Lutheran "megachurch." Such times as these can be rather nerve-racking and uncertain for any congregation.

So with all of this in mind, I began having quiet conversations with some key staff members and some key council members about the possibility not of resigning, but of moving into a pastor emeritus status. I would no longer be the senior pastor, but for the sake of continuity, I would remain on the staff with fewer hours and a rather diminished job description. After nearly three decades, why throw away all these life-giving relationships that had been developed over many years by simply resigning and walking away? To be perfectly honest, I was hoping that one of the other five pastors on our staff at that time would be willing and able, if approved, to assume the role of senior pastor. This arrangement, while not advisable for all congregations, would accomplish two things. We would avoid all the disruption that can happen with a somewhat abrupt departure, and I would still have the privilege of serving the congregation I have loved for a few more years before full retirement. My hope was to retire in "slow-motion"— initially working half time, then perhaps a year or two at one-third time or one-quarter time, and finally, after three years or so, I would turn in my resignation and officially conclude my pastoral ministry at SOTV. By this time, the "new" senior pastor would be well-established, and the transition would now be reasonably smooth and complete. This was the tentative plan I had in mind for my future and the future of our congregation.

One of the next steps I took was to contact our bishop, who also happened to be a seminary classmate and a good friend. I had a long conversation with Bishop Peter Rogness one afternoon and laid out a possible plan for the future of our church. I wanted Peter's feedback, and I hoped for his blessing as well. As we talked, Peter reminded me about a few congregations where a long-tenured senior pastor resigned, remained as a member of the congregation, and then—either knowingly or unknowingly—continued to influence the affairs of the church to the detriment and consternation of the new incoming senior pastor. Truthfully, a few of these examples could only be classified as horror stories. When this happens to a congregation, the end result is almost never good.

I was, however, encouraged when Peter said that he surely wanted what was best for our church and that if this was to be our chosen path, he would do all he could to help with a smooth and beneficial transition. We also agreed on two items that would be critical to the church if this plan was ever to be called a success. One, the two pastors involved (me being one of them) would have to fully understand their new and almost totally reversed roles and would have to stringently respect the boundaries of these new roles for the sake of the church and its future. This would be critical to the success of this plan. The second component would be that the congregation accepts this new arrangement as fully as possible. If either one of these two parts of the plan did not materialize, it would be a failure for sure. Going out the door, I asked Peter to be sure to tell me if he saw from his vantage point any "red flags" popping up along the way.

The next logical step was to share my idea with several lay leaders of the congregation, asking for their reactions as well as their input. I was gratified that all of them seemed amenable to the plan. I also asked them to be very tight-lipped about all of this until we had a pretty good grasp of just how all of this might play out in the months ahead. (Churches can sometimes be real rumor mills, as you may know.) They all willingly complied with my request.

At this time, several of these lay leaders who also were serving on the church council were given the task of meeting individually with each of the pastors on our staff to see if any one of them was interested in transitioning to the role of senior pastor. Following these interviews, it became clear that one member of the pastoral staff was definitely interested in the position. Learning of this development, the church council now had another particularly important decision to make. Did they want to further pursue this current pastor as their sole candidate for the job or would they rather open up the position to a much broader listing of candidates provided by our own St. Paul Area Synod and perhaps other synods of the ELCA as well? It should be noted that I attended none of these meetings as it was very important to me that whatever decisions were arrived at, I remained totally impartial in the process. These are big decisions, and as the soon-to-be-former senior pastor, I did not want to be influencing these decisions in any way. These vitally important decisions had to be made by our congregational leadership without any undue influences from me or anyone else. It is also worth noting that had the council wanted to do a much broader search and seek a candidate from beyond the boundaries of SOTV, I would most certainly have had to fully resign and vacate the premises. There is no way this plan would have worked with a totally new person fulfilling the role of senior pastor.

So it was, following a favorable congregational vote to call "one of our own," that as of December 1, 2007, the torch of the senior pastor was passed from me to Pastor Chris Smith, a colleague I had worked with for several years. Bishop Peter Rogness was present at all worship hours that weekend to oversee this transfer of titles, responsibility, and leadership. We had accomplished all that we had set out to do. And it felt like the Holy Spirit also had a hand in all of these important decisions.

I made a conscious decision at this time to keep a very low profile at the church for about six months, just to give Pastor Chris a chance to get more established in his new role and to send a signal to the congregation that a new order of things was now evolving. We also made some very obvious changes, such as me moving into a very small office (which didn't even have a window), while Pastor Chris moved into what had formerly been my office. I also no longer attended any staff, council, or congregational meetings—again, to send a quiet but clear signal that while I was still on the staff and performing various pastoral acts, I was no longer in charge. All of these changes were pre-planned and well-executed overall. I made a solemn promise to myself that if anyone asked me anything about the daily operation of the church and any important decisions that the pastors, staff, or church council had made or were about to make, I would simply tell them that they now needed to talk either with the senior pastor or the current president of the congregation. I was no longer authorized, and in some cases, not even knowledgeable enough to answer their questions or adequately address their concerns even if I had wanted to. Thankfully, there were very few such instances when someone approached me with their questions or concerns. I took this to mean that the transfer of leadership was complete and, for the most part, well-received.

Duane: More on Succession at SOTV

As Paul notes, the succession plan at SOTV worked quite well. It is highly unusual for a congregation to take the approach they did at SOTV. Part of the reason it worked so well was that even before the succession began, there was an excellent working relationship between Paul and Chris Smith. Chris began his ministry at SOTV in 1997 as an associate pastor. As time went on, his responsibilities grew, mainly because he was so talented in organization and administration—which were not necessarily Paul's most pressing interest. In the early 2000s, Chris took on many administrative responsibilities in an informal manner. Then, a few years later, he was named executive pastor, largely to formalize what he was already doing. So, it was

simply natural that he would become the senior pastor at SOTV when Paul
began to think about cutting back his responsibilities to become pastor emeri-
tus. In other words, there was a step-by-step natural evolution from Pastor
Paul to Pastor Chris as senior pastor.

Paul: Pastor Emeritus

From 2007 until I fully retired in July of 2013, I believe this arrangement, serving as pastor emeritus, worked quite well for our congregation. I continued to preach on occasion, while also officiating at a number of weddings, baptisms, and funerals. I helped teach confirmation as needed and, surprisingly, did a fair amount of counseling. As it happened, around this time, I was also called to Luther Seminary to serve for three years as their half-time interim campus pastor, a position which I fully relished. Working with young seminarians was just a joy. Splitting my time between SOTV and the seminary kept me very occupied for those years. I loved every minute.

But, as the saying goes, all good things must come to an end. My three years at the seminary concluded when they called a full-time campus pastor in 2012, and my years at SOTV also were coming to an end. When a pastor has given birth to a church and then invested thirty-three years of his life deeply in that congregation, saying goodbye is never easy. But because I had been allowed to retire in "slow-motion" through some well-thought-out succession planning, it felt quite natural to exit when I did. It honestly felt like the Lord had called me *to* SOTV and *from* SOTV.

One other indication that this plan has been quite successful occurred when a new senior pastor was called to SOTV in the fall of 2016. Knowing of my previous role at the church, Pastor Rick Summy was quick to invite me to his office for a chat. I wanted to meet with him and to state very clearly that I did not want to do anything that would in any way hinder his ministry, which would include me vacating the church for good if one or both of us thought this was necessary. I was assured many times over that he wanted my presence in the congregation, and I assured him that in all decisions that he might ever make, he would have my 100 percent unconditional support. We have since developed a deep and abiding friendship. We now have another long-tenured retired SOTV pastor who has chosen to retain his membership at SOTV as well.

Paul: What It Means to Leave a Congregation

When I left my first congregation, Sylvan Lake Lutheran, in 1980, my wife Margaret told me that I was in mourning for the better part of a year. That may sound a bit extreme, but it was true. Part of my grief was due to leaving a warm and loving congregation and moving to an entirely new location where there was no congregation at all. Whatever community I desired, I now had to create myself. That was a real challenge. Without God's daily help, it would not have happened.

Leaving Shepherd of the Valley was a different experience because I never had to say a final goodbye to the congregation. Even after I was no longer a salaried staff member, I was privileged to see a huge number of friends and parishioners each time we came for worship. Still, I do recall that first winter after turning over the role of senior pastor to my successor. We deliberately stayed away from the church for at least six months to give Pastor Chris a chance to really establish himself. This was a wise move, but at times, I did feel like a lost sheep who was looking again for a flock to join. I once heard a wise person make this statement at a funeral, "If you never want to suffer in life, you should never love." She was talking about the loss of her son in a car accident. But her comment could just as well be applied to departing pastors and congregations. If those relationships have been deep and life-giving, then there should be a real sense of loss as well as some grief. In time, pastors and congregations do move on to the next chapter of their lives, but those relationships will not be forgotten. Nor should they be.

Duane: Completely Leaving the Congregation—or Not

When a pastor retires in the Lutheran church, it is highly recommended by the bishops that the pastor completely leave the congregation. The reasoning behind this recommendation is that retired pastors who remain in a congregation may have a way of influencing things that is not good for the new replacement pastor nor the congregation.

Contrary to this recommendation, both Pastor Paul and I, when we retired, have stayed at Shepherd of the Valley. We have done so with the permission and blessing of the senior pastor, who seems to see our presence as an asset to the congregation, not a liability. If Paul and I are supportive and helpful, this arrangement works well. If either of us undermines the ministry at Shepherd of the Valley, whether knowingly or unknowingly, then our presence becomes problematic. The key is good communication with the senior pastor and other pastors on staff. Another key is simply being aware of this dynamic and getting honest feedback about it from time to time. Both Paul and I acknowledge that staying in a congregation can probably only happen in larger congregations. It just won't work in a small church.

Duane: What Happened at SOTV after Paul Left

Chris Smith became senior pastor when Paul became pastor emeritus in 2007. Then for six years, until 2013, Paul continued to work part-time at SOTV. In 2013, he fully retired. From my perspective, that transition time worked well for all concerned. There was continuity of leadership. The church just kept rolling along. And, best of all, there was little or no conflict between Paul and Chris. During those six years, Chris was able to help the church purchase and install a pipe organ, revamp the sound system, make some major changes in worship, begin a weekly Sunday breakfast, weather the churchwide LGBTQ+ controversy, and complete a major debt-reduction campaign. He facilitated other changes and updates as well, all the while managing a large and complex congregation and staff.

Two years after Paul fully retired, Chris Smith resigned to become an interim pastor at another large church in the Twin Cities. So the two pastors still at SOTV at the time, Randy Brandt and I, became co-interim-senior pastors. As it turned out, we acted as senior pastors at SOTV for a full year. During that time, a call committee was looking for a new senior pastor. In the fall of 2016, Rick Summy was called to that role. I worked with Rick at SOTV until my retirement in 2019.

The peak year for worship attendance at SOTV was 2003, when it was 2,199. For the next nine years, attendance hovered around 2,000 per weekend. Since then, attendance began a slow but steady decline until 2017. Since then, it has slowly risen. All the while, SOTV has remained a vitally active congregation.

Duane: The Emotions of Leaving

I once asked a retired pastor who had been in his call for a very long time what it was like after he left that church. He said, "Honestly, I sometimes feel good, and sometimes, I feel bad. When the congregation thrives, I feel good because it affirms that I set a good course for the church. But I also feel bad because it means they really did not need me. When they do not thrive, I feel good because, in my mind, it's because they are missing my leadership. Yet I feel badly because I must not have done very well in setting the course for the congregation. In other words, I always have these mixed emotions."

It was emotional for me whenever I left a congregation. When I left St. Andrew's, the congregation had a farewell event for my family and me. It was beautiful. Afterward, I came home, sat on the couch with my wife, Phyllis, and wept. I loved my time at St. Andrew's. Now that it was over, I knew that things would be different in my life. I grieved for the relationships I knew would be changing and ending.

It was similar at the end of my time at Shepherd of the Valley. There were a couple of weekends when my ministry was celebrated, and I was treated royally by people as they said goodbye. Then, I retired. This time, though, I knew how I would be feeling. So I was a bit more prepared. Yet, when I preached my last sermon at five different services, I got choked up at the same spot in the sermon each time. You would think that might happen once—but five times? It just shows how powerful my emotions were because I knew it was the end of a chapter of ministry. Things would never be the same for me.

Chapter 15

WHAT I'VE LEARNED

Roger: "Too early old, too late smart" — Old Dutch Proverb

I t's just six words, but I think this old Dutch proverb quite accurately summarizes what it's like to have a hand in helping to grow a church. I don't know anyone who has been a pastoral leader who says that if they were given the opportunity to lead another church, they would not change a thing. An honest person recognizes that in many ways, we sort of stumble into the future. As much as we attempt to carefully figure out what our next steps should be, we're going to make mistakes. I admit to making more than my share. I regret the times I refused to listen to others, wrongly thinking that the path I had laid out was the best way forward when in reality, it ended up wasting time, money, and human resources. On the other hand, I regret not boldly moving forward with a sense of commitment that could have caused St. Andrew's to become an even greater beacon of hope. There were missed opportunities. There were voices that should have been listened to. There were dreams that were not given the chance to see the light of day. With twenty-twenty hindsight, we see exactly where we took the wrong turn when we approached that fork in the road. Too early old! Too late smart!

But life is not lived looking backward. Like Abraham, we follow a God who urges us to leave the land where we live with trust and boldly march into the future, knowing that God will provide the resources we will need to do ministry.

Like Abraham and Moses, we cannot do it all by ourselves. We need to realistically accept the fact that if we are to succeed, we will need to be guided by the power and presence of the Holy Spirit. And we need to tap the faith and commitment of those in our congregation who want to be asked to help and become a part of the solution to the congregation's needs.

Roger: Make Your Needs Known

One of the best maxims of leadership that has helped to shape my ministry is one that is filled with surprise and the opportunity for others to express their commitment and faith. I first heard the phrase "Make your needs known and sources of help least expected will come to your aid" at a church growth conference at the Crystal Cathedral where hundreds of pastors from around the world were hungry for new insights into how to grow their churches. The phrase is quite simple, but it can make a huge difference.

So often, we are too timid to admit that we need help. The downside of taking that approach that we shut others out of the process of helping us find a solution to whatever problem or need we've encountered. Below are two examples of what happens when we open up and let people know that this just might be the time and place where their talents, faith, and commitment can make all the difference.

Roger: A Clogged Drain and a Helpful Plumber

The story of deciding what land to buy for our new campus includes an interesting set of circumstances that some may attribute to dumb luck and others to the work of the Holy Spirit.

The road to making the decision began with a whole series of meetings with two brothers who had decided to put their fifty-acre family farm up for sale. Actually, the decision to sell was one that was forced upon them by some actions of the city that caused their property tax to be changed from agricultural to residential . . . property taxes that were raised much higher than anything they could afford. Simply put, they needed to sell, but as negotiators, they were looking to get as much for their land as possible. St. Andrew's, however, was at a point where it needed to move ahead on securing land upon which to build our new campus. Even though both parties were negotiating in good faith, we could never get to the point where a deal could be struck. Fortunately, we did have another piece of land available to us that was also for sale. It was cheaper, included more acreage, and the sellers were eager to get the property off their hands. It did have one disadvantage—its location. Unlike the brothers' farm property, which had direct access to a major road and was located right next door to Mahtomedi High School, this second property was tucked a block away from any significant traffic flow. It wasn't ideal, but we had to make a decision and get on with building our new campus. So, a congregational meeting to purchase the cheaper and less desirable land was scheduled.

Now, here's where it gets interesting.

It was a Friday morning, and I was struggling with a clogged drain in the kitchen sink. I tried using a plumber's snake, but that did not solve the problem. Finally, I decided that it was time to call the plumber. He was local, a good Catholic, had lived all his life in Mahtomedi and knew much about what was going on in town. After grabbing his roto-rooter from his truck and setting it up to do its job, he leaned against the kitchen counter and said, "I hear St. Andrew's is going to buy the brothers' farm for your new campus."

I said, "We wanted to, it's our first choice, but we could never get to the point where we could make a deal. So, we've got a meeting scheduled on Sunday to buy this other piece of property."

He sighed and said, "That's a dumb idea! You really need to buy the brothers' farm." He said, "I went to school with those guys. Do you want me to call them and see what I can do?"

"Sure," I said, "but you had better hurry because the congregational meeting is scheduled for Sunday, and we're all set to buy the other property."

As he promised, he called the brothers, and after a flurry of phone calls, a meeting was arranged for Saturday morning. The meeting was short, a deal was struck, and now we were able to come to the congregation with two choices: a parcel of fifteen acres along the highway right next to the high school for $150,000 or a thirty-nine-acre piece of property for $90,000 a block away from any real traffic. Wisely, the congregation chose the brothers' farm, and the rest is history. But it might not have happened were it not for a clogged drain and a helpful plumber who had heard of our need. Schuller's maxim rang in my ears, "Make your needs known and sources of help least expected will come to your aid."

Roger: Just a Pile of Pipes

The story I related in an earlier chapter about the magnificent pipe organ that graces the front of the sanctuary at St. Andrew's is a tale of a bunch of dreamers who were willing to take a risk on a pile of pipes stored in a broken-down barn in Traverse City, Michigan. For a while, it seemed as if the dream of restoring that organ was dead in the water. That is, until word got out about the possibility of St. Andrew's acquiring and restoring it. One family of St. Andrew's was so intrigued about the possibilities this historic instrument could provide that they stepped forward and offered to pay the $50,000 to buy the pile of pipes. With their financial commitment, we were on our way to restoring one of the largest pipe organs in the world. But it never would have happened were it not for "making our needs known so that sources of help least expected could come to our aid."

Roger: A Few Other Things I've Learned

- **None of us is smarter than all of us!**

As pastors, we are called to lead, but in reality, no one person possesses all the tools necessary to take a congregation that numbers in the hundreds into multiple thousands. We need to be wise enough to recognize and use the talented people God has placed in our midst and draw upon their expertise, wisdom, and faith. We need to take advantage of members, of staff, and of friends of the congregation who, if asked, will be more than willing to help move the congregation toward achieving its many goals.

- **Plan the work and work the plan.**

Flying blind is a scary approach to ministry. Although there is a certain amount of excitement that accompanies making it up as you go along, well-laid plans save valuable resources and time. A congregation without a plan for its future will find itself becoming stagnant.

- **When is enough enough?**

Success is said to breed success. But the route to success is also filled with subtle booby-traps that can spell disaster. One of them is letting the green-eyed monster called jealousy invade our senses and cause us to lust after the success of other pastors and congregations. Far too many ministries that were flourishing met disaster when they bit off more than they could chew and found themselves in financial trouble. Get too far ahead of yourself financially, and very soon, a blooming ministry is cutting staff and programs.

- **Dream God-sized visions.**

So often, we short-change ourselves and others by bringing our hopes and expectations down to our human ability, leaving God completely out of the equation. What I found over the years is that the bigger the dream, the more willing people were to embrace the opportunity. Scripture is filled with illustrations of how God took those with mustard-seed faith and allowed them to become a part of amazing ventures.

- **Delegate or die.**

The key to freeing up time for the senior pastor to do the things only they can do is to delegate, delegate, delegate. Far too often, we fall into the trap of thinking that we're the only one who can get the job done. It's a fatal trap. It not only keeps the monkey on our back, but it deprives other staff and congregation members of the chance to use their own skills and gifts in developing a ministry. Delegate or die. In a megachurch, the senior pastor has no other choice.

- **Do the things only you can do.**

There are a lot of demands on the senior pastor's time. If the congregation is going to grow, the pastor needs to figure out what to keep on their plate and what should be handed off to someone else to develop and grow. It's not an easy decision. But if the congregation is going to do vital ministry, the senior pastor has to limit their efforts to the tasks most closely aligned with the expectations of this leadership role. Handing off important ministries to other staff carries with it a certain amount of risk, but it is a risk worth taking if it means the congregation will be better served.

- **Keep the main thing the main thing.**

Churches tend to want to be all things to all people. But before we hop on that train, we need to remember why the church exists in the first place. Our job is to proclaim Jesus Christ. No one else other than the churches in a community are called specifically to preach the Word and administer the Sacraments. That is what we are called to do. So we need to make sure that our worship and music, our preaching and teaching, are done in a way that can change people's hearts and cause them to want to follow Christ in their daily life. Christ and the proclamation of the gospel is the reason we exist. Jesus is the main thing that needs to stay the main thing.

- **Acknowledge the power and presence of the Holy Spirit.**

St. Andrew's is a perfect example of what God can do if we allow God the chance to use us. The fact that St. Andrew's grew from a small congregation in a small village on the outer reaches of the Twin Cities is a miracle in itself. None of us could have possibly put all the pieces together by ourselves. It had to be the work of the Holy Spirit. We are called upon each and every day to ask for God's guidance so that the decisions we make and the plans we formulate are in concert with God's will.

- **Preaching must be practical and relevant.**

The pulpit is the most powerful tool a pastor has at their disposal. Lives have been impacted by hearing the Word. People on the edge of despair have found hope and healing as they sit in the pew and hear the Word preached. However, in order to be effective, the message needs to be one that resonates with people. At St. Andrew's, because of our multiple services, each sermon needed to be no longer than fifteen minutes in length. The challenge for the preacher was to be able to unpack, in a limited amount of time, a message that was not only biblically centered but also spoke directly to people. One goal I always sought was to be practical and relevant while still remaining faithful to the truth of the gospel. The other was to lead the listener to the point where they could see how incredible life with Christ can be.

- **Let people see the real you.**

One of the joys of being a pastor is to be invited into the lives of members and friends of the congregation. That joy, however, can never be fully realized if the pastor is so aloof that they become unapproachable. A pastor does not need to be on buddy-buddy terms with the congregation. But we do need to be real enough to be able to laugh at ourselves and to admit that we walk with feet of clay, just like everyone else.

- **Evangelism**

"Go into all the world and make disciples!" Those are our marching orders. That's the goal Jesus has set for each and every person who calls themselves a Christian. A church that doesn't take evangelism seriously is dropping the ball and failing at its most basic task. Making evangelism a priority is not an option. It is basic to every church.

- **Find voices you can trust to tell you the truth.**

All of us need someone who can serve as a sounding board—a person or group of people who are willing to tell us the truth. During my ministry at St. Andrew's, I was fortunate to have wonderful people who were willing to let me know when I was veering off track and who shared some suggestions on how I could do a better job at being their pastor. Covet those relationships. Encourage them to be totally honest. Consider their wise counsel. Many times, it was those gutsy members who were willing to tell their pastor the truth that helped me avoid making a mess of things.

Duane: What I've Learned from Roger

Throughout this book, I've noted here and there some things I've learned from Roger. However, those things only touch the surface. Here are a few other memorable things I've learned from him:

- *Be visionary. I love this quote from Roger: "Without a vision—the people perish, and without a vision—there is no parish."*
- *One phrase that Roger used over and over, especially at our staff retreats, was "There's no second annual anything." I never really took him literally on that because, of course, there are lots of things that are done annually in a church. What I think he meant when he said that is that we should not rest on the laurels of what we did previously with any event or activity. He wanted all his staff to creatively think about ways to enhance every ministry, every year.*
- *Although Roger is a pastor, in many ways, a better description for him is a "church entrepreneur." By that, I mean that he taught me*

that being in the church is not just about faith, it's also about leading with creativity and innovation.
- In the book of Luke (18:1-8), Jesus tells the parable of the persistent
  widow. Roger taught me that persistence can be a virtue, as it is with
  the widow in the parable. If he had an idea that he thought was
  worthwhile, he was very persistent in telling others about it and
  sticking to it, no matter what obstacles he might face.
- Statistics matter. As Merv Thompson, a Lutheran pastor and consultant on church growth, has said, "Numbers don't tell you everything. But they do tell you some things." Roger echoed that same
  sentiment when I worked with him.
- Treat your staff well. For example, when I was hired by Roger at St.
  Andrew's as a naive, young, non-ordained twenty-four-year-old,
  Roger and the church council made a point to include full benefits in
  my pay package, including retirement benefits. Many other churches
  did not include the full benefit package for non-pastors on staff. At
  the time, I could care less about the retirement portion of the package. But now, forty-three years later, as someone who is fully retired,
  I am so glad that Roger insisted I get all those wonderful benefits—
  just like the pastors. The miracle of compound interest on those early
  retirement funds has been a huge factor in my ability to retire.

Duane: What I Learned at St. Andrew's

I spent thirteen years at St. Andrew's working with Roger and others—
including volunteers. They taught me lots of things, some of which, I have
already noted in this book. Here are just a few other brief notable things I
have learned:
- You can never know another person's faith. Although everyone
  needs to be aware of their own faith it is difficult to project that same
  kind of faith onto someone else. How faith works is different for
  everyone.

- *There is huge power in collaboration with others. I saw this in working with others on the staff, in my endeavors with Sunday school teachers, in the performance of musicals, in writing curriculum, and in working together on shared goals. As a result of learning this at St. Andrew's, this premise has become a "north star" for me in living my life, both personally and professionally.*
- *Youth ministry is vitally important. When I came to St. Andrew's, I was coming off a two-year experience of teaching that had left me cynical about youth—especially middle schoolers. After just a short time at St. Andrew's, my view on youth changed 180 degrees because while working with the staff and others, I realized the impact that good, faithful people can have on kids. Most importantly, I saw how that impact may very well last for the rest of their lives.*

Paul: Learning from Alvin Rogness

Dr. Alvin Rogness was a very influential person in my college and seminary days. He was a highly gifted parish pastor and author of several books who was later recruited to be the President of Luther Theological Seminary in St. Paul, Minnesota. I spent five years at Luther Seminary attaining a Master of Divinity degree and a Master of Theology degree. For many of us seminarians, a highlight of the week was hearing Alvin Rogness preach in chapel. He was always inspiring, challenging, and Gospel-centered.

One spring day in the late 1960s, I attended an ordination service in which Dr. Rogness was asked to be the guest preacher for that day. In addressing about sixty newly ordained pastors, Rogness chose to address them as though he himself was a lay person at one of their churches. He said this: "One, I have a right to expect that you will walk with God (like Noah) and that you will also walk with me. Two, I expect that you will know your Bible and that you will also read the newspapers. Three, I expect that you will love the truth and you will also love people. Four, I expect that you will look to the future but also have a healthy knowledge of the past. Five, I expect that you will cry with me and that you will also laugh with me. Six, I want you to function out of freedom but to also reflect a healthy sense of self-discipline. Finally, I expect you to love your work and to not be ashamed to play." These words were spoken about fifty years ago, but I took them to heart throughout my ministry. They still seem very timely and relevant for today.

Paul: "We Should Write a Book"

For a number of years, we, at Shepherd of the Valley (SOTV), had a wonderful receptionist at our church whose name was Alice Mortenson. At least once a week, one of us would say to the other, "We should write a book about the many crazy things that happen here at SOTV!" We would then have a good laugh together. We decided that if we did write such a book, it would have to be sold as fiction because no one would believe it was fact. Like the time we rented the church out to a group of Russian immigrants for a wedding celebration that started on a Saturday at noon and ended thirteen hours later at 1:00 the next morning! Or the time the mother of the bride came to my office and insisted that we remove the chancel cross (sixteen feet tall and suspended by aircraft cables) so that the bottom portion of the cross would not show up in the wedding photos. Then there was the Sunday morning that a couple showed up with two live ferrets sitting on their shoulders and told us that these were "their children." One time, a groom asked if he could include his two dogs in the wedding ceremony (I think they were Great Danes). Another time, a little boy pulled the fire alarm right in the middle of a Pentecost Sunday sermon when a guest preacher was waxing eloquent about the tongues of fire resting on the heads of the disciples. This is just the short list. I still miss Alice and our moments of laughter.

There are many things that life in the parish has taught me. Below are a number of those things.

Paul: People Can Be Generous

People can be amazingly generous with their time, talents, and money if you show them a truly worthwhile cause. Our annual church budget was about $3 million for the later years of my ministry. In addition, we had five separate capital-fund drives prior to each building expansion. We did not hit every goal, but we always came close enough for the project to move forward. We were never afraid to "talk stewardship," and when we did so using sound biblical principles, people almost always responded joyfully and generously. I will never forget visiting one home on a stewardship call. As we sat down at the kitchen table, the husband looked me in the eye and said, "Well, how much do you want?"

When I regained my composure, I said, "How about $25,000 over three years?"

He replied, "No problem." It was one of the most enjoyable stewardship calls of my career. But I will always wonder how big that number could have been.

Paul: People Want to Make a Difference

People want to make a difference in their communities and their world. They want to roll up their sleeves and get their hands dirty. In addition, they don't want to sit around "chewing the fat." My goal was always for meetings not to exceed ninety minutes. My motto was "more doing and less chewing." I well recall one Saturday when about thirty volunteers came to help us put two coats of paint on the walls of what is now the Great Hall. It took about fifty-five gallons of paint and a lot of rollers. I could not help but notice the next morning how many people came to admire their work and proudly show it off to other members of their family. Such projects create real ownership among the members and provide the benefits of "sweat equity" while also taking some pressure off of the church budget. It appears that there are some folks in nearly every church who cherish the building and grounds dearly and want to care for them, almost like a parent cares for a child.

Paul: People Want to Be Connected to Others

People today long for genuine fellowship and "connectedness" in their lives. We live in such a fast-paced world that can also be so depersonalized. About a year ago, I called my bank to ask about my account. The woman on the phone did not ask for my name. I realize that she likely had all my personal data on her screen and that she only needed an account number. To her credit, she did answer my questions. But it still felt like a very impersonal moment. I always found it very gratifying to learn that many individuals and families found real fellowship at our church. Relationships were developed that have now lasted for several decades. I always contended that the coffee-and-donut hour or the traditional potluck after worship were just an extension of what happens in the sanctuary. I always said that one of the real benefits of belonging to a healthy congregation is getting to work, worship, sing, pray, talk, learn, laugh, cry, and dine with some of the nicest and most caring people you would ever want to meet in your lifetime. We are told that loneliness is almost an epidemic in today's society. So go find a healthy congregation and make some life-giving friendships.

Some years ago, Margaret and I returned to my first parish in Pontiac, Michigan, where I served from 1972 to 1980. They were celebrating the twenty-fifth anniversary of the church, and they had asked me to preach. I was amazed at how quickly we once again engaged in the lives of these saints of God after being gone for a number of years. It was almost like we had never left. It is a profound truth that the communion of saints, to which all God's people belong, transcends time and space and even death itself. The names of all the deceased were read aloud on a recent All Saints Sunday, and I was reminded that the fellowship we claim never ends. It is designed for now and forever, for time and for eternity.

Paul: Leadership Lessons

For Christians, the word leadership can be a bit tricky because there are times when you best serve by leading and other times when you best lead by serving. Another way to say this is to acknowledge that there are times when you walk behind your congregation, times when you walk alongside your congregation, and times when you walk out in front of your congregation. The wise pastor will know when to use each of these three approaches. And for goodness' sake, never "railroad" your ideas, no matter how wise or beneficial you think they may be for the congregation. Railroading will almost always result in pushback, and this can sometimes get ugly. Good communication is also critical. If people are well informed and have a good grasp of the facts, change and innovation in the parish can happen much more readily. Perhaps the most important word here is "trust." If a congregation trusts your leadership, you can often do lots of good things in a fairly short period of time. When that trust is not there, very little will be accomplished. Trust is like building a house; lay a solid foundation and then add one board or one brick at a time. Over time, you will see the fruit of your labors.

Paul: Synod Officials

Synod officials are there to help, but don't expect too much from them. A part of the problem is that their job descriptions are often just plain unrealistic. One of the bishops of our church who was also a good friend and mentor once told me what his job consisted of: one-quarter office, staff, and desk work; one-quarter attending national church assemblies, councils, and conferences; one-quarter (or more) working with troubled pastors and congregations; and one-quarter serving on various boards for our many Lutheran colleges, seminaries, social services agencies, camps, publishing houses, and ministerial associations. Another bishop friend of mine once said that our synod offices need a "people bishop," a "paper bishop," and a "telephone bishop." Some years ago, a local congregation was so divided that they actually had two call committees going simultaneously seeking a new senior pastor, and yet, the synod was totally unaware of this. When it came to a vote, the congregation was split right down the middle. Our synod did give us help in calling some of our pastors, but beyond that, I learned not to rely too much on the good graces of synodical leadership.

Paul: Balance in Ministry

I have learned that keeping a balance in ministry is vitally important. Most young pastors fresh out of the seminary are eager to make their mark on the world. To a point, this is commendable. I, too, will readily admit that for a number of years, I was "married" to the church. Why not? If you do well in ministry, you get lots of strokes and lots of kudos, which can become almost addictive if not held in check. But, as the saying goes, lots of pastors' families have been sacrificed on the altar of clergy ego and pride. Hard as it may be, we must not neglect spouses, children, extended family, and close friends.

Paul Tournier, a Swiss author and theologian, has noted that "God gives each of us just enough time to do what God wants us to do on any given day." This statement, of course, implies that we wisely order our time and our priorities that we learn to distinguish between the urgent and the important, that we plan as far ahead as possible to avoid conflicts, unpleasant surprises, and confusion, and, if needed, that we seek professional help and guidance. St. Paul reminds us in Ephesians 5 to "be careful then how you live, not as unwise people but as wise, making the most of the time."

Duane: Amen

Paul was an extremely hard and dedicated worker. I am sure balancing church life and home life was an issue for Paul. Sometimes, he would spend all day and much of the evening working at church.

In fact, Paul was at church so much that sometimes he took cat naps in his office. But he had a little secret. He once told me that his secret was that while sitting in his chair, he laid his head down on his desk to get a few winks. Then, just in case someone came to his door and said something to him, he could easily lift his head and say loudly, "Amen," as though he had finished a prayer.

Paul: The Challenge of Being Prophetic

The prophetic role of the church has almost always been problematic. People don't always want to hear what they most need to hear. There is an old joke among clergy that it is tough being a prophet in a non-profit organization. To put it another way, the church is sometimes called upon to comfort the disturbed and disturb the comfortable. To be truthful, prophetic words are often met with resistance if not outrage and even violence.

It has been said, half-jokingly, that at least some of the prophets of the Old Testament did not live long enough to collect their Social Security. Most often, they were not well-loved. Their prophetic words, which had little to do with predicting the future, were basically a call to the people of Israel to repent of their sins, turn from their ungodly ways, renounce all idol worship, seek justice for the oppressed, care for the poor, the widowed, and the orphaned—and in general, to embrace once more the statutes, commandments, and ordinances of God. Indeed, much of the Old Testament is the story of God's people frequently moving back and forth between spiritual fidelity and infidelity, righteousness and unrighteousness, punishment and restoration, just and unjust behavior, captivity and freedom, and sinfulness and grace.

Prophetic ministry can be of two kinds. First, prophets call people to change their beliefs, their hearts, their attitudes, their values, and their priorities. This is of primary importance to the prophets. But second, prophetic ministry should also involve profound issues of social justice, economic opportunity, and racial equality. To find examples of this form of ministry recently, we only need to look at people like Martin Luther King, Jr., Dietrich Bonhoeffer, Nelson Mandela, William Wilberforce, Roald Wallenberg, Susan B. Anthony, Rosa Parks, and Mahatma Gandhi. Notice that half of this group died untimely deaths for the sake of their causes, while the other half also suffered their share of persecution. But all lived and sacrificed for a noble, God-given cause involving equality, justice, human rights, peace, and truth. Today, we honor them for what they were able to accomplish in their lifetimes but note as well that at the time, their messages were not well-received by many and that in some cases, they were met with extreme threats, hatred, and violence.

I often ponder the work of the church today in the light of the great judgment scene found in Matthew 25. As you may recall, the sheep and goats were separated and judged on how well they had fed the hungry, clothed the naked, welcomed the stranger, healed the sick, and visited those in prison. The story does not imply that we are saved by our good deeds but rather that good deeds should naturally flow from a heart and a life that is filled with thanksgiving for all that God has done for us. Note that neither the sheep nor the goats were too aware of how much good they were or were not doing. We do not do good works in order to earn God's favor—we do good works because we have already received God's favor. This understanding of God's grace in our lives has been the primary motivation of the church for centuries—to do as Micah compels us: to do justice, to love mercy, and to walk humbly with our God. And may it always be so.

Paul: Let People Know You Are Human

People will respect your title as pastor and your office, but they also need to know that you are human as well. There are too many stories of clergy who, for whatever reason, remained aloof and distant from the very people they were called to serve. Until fairly recently, some seminaries taught classes in how clergy should set themselves apart from and even above their congregants. This is a mistake. My best advice is to just be yourself and be genuine, caring, and transparent. Members of any parish do not care how much you know until they know how much you care. People today can readily detect phoniness. It helps if you are something of an extrovert because you will be called upon to relate to people of all ages and in all walks of life. If meeting people for the first time or initiating a conversation is something you would rather not do, perhaps parish ministry is not for you. Once again, looking at the New Testament, we find that every image of the church described by Jesus or in one of the epistles (letters) is relational. You can't escape it.

Paul: Forgiveness

I have learned to forgive myself. Pastors can sometimes have strong tendencies toward perfectionism. But this goal will not serve you well in the parish. Remember that the church is both a divine and a human organism. As pastors, we will make mistakes, and most will be completely unintentional. But they will be mistakes, nonetheless. We all have feet of clay, and when things are said or done that cause hurt or pain, we need to forgive others and ourselves. I often think of Jesus and the twelve disciples. Even Jesus could not keep the whole group happy and cohesive. Peter denies and Judas betrays. Others fight over who will be most prominent in the coming kingdom. Forgiveness is the salve of life. Apply it often to self and to others. Do good work but just know that there will be days when self-forgiveness will be a huge blessing.

Paul: Retirement Isn't Easy

I have learned that it is harder to retire than I thought it might be, at least in the first couple of years. And this is for two reasons. One, when you do ministry well, it's energizing and satisfying. The pastor is welcomed into the lives and homes of people during the most significant moments in their lives: baptisms, weddings, confirmations, funerals, anniversaries, and other crucial events. To be there and to be helpful to people at such times is just very satisfying and fulfilling. The other reason it is hard to retire is because people still want you to be their pastor. But this is a temptation retirees must resist. Retired pastors need to trust that there are many other fine pastors of a younger age who are more than willing to step up and carry on the same high-quality ministry that you have hopefully demonstrated for so many years. Some folks may be disappointed and even hurt when you tell them "No," but they will survive, and they will also discover a new crop of pastors just as capable and competent, if not more so.

Paul: The Unsung Heroes of the Church—Clergy Spouses

Whatever success we pastors have had, we must, in our most honest moments, acknowledge that this would not have been possible were it not for a supportive, caring, and very understanding spouse. Remember, too, that congregations can learn a lot from a spouses' life and witness. One story comes to mind immediately. When we went to our first parish in Michigan, all the women were wearing dresses or skirts and blouses on Sunday morning. That Sunday, Margaret came to church in a beautiful blue pantsuit which was considered stylish but casual at the time. The very next Sunday, at least two-thirds of the women in the church came wearing their pantsuits! It was quite a learning moment for both Margaret and me. Without saying a word, within two weeks' time, Margaret had already changed the mood and culture of worship at Sylvan Lake Lutheran Church.

Paul: How to Handle Criticism Gracefully

Criticism inevitably comes our way when doing parish ministry. We are, after all, flawed, broken, self-centered human beings, and there are bound to be some disharmonies even in the most healthy and functional congregations. Over the years, I discovered several techniques that often mitigated some of the hurts, tensions, and divisions that can occur in the course of any ministry of the church.

The first rule of thumb is to always differentiate between the criticism itself and the one offering the criticisms. No one likes to be criticized, but it was helpful to try to ascertain just how valid (or invalid) the criticism was and how intense the feelings were that brought it about in the first place. But most of all, I found that sometimes these events, irksome as they may be, were also opportunities for some real ministry. Every time I got a complaint or a critique, directly or even indirectly, I responded as soon as my schedule allowed. The worst thing a pastor can do is to ignore these negative overtures. Whether it was a letter, an email, a voicemail, a text, or even just a note on my office door, I tried hard to get back to this person as soon as possible. Also, if I thought the issue was serious enough, I would invite a person to my office or offer to visit their home—or, better yet, meet for coffee at a restaurant, which always felt more like neutral ground for both of us. I did this because I wanted to hear them, greet them face to face, (gently) correct any misinformation they may have gotten, and perhaps even inquire as to the source of such information. I wanted them to know that I valued them as a person and certainly as a member of our congregational family. Oftentimes, these meetings were amazingly healing. Everyone wants to be taken seriously. Such meetings could be hugely beneficial for both the parishioner and for me.

There were also times (though not many) when people were angry enough that they chose, for whatever reason, to leave the church. I did as much "damage control" as I possibly could, but their minds were already made up. In these cases, I went out of my way to thank them for whatever years of service they may have given the church, sent them forth with my full blessing, hoped they would soon find another congregation that would suit their needs and welcome them warmly, and finally, mentioned that should they ever change their minds, the doors to our church would always be wide open to them. I can think of several households that left our church for some months or even some years that eventually came back to rejoin us. Of course, they were welcomed with open arms.

As a footnote, I well recall an incident from my first church years ago in Pontiac, Michigan. I had apparently offended a parishioner in some way that was never fully revealed to me. I simply received a short note in the mail saying that he and his family were leaving the church and that I should not even try to persuade them otherwise. I honored their wishes. I felt badly about the situation but could do nothing to correct it. About a year and a half later, I met this man's wife in a restaurant. When she approached me, she said, "I owe you an apology." "What for?" I asked. This woman then went on to tell me that at the time of their leaving the church, her husband had lost a father to suicide, had a sister who was gravely ill with cancer, and was himself having health issues in addition to almost losing his job with one of the big three automakers in Detroit. The woman went on to tell how all of this was such an embarrassment to her husband that he just could not come to church anymore, where, in her words, "everyone else seemed to be having a near-perfect life."

I learned a huge lesson that day. Never judge your critics too harshly, if at all. You never know how heavy are the burdens they may be carrying. It also made me think about how the church presents itself to the world. The church is not a museum for saints. It's a hospital for sinners. Over time, I once again befriended this family, though they never returned to our church. Without wanting to sound patronizing, one of my mottos for ministry was this: kill them with kindness. It's surely an overstatement, but there is a real element of truth and goodness in those four words.

Duane: What I Learned from Paul

Paul had a huge impact on me as a pastor and as a person. Briefly, here are some things I've learned from him beyond what I've already mentioned earlier in this book:

- *Humor is important in relationships. I knew this even before I met Paul. But being with Paul reinforced for me how humor can disarm people and enhance relationships. He has that gift. I've tried to emulate it.*

- *Take things in stride. Paul had a couple of sayings he repeated often to remind himself and others not to get too uptight when problems arise. One saying was: "ministry is really a series of ongoing interruptions." The other dictum was: "The New Testament is a bunch of folks writing a bunch of letters to a bunch of churches that were having a bunch of problems. Get used to it!"*

- *Keep your calendar close at hand. I don't remember Paul ever missing a meeting (although he sometimes was late). Perhaps this is because he always carried his calendar with him in his shirt pocket. At the beginning of every week, he would write down his weekly events and other important things on a small piece of paper that stuck out of his shirt pocket about a half-inch. Then all week long, he carried that piece of paper close to his heart, referring to it whenever contemplating his calendar. It became a type of trademark for Paul. Even though it looked a little odd, it worked for him.*

Duane: What I Learned at Shepherd of the Valley

The staff and congregation at SOTV taught me a lot. Here are just a few more things besides what I've mentioned earlier in this book:

- *The focus of my twelve-week sabbatical in 2005 was to find Lutheran churches that had good small group ministry and to find out how they did it. What I learned, much to my surprise, was that most churches talked about and hoped to do small-group ministry, but they didn't actually do it. Successful small-group ministry was virtually non-existent. In other words, every church wants to do good small-group ministry, but very few, if any, actually do it.*

- *Office location matters. I had many different office locations at both St. Andrew's and Shepherd of the Valley. Where my office was located often made a huge, almost unconscious, difference in the kind of ministry I did. For example, at SOTV, there were two office areas. What I found was that when I was located in the Children, Youth, and Family area, I saw things from the perspective of those staff people. So, naturally, my focus was on that ministry. However, when I was in the other office area, my interaction was with the other pastors and administrators who officed there. Again, naturally, my focus was on those ministries—simply because of the location of my office. This separation of offices sometimes led to misunderstandings, miscommunication, distrust, and an "us and they" feeling.*

Duane: Learning Never Stops

After I left St. Andrew's, I kept in touch with Margaret (the kindergarten Sunday school teacher I mentioned in chapter 9). Several years after I left, she wrote this to me:

> A little girl, about five, asked me if I taught Sunday school. I said, "Not this year." She said, "Oh, yes, you're too old to teach." I gently took her by the shoulder and said, "Don't ever forget this: you are never too old to teach, and you are never too old to learn."

Once again, Margaret came through with some wisdom. Learning happens throughout our lives. As this chapter suggests, even throughout the lives of seasoned pastors. You're never too old to learn.

Paul: What Will Never Change

One thing that I am sure will never change in ministry is that people will always be hungry for the Bread of Life, even if they are not always aware of it themselves. I used to sit in my office some Saturday evenings and Sunday mornings and literally watch two thousand people come for worship. I thought to myself, why do they come so faithfully? They could be golfing, sleeping, shopping, or just vegetating in front of the TV or computer. I think I know the answer. Most of these same suburbanites have a job, a home, a car, maybe a boat or a cabin, a portfolio of some size, a family, likely a spouse, a few kids, and a dog or a cat. But sometimes, life begins to look like this: eat, sleep, work, repeat. Eat, sleep, work, repeat. They soon begin to ask themselves, "Is this all there is? Where is the real meaning, the real purpose, the real depth, and the real substance in life?" In fact, that is something we all crave. Someone has noted that the two most important days in your life are the day you were born and the day you discover why you were born. It's as if people are saying, "Give me a good reason to go on living. I have attained so much, and yet, I feel unfulfilled and undernourished. Feed my soul, feed my spirit—not just my body." If the church is doing its job and if its preaching is Gospel-centered, Bible-based, and life-giving, then the hungry will be fed, the people will be nourished, and life will take on all kinds of new and exciting possibilities.

It is a two-thousand-year-old story, but it remains ever new. God created us to be God's people and the body of Jesus here on earth. When we take the time to develop this relationship, it literally can become life-altering and life-giving. Peter put it so well in his letter to the exiles of the Dispersion: "You are a chosen race, a royal priesthood, a holy nation, God's own people, in order that you may proclaim the mighty acts of him who called you out of darkness into his marvelous light. Once you were not a people but now you are God's people" (I Peter 2:9-10).

The church has gone through many hills and valleys in the past, and God always finds a way to revive and refresh people. As the saying goes: it's always darkest before the dawn. And it's better to light one candle than to curse the darkness. We do not do this work alone. If we did, we would be chasing after the wind. But God has promised to be in the midst of us and to guide us into the future, no matter how bleak or how promising that future may be.

ACKNOWLEDGMENTS

Special thanks to our spouses, Phyllis Paetznick, Margaret Harrington, and Carolyn Eigenfeld, for their patience and insights as we have put together this book.

There are others who helped along the way and to whom we give thanks: Chuck Tindell, for his encouragement and mentorship from day one; Charles Quinn, Joe Gonnella, and Dan Ferber for their feedback as we were writing; former colleagues in ministry John Keller, Mary Lund, and Chris Smith for their feedback and clarification of certain stories; other former colleagues Mark Wickstrom and Sue Lennartson for help in the publication process; Scott Tunseth, Rory Groves, and Todd and Heather Zeissler for their guidance on publishing issues; and others who did some manuscript reading and gave wonderful feedback along the way, namely, Edie Cook, Jay Boekhoff, Ann Boekhoff, and Cathy McLoone.

PHOTO GALLERY

Roger & Carolyn Eigenfeld   Paul & Margaret Harrington

Duane & Phyllis Paetznick

Roger's family when they came to St. Andrew's in 1972
Whitney, Jacqui, Carolyn, Lauren, Roger, Kirsten, & Peter

Paul & his family at the first groundbreaking in 1984
Mat, Annika, Margaret, Becca, & Paul

Duane & his family on his last day at St. Andrew's
Duane, Brandon, Adam, & Phyllis

St. Andrew's 1800 seat sanctuary with pipe organ from the balcony

Groundbreaking the first building at SOTV in 1984

St. Andrew's sanctuary at Christmas

The pipe organ at St. Andrew's

Building the first sanctuary of Shepherd of the Valley - 1985

Aeriel view of Shepherd of the Valley - today

Aerial photo of the St. Andrew's campus

The pastors of Shepherd of the Valley in 2005 - Paul's "dream team" - Duane Paetznick, Deb Stehlin, Paul Harrington, Bonnie Wilcox, Mary Lund, Randy Brandt, and Chris Smith